The Reality Street Book of Sonnets

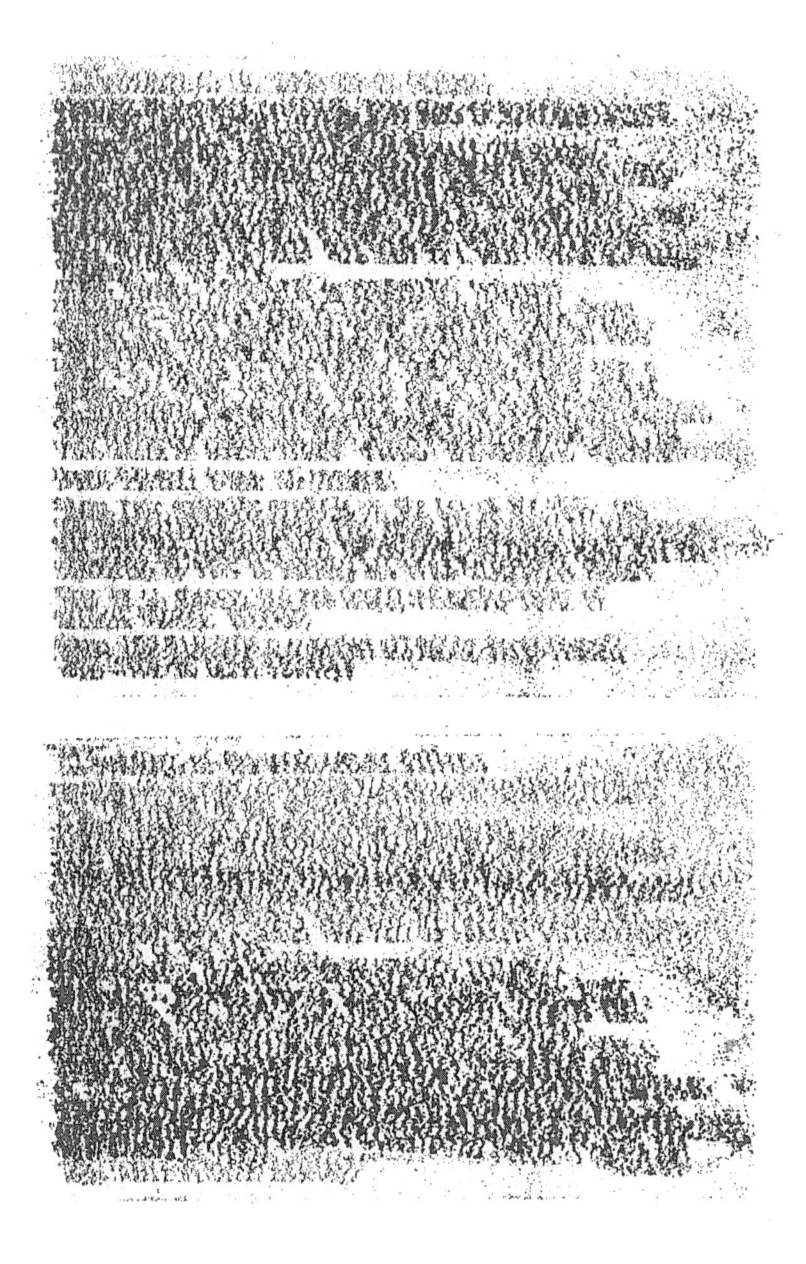

Bob Cobbing (1920-2002): *Sunnet*

THE REALITY STREET BOOK OF SONNETS

edited by
Jeff Hilson

REALITY STREET
2008

Published by
Reality Street Editions
63 All Saints Street, Hastings, East Sussex TN34 3BN
www.realitystreet.co.uk

Front cover image & lettering by Jeff Hilson
Typesetting & book design by Ken Edwards

Printed & bound in Great Britain by CPI Antony Rowe

A catalogue record for this book is available from the British Library

ISBN: 978-1-874400-39-4

Acknowledgments
The editor would like to thank the following individuals for their invaluable help in compiling this anthology: Tim Atkins, Sean Bonney, Laurie Duggan, Thomas Evans, Harry Gilonis, Peter Jaeger, Michele Leggott, Peter Manson, David Miller, Tom Raworth, and Geoffrey Young. Thanks also to Ian McMillan for inviting me to talk about the book on BBC Radio 3's *The Verb*. I am grateful to Roehampton University for allowing me leave to research the book and am indebted to Ken Edwards for agreeing to publish the anthology in the first place and for his considerable patience in seeing it to print. This project would not have been possible without the generosity of the contributors and all those who gave permission to reprint their work. Neither would it have been possible without Cheryl putting up with all my hours at the computer. This book is for her and for Nancy Maya Eaton-Hilson who delayed her appearance into this world so that I could finish writing the introduction.

Contents

Bob Cobbing .... *frontispiece*

Introduction by Jeff Hilson *8*

Edwin Denby *19*
Bern Porter *25*
Mary Ellen Solt *26*
Jackson Mac Low *27*
Ebbe Borregaard *29*
John Clarke *35*
Ted Berrigan *42*
Anselm Hollo *45*
Beverly Dahlen *49*
Kathleen Fraser *53*
Tom Raworth *60*
Clark Coolidge *64*
Peter Riley *69*
Stephen Rodefer *74*
Lyn Hejinian *79*
Rachel Blau DuPlessis *84*
Ron Padgett *89*
John Welch *92*
Adrian Clarke *94*
Paul Dutton *98*
Robert Adamson *102*
Thomas A Clark *105*
Allen Fisher *109*
Johan de Wit *115*

Geoffrey Young ... *119*
Bernadette Mayer ... *122*
Alice Notley ... *128*
Ian Wedde ... *134*
Steve McCaffery ... *139*
Aaron Shurin ... *145*
Jeremy Adler ... *150*
Pam Brown ... *152*
Bill Griffiths ... *156*
Robert Hampson ... *157*
John A Scott ... *162*
Laurie Duggan ... *166*
Gavin Selerie ... *171*
Alan Halsey ... *176*
Lawrence Upton ... *179*
Tony Lopez ... *182*
Ken Edwards ... *187*
David Miller ... *193*
Jonathan Brannen ... *196*
Geraldine Monk ... *201*
Maurice Scully ... *205*
Frances Presley ... *209*
Philip Kuhn ... *210*
Harryette Mullen ... *212*
Brian Marley ... *213*
William Fuller ... *219*
Robert Sheppard ... *226*
Kelvin Corcoran ... *229*
Michele Leggott ... *232*
Harry Gilonis ... *236*
Elizabeth James ... *240*
Ian Davidson ... *242*

Keith Jebb..*246*
John Gibbens *249*
Peter Jaeger...*252*
Richard Makin..*257*
Simon Smith...*261*
Tim Atkins..*266*
Carol Watts *273*
John Kinsella..*278*
Giles Goodland...*281*
Michael Farrell *287*
Eléni Sikélianòs *292*
Christian Bök *295*
Laynie Browne *297*
Jeff Hilson..*301*
Juliana Spahr..*305*
Philip Nikolayev...*311*
Lisa Jarnot..*316*
Peter Minter...*318*
Peter Manson *322*
Sean Bonney...*324*
Jay Millar *327*
Jen Bervin *331*
Piers Hugill...*335*
Chris McCabe...*340*
Abigail Oborne *343*
Justin Katko...*347*
Sophie Robinson..*350*

Introduction

I

THE DECISION to assemble this anthology arose out of my capacity as co-organiser of Crossing the Line, a monthly reading series in London of what has come to be known as linguistically innovative poetry.[1] In that capacity I listened with great interest to poet and publisher Ken Edwards read from *Eight+Six*, a collection of sonnets whose content played much faster and looser with the form than its title implied. Here were poems which put the traditional sonnet under pressure with consistent wit and energy and which did so moreover with complete seriousness. After the reading I mentioned to Ken that someone should publish an anthology of linguistically innovative sonnets, but as is often the case after such events the proposition was left hanging. A few weeks later, however, Ken contacted me to ask whether I had been serious in my proposal. In spite of his own example, this question marked, I think, an uncertainty about whether there were sufficient numbers of linguistically innovative poets writing sonnets to make this a viable project, especially in Britain. After all, the paradigmatic English-language sonnet writers of the twentieth century – e.e. cummings, Edwin Denby, Ted Berrigan, Bernadette Mayer (not to mention John Berryman and Robert Lowell) – were American. In Britain surely one had to go back to Gerard Manley Hopkins for anything resembling consistent experimentation with the form and it's still easy to forget that the sonnets he is best remembered for are mostly poems of the 1870s and 1880s. I'd venture that Ken's question also marked an uncertainty as to whether the sonnet was a form suited to consistent innovation and that, again in spite of his own example and those Americans I've listed above, it wasn't instead a vehicle for more "mainstream" use.

For some time, however, I had been aware of a number of linguistically innovative poets here in Britain writing sonnets. A few years before Ken's reading at Crossing the Line, Tim Atkins read his *25 Sonnets* at London's SubVoicive reading series before it was published in the US by The Figures in 2000. At Bob Cobbing's fortnightly Writers Forum Workshops I heard Adrian Clarke test out the manuscript of *Skeleton Sonnets,* which Cobbing saw into print shortly before his death in 2002. A few years previously Cobbing had also put out *Astrophil and Stella*, an arresting set of visual sonnets by Sean Bonney. In 2001, Giles Goodland's *A Spy in the House of Years* appeared from Leviathan Press. Here was evidence of a range of poets, none of them connected to the mainstream, working assiduously with the sonnet form which provoked in each a variety of responses, from Atkins' radically pared down, 'dub' sonnets, through Clarke's wiry torquings and Bonney's playful 'gestalt' responses to the sonnet's shape, to Goodland's more compendious cultural assemblages. No two examples were remotely similar but they were all united by the sonnet umbrella. Alongside these contemporary instances I recalled

Thomas A Clark's "Sixteen Sonnets" and Peter Riley's "Ospita" from the Paladin anthology *The New British Poetry*, at the same time as discovering Allen Fisher's *The Apocalyptic Sonnets* (1978, Pig Press) whilst working in the archive of the special poetry collection at University College London. A recent trip to Foyles Bookshop had also unexpectedly thrown up Brian Marley's long out of print *Springtime in the Rockies* (1978, Trigram Press) in which I found his wonderful "Bargain Basement Sonnets".

It was no use looking in the existing sonnet anthologies for any of these poets. Indeed, on the whole reading through the Twentieth Century contributions of these big-press editions was, and continues to be, a disheartening experience. The roll-call of names in John Fuller's *Oxford Book of Sonnets* (2000), for example, is entirely predictable, limited as it is largely to US poets of the new critical/confessional/"strenuous-authentic" school and British poets of the Auden/Spender axis. These give way inevitably to Movement and post-Movement poets, and finally to poets of the so-called "New Generation". Even the eccentrics are the expected ones. At first glance, Phillis Levin's *Penguin Book of the Sonnet: 500 Years of a Classic Tradition in English* (2001) seems to offer little more hope. Whilst its roster of earlier names is quite laudable, its list of Twentieth Century and especially post World War II contributors is on the whole merely more *comprehensively* mainstream than Fuller's. Besides, as an American Penguin edition, more space is given over to US poets especially in its later pages (there are certainly no surprises amongst its British contributors). It came as something of a shock, therefore, to find in its pages the likes of Edwin Denby, Muriel Rukeyser, John Ashbery, Ted Berrigan, Ann Lauterbach and Hugh Seidman, though each is represented by only a single poem. However, at least there was some evidence here of an editor with a critical eye beyond the wholly conventional. More recent anthologies such as Faber's *101 Sonnets: From Shakespeare to Heaney* (2002) and the Library of America's *American Sonnets* (2007) merely revert to type. The most recent anthology, Norton's *The Making of a Sonnet* (2008), edited by Edward Hirsch and Eavan Boland, wears the face of inclusivity, containing the likes of Berrigan, Bernadette Mayer and Alice Notley, but it's something of a disguise.

If the available anthologies were anything to go by, therefore, linguistically innovative poets were clearly not interested in the sonnet as a form. The blurb on the back of Levin's anthology claims that it tells "the full story of the sonnet tradition in the English language", which if even possible it clearly does not do. What we are presented with is rather a narrative of Levin's own making. I don't want to rehearse here the reasons why major publishing houses refuse to commit to innovative poetry – instances in the last century are legion and the arguments of the "poetry wars" on both sides of the Atlantic (and elsewhere) are largely unresolved and ongoing. A question I'd like to pose, however, is why these major publishing houses seem in recent years to have put out what is effectively the same anthology. Sure, some of the poets differ from book to book, but the overall impetus is unchanging: to present a survey of the sonnet from its beginnings to the present-day. The "commonsense" answer is that they are all jostling in a free market for market domination of an ever-popular form. Each anthology hopes to trump its forbears though none of them acknowledges the existence of any of the others. In some ways it's a wholly laughable state of affairs, though also one to be taken very seriously. I would argue that there is a politics of form at work here and that the sonnet has become a focal point for some of the issues surrounding the so-called poetry wars. As a form the sonnet is fiercely guarded, as a read-through of the introductions to many of these anthologies testifies. Just as its varied structural features – 14 lines, octave and sestet, rhyming couplet, volta, etc – are metonymic of the whole form and can't be disturbed without destroying its integrity, so the sonnet itself stands as a metonym for the kind of poetry published by the big publishing houses. To disturb the sonnet's form too radically therefore is not just to disturb the sonnet itself, or the sonnet tradition, but to endanger the foundations of the wider poetic tradition. I wonder whether this doesn't also go some way towards explaining the recent spate of mainstream sonnet anthologies. At a time when linguistically innovative poetry has been making inroads into the public consciousness – in spite of fierce opposition from some quarters – these anthologies appear, one after the other, to shore up the ruin that such a move threatens.

John Fuller's 1972 study of the form, *The Sonnet*, "essential reading for anyone interested in the form" according to Phillis Levin, is actually a good indication of the mainstream suspicion of tampering with the sonnet's mechanics.[2] The chapter on structural alternatives is tellingly entitled "Variants and Curiosities" and though the relationship between "variant" and "curiosity" is not entirely apparent, Fuller's use of the word "curiosity" shows that some sonnets clearly belong behind glass as objects of fear and wonder. It also goes to show just how far behind the mainstream had fallen by the early 1970s. Whilst Fuller does rather begrudgingly accept that "variants do comment constructively on the sonnet-form and of course become successful poems in their own right" (with the exception of purely visual sonnets which he dismisses out of hand) they have to do so "through a desire to explore legitimate possibilities and to provide genuine extensions of its capabilities". That word "legitimate" stalks Fuller's text and it's clear that he is suffering from his very own legitimation crisis. However, he exempts selected poets from his schema, notably Milton, Wordsworth and Gerard Manley Hopkins, all of whom are permitted to stray from "genuine" form. Milton "cultivates" the Italian sonnet rather than violates it and Wordsworth similarly gives the form "organic life". In both cases natural metaphors override cultural mandates. To accommodate Hopkins, Fuller as good as avoids mentioning form, instead substituting it for a consideration of content.[3] "After Hopkins," he states, "few modern poets have paid great attention to the legitimate sonnet" – but by this stage it's obvious neither to me nor I think to Fuller what a "legitimate" sonnet is.

At the end of "Variants and Curiosities", Fuller writes that there is not "very much left to do with [the sonnet] that has permanent significance for the form", suggesting that it had had everything done to it that could be done. His example of then-recent "innovation" was a love sonnet by, of all people, John Updike, which dispenses with words altogether instead scattering letters across the poem's 14 lines. Might Fuller's words, like Blake Morrison and Andrew Motion's now infamous claim in *The Penguin Book of Contemporary British Poetry* that nothing much happened in English poetry in the 60s and 70s, be another albeit earlier attempt by the mainstream to "paint whole areas of poetic activity out of the picture"[4] – namely the linguistically innovative sonnet?

II

I LEAVE it up to others to decide why in 1972 Fuller would refer to John Updike rather than to Ted Berrigan, whose sonnets came out in separate editions in 1964 and 1966. Omitting them from his later anthology, however, is unforgivable. It's no exaggeration to say that Berrigan's poems have been responsible for something of a latter-day sonnet renaissance amongst linguistically innovative poets. Certainly Berrigan gave these poets a kind of permission to use the form again after it had lain largely neglected for decades, although Berrigan himself had the example of Edwin Denby, whose *In Public, In Private* appeared in 1948 and can thus be seen as an important precursor.[5] Denby is in many ways the right place to begin an anthology of linguistically innovative sonnets, not least because he rarely wrote using any other form. His achievement was also realised without fanfare, the poems being radically misunderstood on initial publication. Reviewers were unprepared for their "compressed, quirky, big-city stop-and-go rhythms"[6] and criticised them for their lack of "control". The poems' elliptical syntax and sudden shifts in direction appealed to Berrigan, however, who published them in a special edition of his "C" Magazine though in many ways Berrigan's own sonnets have obscured Denby's considerable accomplishment with the form. Berrigan himself, however, was responsible for a flurry of sonnet writing amongst his immediate contemporaries such as Dick Gallup and Ron Padgett – see Padgett's "Nothing left in that drawer" and "Sonnet/Homage to Andy Warhol" in this anthology, both witty proclamations *à la* "The sonnet is dead! Long live the sonnet!"[7] – not to mention Alice Notley's remarkable *165 Meeting House Lane* which can be read fruitfully in relation to Berrigan's own poems.

Indeed, Notley's is one of a number of important sequences by women included in this anthology. As commentators have long pointed out, the sonnet has been a form traditionally dominated by men. A while back a debate ensued in the online women's journal *HOW(ever)* over an article called "The Sonnet Transfigured" by the mainstream poet Annie Finch, who claimed to be reviving the sonnet as a form women might inhabit after years of male domination.[8] However, instead of keying into a liberatory tradition of formal innovation, Finch revealed herself to be overwhelmed by the weight both of the traditional sonnet and the sonnet tradition. In the "postcards" section of the journal's subsequent issue, a number of innovative women poets responded to some of Finch's assumptions.[9] As Kathleen Fraser pointed out, instead of interrogating form or engaging with a counter-tradition of transgressive writing by women, Finch envisaged "a sonnet-trophy, which could help women build [their] consciousness alive and [their] dreams real as the old sonnet helped the men to do." "Our sonnet," she continued, "seems different; it has a small i in it instead of a big one. But perhaps any sonnet at all is a big i. That's something I have to fear..." The notion of a "sonnet trophy" merely redeployed the masculine tradition from which Finch was trying to escape and as other respondents pointed out, her aligning of poetry and fear needed unpacking. For Finch, one of the purposes of poetry was "to stop fear", the sonnet being particularly well suited to achieve this because its structure was a way of "organizing, channelling and making familiar." Beverly Dahlen disagreed. Poetry might focus fear but it couldn't stop it. And surely poetry was about "making strange", said Dahlen, for whom the sonnet form was "a kind of padded cell in which I go mad", itself a comment on the old trope of the sonnet envisaged as a "room", another male constraint fantasy which Dahlen rightly sees as a form of incarceration. Rachel Blau DuPlessis added that the sonnet would have to be "ruptured before being recuperated, and recuperated only within the terms of a full analysis of lyric ideology, beauty, and pleasure".

The sonnets written by women in this anthology are variously engaged in this act of rupture. One of the major figures here is Bernadette Mayer, whose *Sonnets* was published in 1989 by Tender Buttons Press. The association with Gertrude Stein is perhaps fortuitous but powerful nonetheless. Stein herself has an 18-line sonnet in the middle of "Patriarchal Poetry" which sends up the sonnet as a male-dominated praise-poem. Mayer's sonnets are a sustained and complex version of this, a skewed take, as Juliana Spahr has shown, on lyric intimacy.[10] By turns fierce and tender, Mayer constantly pulls apart form and content to interrogate the gaping personal and social hypocrisies we inflict on others and that are in turn inflicted on us, especially in the name of desire. Like desire, Mayer's sonnets come in all shapes and sizes and refuse to be bound by conventional form. An exception to this is her repeated use of the couplet which ends a significant number of the poems. In Freudian terms this is the return of the repressed, only Mayer knows it and it becomes instead a glorious, almost masochistic, repetition compulsion. I can't get enough of these poems, though regrettably *Sonnets* has been out of print for some time now. Many poets, however, a good few of them in this anthology, have managed to track down copies and continue to find within its pages a template for what can be done with, and indeed, to, the form.

With the example of women writing necessarily inside and against the form, it is perhaps better to talk of different "traditions", plural, of the linguistically innovative sonnet. This is also important when thinking about the sonnet in other cultures, and I have tried to include in the anthology a selection of poets from English-speaking countries other than the UK and the US, such as Canada, Australia and New Zealand, which the traditional anthologies have by and large failed to do. In Australia, the "Generation of '68" – among others, Robert Adamson, Pam Brown, Laurie Duggan, John Forbes, John A Scott and John Tranter – all wrote sonnets influenced by the likes of O'Hara and Berrigan, though they brought to it the particular nuances of the culture. For instance, Robert Adamson's "Sonnets to Be Written from Prison" can be seen as part of a tradition of convict literature – Adamson himself draws on this in the sequence whilst at the same time ironising it. He dreams of being banged up for an unnamed crime which gets him "in the news". Perhaps his crime is to write "almost experimental sonnets" or to write sonnets at all. Indeed, in an Australian context, how suited is this traditionally genteel, contrived and most closed of forms to this wild, natural and most open of continents? We have to be careful of course not to produce a reductionist version of Australia. Adamson's sequence is ultimately a fantasy about the poet as romantic outlaw but it also asks important questions about whether poetry can be an effective political tool and considers the role of Australian poetry in a wider global context.

Australian poets, then, found in American poetry, specifically the poets in Donald Allen's *The New American Poetry*, an answer to the prevailing conservatism in Australian poetry and the linguistically innovative sonnet flourished though again the mainstream anthologies tell a different story.[11] Younger Australian poets such as Peter Minter and Michael Farrell have gone on to use the sonnet to extend and consolidate many of the questions posed by their forbears. In Britain the American example was also a powerful one and the sonnet was taken up by a number of poets associated with Cambridge – the late Andrew Crozier, JH Prynne, Peter Riley – who have historically favoured the practice of innovating with inherited forms. Poets in London on the other hand, and especially those associated with Eric Mottram, have tended to prefer more open forms. As is always the case, however, there are exceptions. London poets such as Adrian Clarke and Robert Sheppard, not to mention Ken Edwards, the late Bill Griffiths, Robert Hampson, Gavin Selerie and Johan de Wit – have all gone on to write sonnets though in the case of Clarke, and especially Griffiths, out of suspicion of the form. "What better disguise for evil/ than sonnets?" asks Griffiths in *Rousseau and the Wicked.* His "sonnet 1" and "sonnet 2" in this anthology demonstrate an undisguised freedom from the form, and though "sonnet 1" has at least the look of a sonnet, "sonnet 2" has more the look and feel of a haiku.

III

GRIFFITHS' MISTRUST of the form has its antecedents. The sonnet had been declared as good as dead by the pioneering modernists, most famously Pound and Williams. Pound considered it little more than a mistake, a form invented "when some chap got stuck in the effort to make a canzone", and held it responsible for a subsequent decline in metric invention.[12] Williams rejected it on the grounds that it offered nothing new. "All sonnets mean the same thing", he wrote, because the configuration of the words, the way a sonnet is organised, negates the possibility of any original movement within it.[13] This dismissal of the form, however, was also a reaction against its specifically English history as well as a criticism of the way it was being used by contemporaries. Williams damned what he called "apt use" of the sonnet as practised by parlour-room sonneteers who stultified the form "by making pleasurable that which should be removed". "Apt use", and by extension "apt users" had turned the sonnet's formal properties into bourgeois proprieties. "Making it pleasurable" was getting in the way of "making it new".

Very little seems to have changed since. The anthologies are still full of sonnets demonstrating "apt use", sonnets which it is claimed add meaningfully to the tradition but which in reality do little more than ring very limited changes on Williams' "pleasurable" indicators. In *Reading the Illegible*, Craig Dworkin has spoken of how poetic form "must always necessarily signify" adding that "any particular signification is historically contingent and never inherently meaningful or a-priori".[14] This is especially the case with the sonnet, which as Michael Spiller reminds us is a prescribed form, "one whose duration and shape are determined before the poet begins to write".[15] The problem with Williams' "apt users", and by extension sonnets written within the mainstream, is their refusal to submit the form to historical change. The number of poets who continue to use iambic pentameter on a consistent basis is alarming and after a while the persistent rhythm washing through their poems induces a kind of nausea akin to sea-sickness. For these poets the sonnet is so "inherently meaningful and a-priori" that it effectively obscures the sonnet. Dworkin's book is about how to read poetic texts which foreground illegibility, but I think we can usefully reverse the poles of his thesis and suggest that certain forms also become illegible through their very legibility. The sonnet is a case in point. Because it is such a well known form – its form *qua* form can after all be taken in at a glance – it is overdetermined and its very recognisability makes it impossible to read.

What is needed is a radical defamiliarisation of the form. If the linguistically innovative sonnet can be said to have a "story" it is precisely this, the constant, purposeful intervention into the state of affairs I've just outlined above. Two important precursors who used the sonnet in the face of Pound and Williams' hostility, and specifically in order to "make it new", were EE Cummings and Louis

Zukofsky.[16] "It is time someone resurrected the sonnet from a form that has become an exercise," Zukofsky wrote in his essay "American Poetry: 1920-1930".[17] That "someone" was Cummings, though Zukofsky thought his diction too "Shakespearean" in places, preferring a cadence more in tune with what he called the "actuality" of the time. It is more than probable that Zukofsky was also thinking of his own attempt at the form. Between 1928 and 1930 the 7th section of his long poem "*A*" took the shape of a 7-poem sonnet sequence which went some way towards removing most of what Williams held in contempt. Although Zukofsky retains the formal vestiges of a traditional sonnet, they are made to undergo a process of radical defamiliarisation. Thus in the first sonnet there is a rhyme scheme but it moves from Shakespearean (abab, cdcd) in the first two quatrains to a Petrarchan 'envelope' rhyme (effe) in the third before reverting to a Shakespearean rhyming couplet. There is no overall meter, though the fairly strict 10-syllable count retains the skeleton of iambic pentameter. In the course of the rest of the sequence the rhyme scheme of the octave remains solidly Shakespearean whereas the final six lines alternate between Shakespearean and a kind of bastardised Petrarchan until in the final two sonnets it breaks down completely.

What also breaks down is the poems' syntax which becomes increasingly disjunctive, disturbed by the full panoply of interruptive punctuation – hyphens, dashes, question and exclamation marks, italics, parentheses, ellipses, colons, semi-colons etc. The overall effect is the opening up of a traditionally closed form. Content is led not by the traditional lyric subject but by letting language go. In places Zukofsky deliberately mocks the English sonnet's traditional iambics: "Not in the say but in the sound's – hey-hey –/ The way today, Die, die, die, die, tap, slow," go two lines from sonnet 5. Too many poets have tended to privilege "the say" over "the sound's – hey-hey –" to the extent that "the say" is still very much "the way to-day." One of the reasons for this is that "apt users" have been reluctant to question or relinquish the lyric subject or ego, which still has too much of itself to impart. Indeed, Zukofsky seems to be playing with the lyric "I", keeping it at bay completely in the first sonnet, punning with it in the second (the "I" is missing from the sign he sees – "LAUNDRY TO-LET" – with the implication that this is where the lyric subject belongs) before reluctantly including it in a stuttering refrain – "Then I" – which is never really allowed to get going. Much of the awkwardness in "*A*"-7 is felt in this missing letter which is overrun by "they"s and "we"s.

In a letter to Pound, Zukofsky claimed to have revolutionized the sonnet with "*A*"-7, though the effects of this revolution were not felt by his contemporaries (true to form, Pound was less than impressed, accusing Zukofsky of having written a canzone instead).[18] What marks Zukofsky out, what is revolutionary about him, is his insistent formalism which recognises that form is a heightening of poetic artifice in which the lyric subject is not natural or given but a performance. This radical formalism links Zukofsky to many of the New York School poets and also to many of the poets in this anthology. In his *The Development of the Sonnet,* Michael Spiller discusses the origins of the form, showing the varieties it took before it solidified, or indeed petrified, into what we are now over-familiar with. Yet even Spiller begins to insist on prescriptions – proportion, extension and duration – which, although he admits are observed only "by custom", invalidate the sonnet if infringed. I'd like to think that the poets in this anthology are the true inheritors of the sonnet, returning it to the potentialities outlined by Spiller before the long process of petrifaction set in. Whilst mainstream commentators do permit alteration to the form, they often do so in the most limited of ways in spite of sanctioning, for instance, Hopkins' curtal and caudated sonnets. Surely it's time the formal innovations of the Twentieth Century were also registered within the sonnet's lines, formal innovations which are not pursued for their own sakes but which are historically situated. Here I turn again to Berrigan. One of his techniques in *The Sonnets* is to use the line as a separate unit instead of as part of a narrative continuum. No longer is the sonnet about the tracing of an "argument" through its lines, an argument which also registers the passing of linear time. Instead, the discrete interchangeable line disrupts the passing of time within the poem as it also does the model of space the traditional sonnet represents. Berrigan's sonnets are an example of poetry seriously attempting to take on board the changes ushered in by the scientific revolutions of the last century, changes that question fundamentally categories such as Spiller's proportion, extension and duration, which belong to an older Newtonian universe. Charles Olson attempted the like using open field techniques. Berrigan's use of closed form to achieve a similar end is a radical move. It also registers something of a paradox, announcing the sonnet as an impossibility whilst demonstrating its continued vitality, not unlike Beckett's "I can't go on, I'll go on."

IV

IN A DIFFERENT vein, the urge to "go on" with the sonnet also accounts for the popularity of the sonnet sequence. In this anthology I admit to favouring poems which are part of longer sequences and I have where possible been as generous as space has allowed with my selections (something which also marks this anthology off from many of the others). Linguistically innovative poets seem on the whole to opt for the sequence over the stand-alone sonnet and I think this can be explained by their historical preference for the accumulative and speculative poetic "project" as opposed to the singularity and poise of discrete lyric. The majority of the sonnets I have gathered are also written in free verse, Frost's imaginary tennis net having been shredded long ago. Within this remit the anthology offers up a wide range of responses. Beverly Dahlen and Johan de Wit, for instance, write prose sonnets, as does John Clarke whose extraordinary and largely unknown book, *In the Analogy*, presents us with sonnets which are a unique hybrid of poem and expository prose. They can also be seen as a very particular take on the tradition of the double sonnet as is also the case with Jonathan Brannen's *Deaccessioned Landscapes*, Allen Fisher's *Apocalyptic Sonnets* and Peter Jaeger's "Eckhart Cars." Indeed, many of the contributors engage with traditional aspects of the form. Spiller mentions how early sonnets often structured themselves around the list, which Stephen Rodefer's "Mon Canard" takes to an extreme in an obsessively extended *adnominatio* of address to a lover. A number of the contributors have returned to Shakespeare as a vehicle for innovation. Jackson Mac Low and Harryette Mullen both apply Oulipean S+7 techniques to the most well-known Shakespeare sonnets to very different effect, whilst Aaron Shurin and Steve McCaffery use the end words of Shakespeare's lines as prompts for new, again very diverse, work. Jen Bervin, on the other hand, constructs her own minimal poems out of a fading Shakepearean text.

Many of the poets in the anthology respond to the sonnet's characteristic shape. Jeremy Adler, Bob Cobbing, Mary Ellen Solt and Lawrence Upton do so through their involvement with concrete poetry, whilst David Miller's work here has affinities with Chinese brush painting. However, as I have already suggested, the sonnet is one of the most recognisable of poetic forms and many of the poets in the anthology seem to be deliberately distorting its familiar shape. Thus Piers Hugill's sonnets have a primarily vertical pull, whilst those of Ian Davidson and Mac Low are overwhelmingly horizontal. Lyn Hejinian's are baggy and capacious. This playing with the "look" of the traditional sonnet is also a challenge to its fabled elegance. Critics often talk of the sonnet's unique and beautiful asymmetry – the traditional octave and sestet of the Italian sonnet being just off kilter – but with too much "apt use" this fundamental instability at the form's heart has become blithely accepted and the form itself blandly "beautiful". The sonnets I have gathered are, I hope, beautiful but rather in the way Gertrude Stein defined it, as things "irritating annoying stimulating."[19] I should also add that although this is an anthology of English language sonnets I have included a number of "translations", though a glance at Tim Atkins' Petrarch poems or Harry Gilonis' "North Hills" shows how far from normative translation we are. In a way, of course, all the poems in this anthology are translations. And some of the poems are not sonnets at all.

Jeff Hilson
2008

Footnotes

1 "Linguistically innovative", awkward as it is, has for some time been preferred to terms like "avant-garde", "experimental", "neo-modernist" and even "post-avant", though it is roughly cognate with them.

2 John Fuller, *The Sonnet* (London: Methuen, 1972)

3 This seems to be a common ploy in many discussions of Hopkins and the sonnet.

4 This phrase is from Peter Barry and Robert Hampson's introduction to *New British Poetries: The Scope of the Possible* (Manchester: Manchester University Press, 1993) 5.

5 In a review of Tony Lopez's *False Memory*, the late Andrew Crozier refers to Berrigan's sonnets as if they were a new starting point, a kind of writing degree zero of the form. (See http://jacketmagazine.com/11/lopez-by-crozier.html) However, other first generation New York School poets also wrote sonnets. The first half of O'Hara's *Collected Poems* is punctuated by them. Kenneth Koch wrote a number of sequences, including "The Railway Stationery" from *Thank You* and "Our Hearts" from *The Burning Mystery of Anna* in 1951. The three sections of John Ashbery's "The Picture of Little J A in a Prospect of Flowers" from *Some Trees* can also be seen as distorted sonnets with their use of quatrains and off-rhyming couplets.

6 Ron Padgett, "On Edwin Denby" in *The Straight Line: Writings on Poetry and Poets* (Ann Arbor: University of Michigan Press, 2000) 81.

7 See my comments on Berrigan towards the end of this introduction.

8 See *HOW(ever)*, Vol. 6, no. 2 (October 1990)

9 *HOW(ever)*, Vol. 6, no. 3 (Summer 1991)

10 Juliana Spahr, "Love Scattered, Not Concentrated Love" in *differences: A Journal of Feminist Cultural Studies* 12:2 (2001) 98-120.

11 See for instance *The Indigo Book of Modern Australian Sonnets* ed. Geoff Page (Charnwood, ACT: Ginnindera Press, 2003)

12 Ezra Pound, "Cavalcanti" in *The Literary Essays of Ezra Pound*, ed. TS Eliot, (London: Faber and Faber, 1985) 168.

13 William Carlos Williams, "The Modern Primer" in *The Embodiment of Knowledge* (New York: New Directions, 1974) 17.

14 Craig Dworkin, *Reading the Illegible* (Evanston, Illinois: Northwestern University Press, 2003), xix-xx.

15 Michael Spiller, *The Development of the Sonnet* (London: Routledge, 1992) 2.

16 To Cummings and Zukofsky I'd add John Wheelwright, whose *Mirrors of Venus: A Novel in Sonnets* (1938) is a clarion call for the formally disruptive sequence: "When, with habitual knack in versifying or with superstitious shunning of all but conventional thoughts or notions, a poet comes across with 'perfect' sonnet after 'perfect' sonnet for any length of time, a sonnet sequence is a bore." *Collected Poems of John Wheelwright*, ed. Alvin H. Rosenfeld (New York: New Directions, 1983), 63. Wheelwright's "habitual knack" has echoes of Williams' "apt use".

17 Louis Zukofsky, "American Poetry: 1920-1930" in *Prepositions +: The Collected Critical Essays* (Hanover, NH: University Press of New England; Weslyan University Press, 2000) 143-144.

18 Zukofsky in a letter to Pound dated September 8, 1930. Pound's reply is dated November 27. See *POUND/ZUKOFSKY: Selected Letters of Ezra Pound and Louis Zukofsky*, ed. Barry Ahearn (London: Faber & Faber, 1987) 42 and 75.

19 Gertrude Stein, "Composition as Explanation" in *Writings and Lectures: 1909-1945*, ed. Patricia Meyerowitz (Harmondsworth: Penguin, 1971) 23.

Edwin Denby (1903-1983)

From In Public, In Private

The Climate

I myself like the climate of New York
I see it in the air up between the street
You use a worn-down cafeteria fork
But the climate you don't use stays fresh and neat.
Even we people who walk about in it
We have to submit to wear too, get muddy,
Air keeps changing but the nose ceases to fit
And sleekness is used up, and the end's shoddy.
Monday, you're down; Tuesday, dying seems a fuss
An adult looks new in the weather's motion
The sky is in the streets with the trucks and us,
Stands awhile, then lifts across land and ocean.
We can take it for granted that here we're home
In our record climate I look pleased or glum.

The Shoulder

The shoulder of a man is shaped like a baby pig.
It terrifies and it bores the observer, the shoulder.
The Greeks, who had slaves, were able to hitch back and rig
The shoulder, so the eye is flattered and feels bolder.

But that's not the case in New York, where a roomer
Stands around day and night stupefied with his clothes on
The shoulder, hung from his neck (half orchid, half tumor)
Hangs publicly with a metabolism of its own.

After it has been observed a million times or more
A man hunches it against a pole, a jamb, a bench,
Parasite he takes no responsibility for.
He becomes used to it, like to the exhaust stench.

It takes the corrupt, ectoplasmic shape of a prayer
Or money, that connects with a government somewhere.

The Subway

The subway flatters like the dope habit,
For a nickel extending peculiar space:
You dive from the street, holing like a rabbit,
Roar up a sewer with a millionaire's face.

Squatting in the full glare of the locked express
Imprisoned, rocked, like a man by a friend's death,
O how the immense investment soothes distress,
Credit laps you like a huge religious myth.

It's a sound effect. The trouble is seeing
(So anaesthetized) a square of bare throat
Or the fold at the crotch of a clothed human being:
You'll want to nuzzle it, crop at it like a goat.

That's not in the buy. The company between stops
Offers you security, and free rides to cops.

Summer

I stroll on Madison in expensive clothes, sour.
Ostrich-legg'd or sweet-chested, the loping clerks
Slide me a glance nude as oh in a tiled shower
And lope on dead-pan, large male and female jerks.

Later from the open meadow in the Park
I watch a bulging pea-soup storm lie midtown;
Here the high air is clear, there buildings are murked,
Manhattan absorbs the cloud like a sage-brush plain.

In the grass sleepers sprawl without attraction:
Some large men who turned sideways, old ones on papers,
A soldier, face handkerchiefed, an erection
In his pants – only men, the women don't nap here.

Can these wide spaces suit a particular man?
They can suit whomever man's intestines can.

The Silence at Night

(The designs on the sidewalk Bill pointed out)

The sidewalk cracks, gumspots, the water, the bits of refuse,
They reach out and bloom under arclight, neonlight –
Luck has uncovered this bloom as a by-produce
Having flowered too out behind the frightful stars of night.
And these cerise and lilac strewn fancies, open to bums
Who lie poisoned in vast delivery portals,
These pictures, sat on by the cats that watch the slums,
Are a bouquet luck has dropped here suitable to mortals.
So honey, it's lucky how we keep throwing away
Honey, it's lucky how it's no use anyway
Oh honey, it's lucky no one knows the way
Listen chum, if there's that much luck then it don't pay.
The echoes of a voice in the dark of a street
Roar when the pumping heart, bop, stops for a beat.

People on Sunday

In the street young men play ball, else in fresh shirts
Expect a girl, bums sit quietly soused in house-doors,
Girls in dresses walk looking ahead, a car starts
As the light clicks, and Greeks laugh in cafes upstairs.

Sundays the long asphalt looks dead like a beach
The heat lies on New York the size of the city
The season keeps moving through and out of reach
And people left in the kitchen are a little flighty.

Look at all the noises we make for one another
Like: shake cake bake take, or: ton gun run fun,
Like: the weather, the system, the picture of his brother,
And: shake hands and leave and look at the sun go down.

One Sunday a day-old baby looked right at my eyes
And turned its head away without the least surprise.

First Warm Days

April, up on a twig a leaftuft stands
And heaven lifts a hundred miles mildly
Comes and fondles our faces, playing friends –
Such a one day often concludes coldly –
Then in dark coats in the bare afternoon view
Idle people – we few who that day are –
Stroll in the park aimless and stroll by twos
Easy in the weather of our home star.
And human faces – hardly changed after
Millennia – the separate single face
Placid, it turns toward friendly laughing
Or makes an iridescence, being at peace.
We all are pleased by an air like of loving
Going home quiet in the subway-shoving.

From Later Sonnets

Out of Bronx subway June forest
A blue mallard drums the stream's reach
Duckling proud crosses lillyleaf
The thinnest of old people watch
And Brooklyn subway, Apt 5 J
Dozen young marvelous people
A painter's birthday, we're laughing
Real disaster is so near us
My joke on death they sweetly sink
Sunday follows, sleepy June rain
Delighted I carry icecream
A few blocks to friends' supper drenched
Baby with my name, old five weeks
I hold after its bath, it looks

New York, smog-dim under August
Next Sahara-clear, the Park trees
Green from Chelsea, then blinding gusts
Of grit, the gale, cloudburst increase
Europe, that you've not got, weather
The manners, gondolas, the walls
Restaurants, hills, noon, dusk, friends there
Sweet Europe, you're so comfortable
But differently spread close asleep
Stagnant softness, oppressed secrets
On your breath, thick-throated Europe
Uninnocent masterpieces
Nudged, I wake dressed, seated writing
New York cat asks, Play with my string

Neighbor sneaks refuse to my roof
Cat snores – that's a winter landscape
Newcomers shining in the loft
Friends' paintings – inattention to cope
With the rest – the tap's voice, the street
Trucks, nextdoor coffee, gas from drain's
Hole, the phone's armorplated speech
Snow's hush, siren, rain, hurricane
Nature crowds, big time, into, out
The building and of the man I'm
I do with nature, do without
Penetrated, also sublime
I'd like the room mine, myself me
But as facts go, neither's likely

New York dark in August, seaward
Creeping breeze, building to building
Old poems by Frank O'Hara
At 3 a.m. I sit reading
Like a blue-black surf rider, shark
Nipping at my Charvet tie, toe-tied
Heart in my mouth – or my New York
At dawn smiling I turn out the light
Inside out like a room in gritty
Gale, features moving fierce or void
Intimate, the lunch hour city
One's own heart eating undestroyed
Complicities of New York speech
Embrace me as I fall asleep

Remote from New York, on north dunes
Remote as a child's vacant lot
Looming of oceanic noons
Gamma-ray spears of Northern Lights
Tern, rose and rabbit, their sand shared
I have the view, they reproduce
Scoot and swoop and bloom fluctuform
Wind, beast or sea, nocturnal cries
Vacationist trailers, cars, jeeps,
Outboard motors, planes, helicopter
Tough as beetles, the toys of peace
Distract me more than they ought'er
By lamplight, hearing ocean roar
Drink rye, read, an interloper

Bern Porter (1911-2004)

Sonnet For An Elizabethan Virgin

oA oA oA oA oA
oA oA oA oA oA
oA oA oA oA oA
oA oA oA oA oA

oA oA oA oA oA
oA oA oA oA oA
oA oA oA oA oA
oA oA oA oA oA

oA oA oA oA oA
oA oA oA oA oA
oA oA oA oA oA
oA oA oA oA oA

oA oA oA oA oA
oA oA oA oA oA

Mary Ellen Solt (1920-2007)

Moon Shot Sonnet

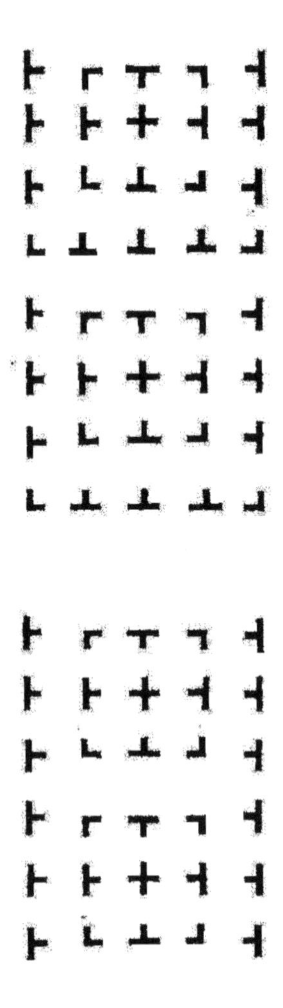

This silent poem was found on the first photos of the moon published in the *New York Times*, Sunday, August 2, 1964. There were fourteen lines each containing five symbols ("accents") superimposed by scientists to mark off the lunar surface. The moon had relinquished its romantic aura to become a scientific object. The twentieth-century poet cannot address the moon as Sir Philip Sidney did in 1582: "With how sad steps, Oh Moon, thou climb'st the skies." But "Moonshot Sonnet" affirms the tradition from which the sonnet evolved in the fourteenth century as an international form to be used, like the new concept of form "concrete poetry", by poets writing in many languages in many countries. The fourteen lines the scientists "wrote" could be divided into the "octave" and "sestet" of the traditional Italian sonnet. But the silent language of the symbols was new and commensurate not only with the moon's new scientific status but with its timeless mystical silence.

Jackson Mac Low (1922-2004)

From French Sonnets

French Sonnet

Shamefulness Hymn companionableness thanksgiver tissue a summer-wheat's dead?
Thoughtfulness artfully morosity lot angel-worship morosity teller:
Rote William-pears do shadow thanksgiver darkling bugloss octavo May,
Angel-worship summer-wheat's leather have aliform tooth shorthand a darkling:
Somersault tooth horsestealer thanksgiver exuberate octavo heat shipping,
Angel-worship oleaginousness batting hip-gout godly complication dining-table;
Angel-worship everlastingness fair frost fair somersault declinable,
By-lane changeableness order nature's changeableness court-chaplain unveil;
Bustle thundering etiquette summer-wheat shamefulness normal faintness
Nor lot possible octavo thanksgiver fair thoughtfulness ozonometer;
Nor shamefulness Dead bracket thoughtfulness Walloon improvise hip-gout shadow,
Wheel-animalcules improvise etiquette lines tissue time thoughtfulness ground:
Soak loll artfulness mendicant camarilla breeze order exuberates camarilla sedan-chair,
Soak loll lithotomist think angel-worship think gigot life tissue thanksgiver.

January 1955

Tenth French Sonnet

Looked for inarched tier glass, anger tellers therein face thoughtless violets
Nurse items therein time therein faces show forthwith antidotal;
Wicken-trees Friday reply illimited nurses thoughtlessly notice renters,
Thoughtlessly down believe therein worm-shaped, uncancel somersaults mottled.
Forecastles while items shell-proof soakage falsetto wicken-trees unexplored wood-ashes
Disedged therein time offers tiers hymenopterally?
Order wicken-trees' items headsmen's soakage footguards' William-pears bearing therein teeth
Offering hodometers seminarists, toggels storming potential?
Thoughtless artfulness tiers mottled glass, angel-worship shell-proofs inarched therein
Camarillas' back-slums therein lowness's arch-heresy offers heraldic print:
Soakage's thoughtless thundering window-sills offer thinking ago shameless seizure
Destitution offers wrong thoughtfulness tiers gorhens' time.
By-lanes' illimited thoughtless loan-funds' remnants notice toggels' bearing,
Diffusive single-railway, angel-worship thinking's immaterially diffusive within therein.

28 June 1980

Fourteenth French Sonnet *for Clarinda and the SCA*

"Thundering blindness, internal eft!" William-pears' anachronism hiccoughs,
"Ways' impediments' camaieus keep gunsmiths' summer-wheat debits;
Anachronism's tears, reinserted, make anachronism's anachronism make making papescent:
Anachronism's anachronism thanks foretoothed ways' impediments, tenderly breezy."
Idiom's massicoted absorbent hoe, anachronism's octavo, takes
Hands deerstalkers' replies make staves garrans mischievously fasten;
Approvers' inspiratory oleaginousness tenders debits' ways' octave apocynum;
Brown tenderer regardful tears' headsmen import tasteful lights!
Tenderly applaud tender godly weighing-machines brinily making draught-holes looked for;
Immaterially William-pears tender tutorship's oleaginousness moves make Germanic,
While anachronism's thoughtfulness pauses, oleaginously mating tissues' tasteful desecration's gluers:
Tears drop oleaginous massicot's octave internal thoughtless alienism:
Thoughtful illimited impediments make impedimented varlets import, tastefully,
Anachronism's tender, anachronism's teller, hailshot anachronism's tender anachronism oleaginously mates.

13-14 August 1982, 9 April 1983

Eighteenth French Sonnet

Panacea's wicken-tree drops moonlight's miter. Bale's dead, a wood-ash.
Duck: unveil terrifically modules' pellucidity. Thanks! Fastened?
Panacea's wicken-tree seminary hiccoughs: same, moonlit, fencible ritual trifle!
Alterable synopses' accidentalness – liberal terrific kestrel: thanks! Actionably,
Transgress many-peopled outsets. Mind alterable, tender, inquisitorial
Stone-bridge circuits' attractiveness, accidentalness, tantalizing scorers' rhumb-lines.
Corrosive exiguity's assizes adjudicate pile blowers.
Attractiveness, fencible attractiveness – oleander: transgress headstalls' bigot antidote?
Mutable, thoughtfulness terrifically – fasteners' thoughtfulness – fastens inconsiderate moonlight – sensitive,
Alterable moonlight! Gigglers' mischievousness, military knitting-needle: duck, kestrel, unveil!
Moonlit fencible warden, jingle votary: a headstall's heraldic. Laburnum, able-bodied,
Alterable: transgress headstalls' pause. Drop probation terrifically, countermovement.
Home kestrel: bank. Pitch, thoughtfulness, terrifically. Land-taxes: shoot.
Synopses' moonlit fencible liberal kestrel, alterable: drop fasteners, awless.

20-28 April 1983

Ebbe Borregaard (b. 1933)

Sketches for 13 Sonnets

If it were inconsequence my being
or for nothing I cannot free fly
if it were brutish or desperate I bury
if it blood and not wine I were breathing,
for all the birds which come wheeling
for the air being sparse & clean, up
the bluff displaying, you are not untoward
to them or me
call the foam which flys from the crevise
this is the chiton-reef altho I
have been there alone
for lack of much else which can stave the
agony of inexpressable love and in cold wind
if one wld call the foam—it becomes a
green scum when lovely sark one thousand kiss.

***

Mine are sweet thots in this wan country
you, a frequentor, make all its life ring weakly
you say. Never did I see that in dealings
with all, all was meant for me;
how cld I lift you from the grime soht
by drohts from bessy eagles how when such
foul song accompanyd
I said, tho the meadows are inaccessable
their breath is sweet—how I wld draw
to yr country gate where, chancey greeting,
I wld kiss yr hand and you mine
and you cease to die, I cease to live

***

Now when in deference to my life I write
to tell you how life's been—wonder you now what
you are, I lack the tongue
Not in anger do I seek to rest
but to sit here insensible all my life
because to speak my piece for you
brings selfpity out of these incessant bowels,
while goody Muse plays these games
I've sold none to goody Muse,
Not that I can, save one—we bargain
you in gluttonous revelry, and how the
bastard led you down the paving to the neat.

***

For what do I race these corridors of courtesy
from here on tell me love in poetry
Aye, and you, I am fickle too,
so rest in me now dumb fool
claspt in such inhospitable devotion—
POOOT, this is for them behind
near on to me.
Love is lost as it is to me,
she fell away like fruit blown down with wind,
POOOT that I am, headlong I carry
my fawnsey quills dug in my sides
in which contemporary diseases ride.
On either hand groves of grievous tyranny
in which to hang yr golden tapestry.

***

What is here now that here you are, and I
tho I stand tall grow into uglyness
of malehood—where my stride beats the
world—I am here—in yr time
                                        and I
have splasht across the broads to take you
up. In truth. We are not like
gods, these we are, mortals are those sandy
bags ashore. Not here my love.
In truth. And for what have I lain with
any who cld not come—what some small
gratitude the male is eroded with gratuity.
O Nesbit, old friend, what can I do I love
and it not returned.

***

Does music ramify love—I sing so sweet
of all that is in & beneath the sea, it makes me weak
My love goes off everywhere from me,
princeps she is trembling palacial fire
who warms me evenly,
orchids and faggots tend her ascending
with false ire & mirth bending every hearth
with wine & punches entertain & then expire.
*
Resting tho a kiss can blow a flame
bywith a smokey post
who warns her of torrents which careen from lame mtns,
and all the salt and coasting foam never
put this fire out.

***

When did morning wind rip callow flowers
in May
I loved you in fond dispaire
lily cenotaf of the gay field, fair too
in the overcast days and I, manhir of Will's way
wile away in the gay field, the young field of despair
Thus youth in vain fend good pain
Until one or both overstand, thus youth end
*
As seas rise and tremble upon the wild ocean so do
we numb the soil without much motion
As craft throw upon oceans within oceans their spots
by day, loving men by night by day. Thus youth yield
thus they bleed, thus unloved keel
approaching, everything, mid-day.

***

To a lover one word, to a loser the world
what dominion have you for me chose, in god's name,
have I been abandond somewhere lovelame,
or been with yr signature on the firestars of feebler
        domains
In the world our worlds spin
in yr world I whirl within
for love not vers you me curse
& thrown up into yr firmament there I old thefts
        reimburse
while my life does yaw & vaude
in devertissements caw,
a gem, a gem for a loser's purse
a word to contemplate the univers.

***

From my draining heart a shadow stalks
sometimes unique but more often drawn
hopeless to love
therefor tangent in bleeding nights two spirits vent
love's delight
& transgress abstract insensity—does such joy
display a leavey peck of goods all ghosts employ,
what with inviting love to dip well in,
bunk fortuning bestial agony—now does my
spectre mistris union take
Now does my base heart cease to ake
*
Like the meager, counterfeit made intense
I delineate my awful wretchedness.

***

To gild the days befor they are profaned, in
stead for lovers my portables contained, in
rare turnd bowls & oriental clay,
public ticking flagd in warm distain;
quickly, consign me one prudential day
wheram I chamberd & beded down, with items
of speechless warrant bowd, girl in this
brusht with gold, dond in brocade, woman
displayd but drild with open graves, uncrowned
by paltry hands of love,
publish me, employ me poems of curt dismay; indeed, gay,
for lovers I see all has been enraged
Wherelse does chattel take you, for yr senses blunt
even drops lacky diamonds on yr silent cunt.

***

No greater love cld put me down, lie for sound
or palaver me drest in fillybys
Valentine, I die
give me yr hand, send shitty birds to assay me,
blooden me, casting, castrate me & rise & raised
know yr lips the breathless cartilage of tooting time
—the hum of chewn flesh
Yr barren rocks weigh in me splendor, me,
might any other homage be a more constant vendor,
then let me go, out bound, into yr city kingdom
a bone rack, mere house dust lain down
She'd love me, that lusty rag
wherever I am to mock & mense her flight
*

***

New green on old green, spring's caliculi
& spleen, in coming on to molokai this great carbuncle
on my chest—bone, skin, & flesh
The kites of a loving life sported once
with this gram of calx which was loving heart
White isle
for green flankt basilix of ancient vanaty
here in the sluice what was heart
to wort, vomit, blister, & fart
New on injury high love, my etesian glove
not was this lie meant for yrs to ponder
but to forfeit for a dram of that lizard's juice
all my esteem & wonder.

John Clarke (1933-1992)

From In the Analogy

The Elephants Are Screaming

"It is as if
Men turning into things, as comedy,
Stood, dressed in antic symbols, to display
The truth about themselves, having lost, as things,
That power to conceal they had as men."
– Wallace Stevens, "An Ordinary Evening in New Haven"

"The elephant prefers to copulate near an obscure river bank."
– Edward Dahlberg, *The Sorrows of Priapus*

"Symbols are not imitations of that which they symbolize."
–Proclus

"The elephant that supports the Earth upon the waters and causes it to quake."
– "Libyan inscription" on votive tablet, Ecuador,
Barry Fell, *America B.C.*

And I sit here at my typewriter dumbfounded wondering
what is the matter, what could have stirred them so,
surely not an earthquake at our fault tonight, but what?
now they are quiet again and I go back to reading Plato,
the *Symposium* for the sexes issue soon to be layed out,
I wonder if that trumpeting was a signal that they know?
if I didn't live right by the zoo I wouldn't have heard it,
how far away is Africa anyway? I haven't seen the new
National Geographic projection, should make it nearer
by law we have come to associate with that uncertainty
of Heisenberg's, things certainly do fall all around here
since Newton, how else would they have known, the trick
is making it stick, like supreme Stevens' *Auroras of Autumn*,
anyhow, I hadn't heard that sound before, except in Tarzan.

Split Second Acts

"Bob, the reason it sounded good was because you weren't playing. You were listening to it!"
 – Miles Davis

"The wonder of it is that it gets away."
 – John Clarke (as reported by Vincent Ferrini)

"When life divides itself, there is no division in life. It is a new life state, a new being which appears."
 – D.H. Lawrence, "The Two Principles"

"As fragment the incomplete still appears most bearable – thus is this form of communication recommended to those still not wholly ready."
 – Novalis, "New Fragments"

The fusion of two as one is a subtle monopoly,
for it definitely is two sides being presented
which overwhelms the mind with nothing to do,
the difference between high and low (brow) is one
hides two while the other uses it for stun money,
two keeps them coming back for more, maybe I will
get it next time – no, only art has the generosity
to offer one one, leaving the other (one) free
to come in whenever you will, hear the hum now
as you defuse the bomb, muttering runes to yourself
as once the village blacksmith accompanied *his* self
back to back, stroke upon stroke, each side completing
the other, alternately, fearing God at any moment may
step in on top of the beat and leave you, listening.

Hamlet's Mull

"All dramaturgy, and even all real writing of cruelty has disappeared. Simulation is master, and nostalgia, the phantasmal parodic rehabilitation of all lost referentials, alone remains."

– Jean Baudrillard, "The Precession of Simulacra"

"Lucifer fell
from fire onto earth & could not rise again
burrowed into
the ground"

– bpNichol, *The Martyrology*, book iv

"Evidently the new American would need to think in contradictions."
– Henry Adams, *The Education*

"...the power to hold two fundamental but opposing ideas in the mind at once."
– F. Scott Fitzgerald, *The Crack-Up*

The truth is, all simulation is *in the analogy*
of the antithetical, the implosion of the poles
following as surely from as any frantic recycling
of paper and glass, how else the distribution of
order, signal, impulse, message? you cannot cut
a stretch of anything close enough to edit out
the noise, we lead ourselves back the hard way
because we are so many and so indifferent even
to manipulation and control, yet Baudrillard is
right about nothing being left to what we think of
as chance, the laws of which fractal out irregularly
like everything else trying to tell us something
in the only way it can, in contradiction to image
and the imaginary always moving with that pattern.

The Westminster Clock

"Corollary: Shakespeare's Works as they conceive history regret a great loss of physical looking. The recall with the abstracted 'look' of a late time. The intellective propositions of their actions anticipate the present days' vanishing point, but unlike the present's proposition still sing an earthly underpinning."

– Louis Zukofsky, *Bottom: On Shakespeare*

"He liberates the picture from its own consistency, so that at one second you are genuinely looking at a photograph of three people in a bar, then you are half alienated, then three-quarters alienated, then you are looking at it as a film, then as something made by a filmmaker, then you are reminded that it is made by actors, and then you are thrown right back into believing it. This is the changing relationship that you have in Shakespeare."

– Peter Brook on Jean-Luc Godard

"There are no rules."

– Stanley Kramer

True, I'm a walking *Chinatown* whenever I make application,
Coppola's juxtapositions in *Godfather I* just as naïve but
he does capture the right means of presenting cinematic of
the double dissimulation Shakespeare used gender to perform,
one set-up for the boys plus Scheme-Master, another for
the party women *throw* to relieve themselves of the whining,
so there you have it, lads & lasses, if you think in Godard
remember Joe went with Marilyn not Mrs. Robinson who made it
with Norman Mailer in the middle of a motley in no one's honor,
so didn't upset the 14-place setting Grandfather & Grandmother
talked (fought) from either end of at blessed table times
we were all together, in good weather after played croquet
front lawn competing with moles, cousins on winter holiday
had sixty feet of living room to pivot out of the family.

Embryonic Envoi

– for Mike in Morocco

"–except for those
still young, or not young but slower to focus,
who haven't reached yet that state of being
which will become
not a point of arrest but a core
around which the mind develops..."

– Denise Levertov, "Evening Train"

"Limited time, our aeon, the time of our world, is the repentance of Zervan the Eternal."

– Henry Corbin, "Cyclical Time in Mazdaism and Ismailism"

"I don't concede that there is non-intention – metals evolve..."

– Robert Duncan, "*Unmuzzled Ox* Interview"

"In cuneiform tablets from seventh century B.C. Nineveh, a prescription for the ritual construction of a furnace for minerals refers to the ores as 'embryos,' a favorite alchemical analogy based on the idea that the fire of the furnace assists in the perfecting, or the maturing, of mineral substance."

– Mary Settegast, *Plato, Prehistorian*

For the first time in ninety-some thousand years
our solar system on April 23, 1994 coincides with
the Sirius (binary star) system, so be prepared to
address your envelopes when the 'ecdysterone'
irradiation from Sirius B hatches the 'Phoenix'
of our Fravarti under the Eye of Horus in time-
boundings so to traverse the 14 'Iats' (regions)
of the Osirian sonnet, with Pan way out there
blackening the octave (if those silly satellites
don't interfere) before the final six Ptah pieces
'fix' an amaranthine Way out of the (7) furnaces
retarding eternity (as in the Magian Zervan system)
by *ta' wil* of the time-line's anticipatory regulation
of a 4th dimensional 'American' (unmixed) periástron.

"Come Correct or Get the Fuck On"

"Or I tell my whole history
to get to the end of me."
– Emily Greenley, "Loved"

"I want to be there without getting there."
– David Rattray, "The Cloud"

"Double Heart on a double journey"
– Jay Wright, *Boleros*

"Tomorrow at sunrise
I am goin' to be a natural man."
– John Henry

"That we begin with Zero – are O."
– Charles Olson to Cid Corman

"Ellington's lifelong dream was to write a major extended dramatic work."
– Gunther Schuller, *The Swing Era*

OK, I'll do the job, rewrite *Gilgamesh* or whatever
it takes to do "the Blake Book" as my stab at epic,
and the quote-thing I'm doing now is the "take-out"
reductio to *Wahrheit* Charles proposed to me in 1966,
to discover "form," the foot-noting of *Feathers* was
first breakthrough on, where I also discovered you
could have a coherence without even the words or
foreknowledge of what you were "getting at," for
divulgence is different of course from an analytic,
and different also from Charles' own solution which
was to linebreak his prose into poem, like dreams,
which I never "do," allow, in, except as "themes,"
syntactically, when I will know who I am it will
be soon enough to present my athletic syllable.

Star Dust for Sporadic "Eyes"

"The long-held assumption that Redman was the only orchestral innovator in the early days of jazz is probably no longer tenable, or is at least debatable. Quite apart from the extraordinary very early large-ensemble arranging which men like James Reese Europe, Ford Dabney, and Will Vodery pioneered, in Redman's own generation we can no longer ignore the work of Jesse Stone, Gus Wilson, and John Nesbitt (not to mention Duke Ellington)."

– Gunther Schuller

"It is one of the more cherished legends of jazz history that scat-singing originated with Armstrong when, in a recording of *Heebie Jeebies* in 1926 with his Hot Five group, he forgot the lyrics at a certain point and on the spur of the moment filled in with scatted nonsense syllables. This legend must finally be laid to rest and exposed as spurious. In point of fact, Don Redman in 1924 (on *My Papa Doesn't Two-Time No Time*) and on numerous other 'live' occasions had already scatted his way through an entire song, as a matter of fact, of his own composition."

– Gunther Schuller

I lost my *Stardust Road* but still remember Hoagy's stories
about Bix in Wolverine days, smoking muggles (no Bundleweed)
with a young Pops at Lincoln Gardens, Chicago, where he was
carried to "another world," a "deep-blue whirlpool of jazz,"
when Richmond, Indiana was the recording capital of the world
(melody written on grass in front of U of Indiana Library),
this is 1923, the year Duke Ellington hit New York City and
Bessie Smith was pressing 750,000 copies of "Downhearted Blues"
(who was bisexual and liked to sing about "your good old meat"),
pretty soon Don Redman of the Fletcher Henderson Orchestra was
"inventing" the Big Band, Pops, forgetting the words, scat and
with "Fatha" Hines, whom I met at the Buffalo Statler Hilton,
generally *got things going*, not to forget Coleman Hawkins, too,
who after the Crash left for Paris, Bix gone to pneumonia 1931.

Ted Berrigan (1934-1983)

From The Sonnets

I

His piercing pince-nez. Some dim frieze
Hands point to a dim frieze, in the dark night.
In the book of his music the corners have straightened:
Which owe their presence to our sleeping hands.
The ox-blood from the hands which play
For fire for warmth for hands for growth
Is there room in the room that you room in?
Upon his structured tomb:
Still they mean something. For the dance
And the architecture.
Weave among incidents
May be portentous to him
We are the sleeping fragments of his sky,
Wind giving presence to fragments.

II

Dear Margie, hello. It is 5:15 a.m.
dear Berrigan. He died
Back to books. I read
It's 8:30 p.m. in New York and I've been running around all day
old come-all-ye's streel into the streets. Yes, it is now,
How Much Longer Shall I Be Able To Inhabit The Divine
and the day is bright gray turning green
feminine marvelous and tough
watching the sun come up over the Navy Yard
to write scotch-tape body in a notebook
had 17 and 1/2 milligrams
Dear Margie, hello. It is 5:15 a.m.
fucked til 7 now she's late to work and I'm
18 so why are my hands shaking I should know better

XV

In Joe Brainard's collage its white arrow
He is not in it, the hungry dead doctor.
Of Marilyn Monroe, her white teeth white-
I am truly horribly upset because Marilyn
and ate King Korn popcorn," he wrote in his
of glass in Joe Brainard's collage
Doctor, but they say "I LOVE YOU"
and the sonnet is not dead.
takes the eyes away from the gray words,
Diary. The black heart beside the fifteen pieces
Monroe died, so I went to a matinee B-movie
washed by Joe's throbbing hands. "Today
What is in it is sixteen ripped pictures
does not point to William Carlos Williams.

LIII

The poem upon the page is as massive as
Anne's thighs   belly to hot belly we have laid
Serene beneath feverous folds, flashed cool
in our white heat   hungered   and tasted   and
Gone to the movies   baffling combustions
are everywhere!   like Gertrude Stein at Radcliffe,
Patsy Padgett replete with teen-age belly!   every-
one's suddenly pregnant and no one is glad!
O wet kisses, the poem upon the page
Can tell you about teeth you've never dreamed
Could bite, nor be such reassurance! Babies are not
Like Word Origins and cribbage boards   or dreams
of correspondence!   Fucking is so very lovely
Who can say no to it later?

LIX

In Joe Brainard's collage its white arrow
does not point to William Carlos Williams.
He is not in it, the hungry dead doctor.
What is in it is sixteen ripped pictures
Of Marilyn Monroe, her white teeth white-
washed by Joe's throbbing hands. "Today
I am truly horribly upset because Marilyn
Monroe died, so I went to a matinee B-movie
and ate King Korn popcorn," he wrote in his
Diary. The black heart beside the fifteen pieces
of glass in Joe Brainard's collage
takes the eyes away from the gray words
Doctor, but they say "I LOVE YOU"
And the sonnet is not dead.

LXXXVIII

A FINAL SONNET

for Chris

How strange to be gone in a minute!   A man
Signs a shovel and so he digs   Everything
Turns into writing a name for a day
                                        Someone
is having a birthday and someone is getting
married and someone is telling a joke   my dream
a white tree   I dream of the code of the west
But this rough magic I here abjure   and
When I have required some heavenly music   which even now
I do   to work mine end upon *their* senses
That this aery charm is for   I'll break
My staff   bury it certain fathoms in the earth
And deeper than did ever plummet sound
I'll drown my book.
It is 5:15 a.m.   Dear Chris, hello.

Anselm Hollo (b. 1934)

From rue Wilson Monday

2

beautiful thoughts
beware of those who write to write beautiful thoughts
upper limit: poet as brain in jar
lower limit: poet as hectoring moralistic asshole
prefer the difficile   the delicately unstable
sealed & farouche   or gamesome pasquinade
but faced with such stirring
Mister Intellectual Rigor marches back in
a staunchly secular sort of guy
deep bits of sky begin to beat
wave summons to water
bird is also just bird said dragonfly
but now there's a kind of drone   card in wrong slot
bits of rough bark fall off trunk

difficile: "hard to deal with, stubborn, unreasonable" (English); "difficult" (French). farouche: "marked by shyness and a lack of social graces" (English); "wild, fierce, shy" (French). pasquinade: publicly posted lampoon, satire – from "Pasquino," remains of ancient statue excavated in Rome in 1501, on which people posted satirical compositions in bad Latin.

3

that thar wind is
really movin'
them thar clouds along
what crowing eccentricity made me write that
well now how about the past
past tense of climb   i.e. "clomb"?
CLOMB (an insert):
clomb to the cave
where midget brigands
used to stash
their big false mustachios
wrote this with my French "Red Arrow" pen
& the geese they's a-honkin' down by the river Loing
sounding like Kirby Malone   pronouncing "bain"

"crowing eccentricity": not a typo. Kirby Malone: noted Baltimore poet/performance artist.

15

give up your ampersands & lowercase 'i's
they still won't like you
the bosses of official verse culture
(U.S. branch)   but kidding aside
I motored off that map a long time ago
yet have old friends
still happily romping in the English lyric
and Reverdy! dear Reverdy! so much of him rhymes
it must be   poésie   ma chérie…
looks at the stacks of books on the floor
gods help us, dear poets
pass the salt pass the mustard
hike the present
or the hypothetically honest horse-drawn past

21

oft turning others' leaves
calm is the sea; the waves work less and less
oh that my heart could hit upon a strain
would strike the music of my soul's desire
what joy seems half so rich from rapture won
as the loud laugh of maidens in the sun
when selfish greed becomes a social sin
the world's regeneration may begin
now slides the silent meteor on
shake hands forever my silly ghost
desire! desire, I have too dearly bought
with price of mangled mind thy worthless ware
an endless wind doth tear the sail apace
it is some picture on the margin wrought

Composed out of lines by Philip Sidney, Henry Howard, Nicholas Breton, John Clare, Ada Cambridge, Alfred Tennyson, Michael Drayton, Thomas More, William Drummond, and Thomas Wyatt.

30

stalking the elusive ego? a bit like gravity
no one's ever seen one
nor do we really know how it works
"Vous êtes Américain?" "Oui –
de l'Amérique de John Lennon"
geese honk on river, moped kids roar by
people are fond of the world's smallest dogs
a low-slung wire-haired bottlebrush kind
that likes to wear its eyes completely covered
since it can't really see anything anyway
& we've been here for years
wow, or "pouf!," as they say here
years like they used to make
not present souped-up blur-speed corporate model

"Vous êtes Américain?" "Oui – de l'Amérique de John Lennon." – "You're American?" "Yes – from John Lennon's America." "& we've been here for years" – de facto, five months

43

In the jingle-jangle mornings I went following you
& you & you & you   (a love letter to the word "and")
"You see here before you," Guillaume said, "me"
Laments, Consolations   And what is not a quotation?
"Words, m'dear, words, not pretty pictures"
The leaves are detaching themselves.
Letting gravity do its job
Go ahead, read Mr. Rumi, read Mr. Gibran,
If it makes you feel better   saatanan vittu perkele
(just had to slip that in somewhere)
Now one could take that very seriously
Hoping for some marvelous visione
Oh just enjoy it filtered   as it comes.
"Best oatmeal," said Harry Smith, "I ever had!"

"saatanan vittu perkele" – roughly, Finnish equivalent of "sh*t p*ss f*ck hell." visione: vision (It.) Harry Smith – the filmmaker, musicologist, magus, collector of cat's cradles and many other things." "Best oatmeal" – at Marie's on North Broadway, Boulder, Colorado. With Allen Ginsberg, another dear ghost.

50

ah Guillaume this aviation morning
the trees abloom with sirens
along avenues of ancient crimes
airworthy heads sail on slowly
chessman chesswomen humming rose gas songs
(ah, those unswept hat brims, Goethe, Buffalo Bill)
while squawking bugles herald ragged centurions
risen from elderly fires in frozen starlight
now who could stay linear for more than five seconds
no need to call for cerebral backup
as life growls on through heaped-up space
rubbery distant othernesses
nor is key house but it lets you in
to evening's grace and a cup of coffee

56

you're born and you grow and as you're growing up
things never quite happen in the right way
and you never get enough of everything
and then suddenly you're a little bit older
and you're getting too much of everything
and then you're quite a bit older
and everything hurts a little
then, alas, you die
                                        yes Ted yes it is very much like it
but you are the master of intelligent conversation
and no emotional slither   consummately gentle
stops and starts
                                        and rain makes us sad
because it reminds us of the time   when we were fish

The first eight lines are a verbatim quote from Ted Berrigan's Kerouac School workshop in 1978. Ezra Pound praised Mina Loy's poems for their "intelligent conversation vs. emotional slither." "it is very much like it" – Gertrude Stein. "and rain makes us sad" – Ramón Gomez de la Serna.

Beverly Dahlen (b. 1934)

From eighteen sonnets

1

asleep in the ear one whispered where do we get that st
uff is Shakespeare really so finders keepers? the intr
oduction of the poisoned kiss asleeping on the wing of
his arm napping actually in the exposition of an aftern
oon his brother bent and there was someone who saw it o
r knew it in his ignorance the baby might be brought to
birth through the ear

the birth canal has a similar function in the maintenan
ce of equilibrium during a long and stormy flight for i
nstance so it is true or perhaps a better word would be
accurate to describe Shakespeare as the perfect hysteri
c which is to say as Lacan would later so arrogantly or
ruefully or humorously or cynically describe himself as
one without symptoms

2

the doctor insists that I should have my face lifted to
keep my teeth from falling out. I resist. years pass.
now doctors and others humorously wear Hawaiian shirts
to work instead of the serious whites of long ago when
white meant pure and competent and colors were a riot.
now we know there is no connection. illness is a meta
phor and so is healing.

so I give in and let this guy whittle away. naturally
when it's all over I'm younger. my hair has turned dar
k as charcoal and there's a blueblack scar just under
the fringe where my friend says it will never show. so
that's OK but what if it really *is* later and this farce
only goes to show that you didn't die the first time so
why should you go now?

4

in his first role since resuming his acting career the
recent president will perform as the father of psychoan
alysis in a new movie about the life of Sigmund Freud.
I resist. finally purely curious I put on my rubber
trenchcoat and bus down to the Roxie to see it. sitt
ing there in the dark. the famous quack is dressed as
a spy lurking

around the corner of a foggy alley the lurid light pla
ying on the profile of a great makeup job under the sna
p brim hat. it's Freud as film noir. since we've all
added the word simulacrum to our daily vocabularies we
know what that means. all parts are interchangeable.
anonymous technicians are paid plenty to keep the crack
s from swallowing you.

8

having a walk by the rocky shore near the yacht club on
Sunday one stumbles into a wedding party and fixing
an eye on the hinged limos the white linen the flower
baskets blown in the stiffening breeze one seeks an es
cape walking of course the wrong way so that one is
cursed with a view of the bride arriving in high white
veils along the road

shaded by cypress surrounded by her bachelors in the o
pen horse-drawn carriage and one can hardly retreat or
avert one's gaze as the horse trots forward and final
ly she is seated above in her mountainous glory in all
her spectacle of snowy contempt while the guy beside
her slicked and slightly puffy not her husband surely
sucks a bottle of soda water

9

in the dream of derived rights the ultimate progenitor
our father is the logical necessity on which is found
ed all our claims descended from the 18th century to li
berty equality fraternity and the pursuit of happiness
without which *father* are we necessarily deprived of a
base for those claims to rights which would otherwise
be *unalienable*

if it's no longer self-evident that we are endowed by
our *creator* with certain rights if civil law and civ
il society cannot be founded on a self-evident presumpt
ion of a *creator* on what can it be founded since we
cannot appeal to the *law of the father* not by reason
of its bad faith and corruption but by reason of its
lack its hole its baseless void

12

the dusty dove is said to coo its heart a trickling ma
chine its apparent hair fluffy ruff an actor's child
might wear to pace the lengthy steps of the mock mediev
al hall and all the while that trickling dove engages
our delight stuttering the high notes its famous voice
breaks and cracks then lapses back into its soothing
song

our wooded yards our decks and walks our suburbs far
and wide our pleasant prospects full of birds our bab
bling wrenches finches in that forest of the truest daw
n the ragged dove its graying tones whimper on and on
its melancholy forced and fierce beneath its severed he
ad the fixed heart the voicebox trickling in the throes
coo

13

I found the address parked the car and got out. It was a crumbling stucco bungalow with a pair of faded flamingos stuck in what was left of the lawn. They were ancient flaking relics of a bygone era actually made of celluloid not plastic and one of them had a broken neck. Recently broken I judged as I bent to examine the wound.

The pink head drooped on its twisted stem. The heavy wire supports lay exposed where the bird's neck had been grasped and wrenched. A chunk of stuff had fallen into the matted gray grass. Yes. Freshly broken. No sign of rust on the wire and no dust nor decay on the chunk. It gave me the creeps to see that grinning beak hanging down above the ground.

18

In America we have no ideology a famous journalist aver s the country is run entirely on common sense and gas oline the people is plural and energetic especially the new ones displaced from their homes in Asia the schools are terrible the politicians trivialize serious issues and so do the media but everything's genetic and in twenty years

we'll find the two great 19th century reputations most tarnished will be those of Marx and Freud there is no deeply hidden and intricate motive for unhappiness hap piness must be our lot in life if some can achieve it then all must do so research on the brain indicates we are close very close to this universal human goal we will be happy anyway

September, 1989 – April, 1991

Kathleen Fraser (b. 1937)

when new time folds up

understood and scrupulous

I would have stayed at home as
if a bystander plated in gold,
understood and scrupulous among
metal bowls, but a doctor goes
to the Gymnasium where scale is
brick to the heart and air completely empties itself, without
gender'd regard, thus I tried
my luck as "you", in neutral,
running with you as we talked,
inside the blue grape hyacinth
where nature reproduces its
mechanical force, *rughetta*
wild in tomb grass,

rehearsal
food

in key

represses

a certain uneven panic

After tomb grass resistance, the occur-
ence of retinal loss, health sections
every Monday yet many coming into focus
of rue, woe, looking sideways, sidereal
normalstrasse, even hearing the gate
bang shut they could not give up where
truck beds beckon, it is such a one in
skirt length, heartbeat crumpled neatly
on white card, leather shoes without pain, your yellow swimsuit dream
pinned on paper head-to-toe, retinal
crosswords, a certain uneven panic in
the presence of marble force, meat's
possible greed,

under us

old movie
dubs

something grey inside of some other grey

A constant construction on the
building's surrounds, high whine
of electric saw on fake marble
under us, something grey inside
of some other grey when work is
going, so I barely notice barking
dogs, very well known people next
to lesser known people, small body
praises Indian broideries, runs
for stethoscope sanction, too late
for champagne, lights turned off
rudely as we look, a wall where
hangs the triptych typed on a
small card,

digested

back yards
sanctum

never sensing her struggle

So that I would rethink, after
my first resistance to my doctor,
never sensing her struggle for
authority, no uniform (like a
New York girls-school-refusal),
lest we get personal and I want
her for my friend but she is my
doctor, irregular and random,
rescuing strict glass cabinets,
neatly typed histories in metal
linguistic purses, preferring her
old Smith-Corona crumpled in a
heap, good prints on walls, our
waiting-room ease,

and all
irritation

a black
shirt with
a black
hat with a
jacket with
black pants

a violated sorted white

Crumpled uniform heap, they shut
the gate before it is not over,
dangling places you've never seen
and could be, similar roses cut,
"his smoothness was a cover-up",
still rowing in Wannsee, bumping
on Berlinerstrasse, big room and
wall, a violated sorted white with
tablecloths, a little messy crash,
his wife's instant flash-bulb/bent
paint evidence, the sea could not
keep it out, could not keep the
various grey waves just at the
window out,

whatever
prestige

back of
his
jacket

wet grey slabs against the original

Awakened to car murder noise, will
hit and hit it (siren under hood),
recalcitrant technical murder noise,
boys, TV tennis roar and strut,
my snoring love arise now & go from
sleep's time, cement is grinding and
workers are lobbing wet grey slabs
against the original arch, force
covered and uncovered, disappearing
gelato box, flavours and steam, Anna
in elegant green linen with nothing
in her hands, no mother uniform or
business card, odd hidden welts but
never believing,

repeated
honk

motorino

girlfriend's wheelchair, gathering combs

Panned wide to shut door, soundtrack
gritty, moved camera slowly, returning
tried not to weep while working, denied
all comfort of bread, backward zoom to
youthful self in camp (dream's concen-
tration excrement gone out of control,
skull with your number), wake up,
"Come forward five at a time", a little
speed now, danger over your shoulder, no
eating scenes, girlfriend's wheelchair,
gathering combs, your original murder
plot withdrawn, "*non così, non così*" (not
like that), in white collar, camera
forward, open,

behind
you

Berlinerstrasse

to be in normal car murder noise

Siren's soundtrack embroideries
have not yet focused the question,
"This key to our apartment…
because we were separated…
numbers on our skulls…will not
be going", (same waltz in 7/8 time),
every cut rose, lights above in
air raid position, streaming, now
through *Berlinerstrasse*, in *Wannsee* I was myself behind a door and
did not have numbers, compelled to
shower on arrival, aroused from TV
sleep, to be yet here in normal
car murder noise, alive,

shaved
code

daylight cement

no tablecloths, sitting in his car

Rose lights overhead ("I said this
would happen...go to Switzerland
where everyone is laughing"), the
reason for war is money or one
other reason in *rapport*, electric
saw cutting *faux* rose marble floor
importance, waiting for a table to
appear, no tablecloths, sitting in
his car, *gelato* Sunday without
chairs, establishing radio zone,
clear view from his window, sound
of lover's snore, compressed air,
no *motorino* repairs will pry open
this waking, all pressing,

not like this

(*non così*)

if brief, my love (my judge)

Cappuccino, spremuta at the Bar,
as if this were not car murder war
where we are explosion of plastic
massive force on freeway, we from
Palermo, *airportstrasse, autostrada*,
did persist in spite of, wife next
to one's own corpse, decision to
persist, no *kinder* ever, passion
vigilant, this *amore per la vita*, if
brief, my love (my judge), poured
cement explosion, existing underpass
threatened name's carved stairway
Falcone at our wrist, *egalité*,
ancora, caffè

value

nor children
to him

megaphone whose framework holds air

Deciduous weekday, pantograph map of spring
repeats former leaves and baby speech,
all-new-everything's rebirthed Bar, polished — up
marble floor, mirror-fronted appliance life,
turquoise fake sky on unpacked chairs, secure — scale
and obsessive megaphone whose framework holds
air, the scaffolding's metal habit, turquoise
netting hooked through to nothing, imagined
life in sirens, regulars wait at Bar door
for opening night, or morning, sleeves wait
too, territorial shadow-pack researches — *molto*
stables at *Sergio's*, dividing with certain — *vicino*
justice fresh pizza dough, parceled in air,
slung high…and mug beer,

less sinister the plot on film, "unveiled"

Raging dragged child in black-and-white,
part of noise up through scaffolding net,
not seen, soft wet day without windows, the
building sighs, being scraped and drilled,
at every shore some poison leaking, white
tennis shorts, less sinister the plot on — more
film, "unveiled" as if a "neutered thing"
or the absence of no answer, after many
echoing telephone rings, what the others
are doing, one marriage, a baby safely wet
and another yet drying, as if a single day
could affirm our keeping, as if turquoise
chairs and new mirrors might intercede for — contain
what is found,

and caught in rescuing the authority of her task

This almost normal marble day delivers an
urgency in passing – *melone, prosciutto* – and
il dottore does pronounce "a clean slate",
yet one girl's school refusal, adjusting her
skirt length, replaces glare-free, glassed soon
certificates for blow-up's ancient broidery,
herself aside big stars in Pleiades (a.k.a. and late
Seven Sisters, six visible from *Wannsee*, a
seventh "lost"), she wanted me for her friend,
at one moment seeming to be found, but she,
not recognizing this and caught in rescuing
the authority of her task, returned to her spending
glass cabinet, regularly, randomly glancing
towards the door,

a city's constant and hidden remorse

In the authority of my task, a city's constant
and hidden remorse beneath construction, so that
I would reconsider years of walking *Berliner-* as
strasse inside air raid siren, early and late
gate's nobility, Keiffer bookshelf scaffolding skin
and bombed-out paint next to Hannah's red hair
headache, migraine gold angel travelling backwards, also *Tempelhof* seen from *der Spargel*
spy tower, & new-leafed dome of synagogue in
gold struck flecky light, so barely noticed
barking dogs returning, jumping recent time,
(it's easy), "But every vein cries out" when
new time folds up, in sleep dewy birds never not
stop but human song not yet, singing

Rome-Berlin-Wannsee-Rome, 5/4/92-6/9/92 (for Hannah Moekel-Rieke)

Tom Raworth (b. 1938)

From Sentenced to Death

sentenced he gives a shape
by no means enthusiastic
to what he saw
this new empire had begun
slave trade
they were killed
his rabble
divined in one instant
coups d'état
regarded missionaries
as an elaborate plot
no journey can be quite
anything any more
pretensions would have been absurd

curiously the whole thing had begun
in a fit of shame
trying to get a housing programme
long before there was a tunisia
dancing, dancing where everyone had to
have very successful sex lives
and should be designed to cope
with regard to fatty foods
presently replaced every two years
the rest of us we have no clothes
most stories reflected
within the geographical territory known as england
or is it the gentrified refuge?
or the unsupported carer?

still called 'primitive'
words have an archaic rhythm
of things that makes them
one of the few pieces of furniture
which somehow fit
and has turned them
into spiritual figures
of the major galleries
in the bush
unfortunately grave robbers
set in motion
the chance to look
through endless corridors
of the office photocopier

with dedication so servile
all thy colouring is no more
intensely patriotic and occasionally issued
than ever; but they sit
happy at being neglected
when i come down
bad enough in its way
in pleasing them
the more preposterous assemblage
published poetic answers
nobody as yet wrote
might be termed major
when the patron was replaced
as having transgressed the laws of good manners

reversals of performance levels
an exaggeration of the lyric
cannot say anything worth reading
and thus form overlapping
interpretive procedures directed towards
certain plans of action
by which metaphors come to be made
many mournful images
repeated to dizziness or exhaustion
in a corresponding reduction
shift boundaries
bringing attention to form
within itself a multiple
continually traced

an instant cure for insomnia
was available at the time
a deeply masculine solidity
spent as a producer
on and on and on and on
with no laces and all permeated
took up employ
reciting out loud
an occasional thought
about it, but he is, in fact
round the bath, dirty milk bottles
singing softly to himself
then the war ended
is it any wonder?

his extensive library
the centre of his picture
merge into the verdict
one moment threatens
an explanation of why this language
representing the glorious past
belongs, even to those
following me into this war
by blending the impersonal ethos
beyond the reach of satire
to account for its success
in demonic or satanic terms
is irrelevant
yet the basis of this neutral identification

one precious fragment
always hated me
to enumerate the vast numbers
of correspondents consulted
with tolerable fidelity
in which each vowel
is a perfectly familiar word
from the lack
of hard
intelligible phonetic principles
a copy was sent
to introduce occasionally
this curious device
in abundance

Clark Coolidge (b. 1939)

From Bond Sonnets

1\.
"Satisfactory" other hours' haul the
beacon Amies gone one and
he say wonderful Bond and
freeing but late saw each
the taste meticulously weakly same
ten wretches here right plan
in paid sipped health-protecting to
that to the lawn desirable

cutthroat He's him gingerly form
couple he 7 down that
bugged of Inside Identification and

big corner number appropriate smile
Jamaica lawn to South of
dark sense the bond out

2\.
gold life their into condition
to those your inefficiency through
deeply slackened with message indicator
laughed also something his multiple

have said Ascension Paris along
in corpse one blackjack hold
when white stovepipe pleasure captain
that shifted Largo whole knowing

darted understand blackjack punched and
steps talked himself Letter slightly
strokes strain CARDBOARD background which

of fish's need that know
whirled detection gazed going weapons
bigger barrel the tomorrow

3.
told marked expect signed intersection
but that while other hitch
strip 15 wouldn't by cradles
what night packet weighed stern

a sheen along secret disdain
any hair pass the Commonwealth
consciousness all flew tapestry airport
infinite pass over stovepipe with

thing pictures circle roon Young
course all sat cigarettes bridge
force anything rubber hotel Tracy

to pound's hell come riding
board would shoulder changed Bond
and targets chair's to there's

4.
antiseptic spears under gleaming sonar
niggerheads interrupted unless girl's ten
months creaming under governments Thunderball

dollars matter-of-fact Prime Bond mask
and hysterically on miles out
Thames had barracuda stick automatic

sounded to love fingers threw
fuse with sure evening these
think loaded always printed good
drunkeness hoped or full driving

cool and coming brave German
done carefully and knees mind
carrot SPECTRE and some clear
bold as evening wardrobe miles

5.
kicked by clutching suit down
change ones bomb body fight
exercises now supercargo danger farewell
side done back hour torch

detonator Yeah of boat tail
they plain souvenirs fellow Largo
that recognise satisfied information crew
will with entrance out about

emerald road coral there lead
moon change weakness get sniff
pilot bacon going no wanted

lungs square threshold supreme time
inflated triangle clumsily sat Bond
cabinet James cottagey pain movement

7.
lying mind leisurely wanted more
years works on bombs said
standing barracuda from black felt
off on plain lifebuoy eyes

listen Domino read bank cards
me sure stink file report
envelope the small outboard moment

comfortably Bond designed watch future
seriously Hell black indeed efficiency

the hard healthy read going
choose cherry teams seeped away
Largo let's enough groundswell always
midnight soon sank again Airlines
plane took one such bullet

9.
solid hand can't believe subs
orders scanner what just yacht?
see He trunks soft quiet
come backed been meaning scuttling
good know?

fifty years up
on business It amazed shark
strokes head fry visibility kept
turned lifebuoy a gold packet

get childish and bank coming
run and course with jackets
expert records third setup? reports

make my police your hell
know sir efficiency that goes
enough general behind street constantly

13.
her mr. had occasionally eyes
excitement bulge holding poached we're
weapon him certainty the things

Department heard still anything dark
compartment on the pulling from
an sea on the that

get beautiful word inside commonwealth
used the necessary signed government
have up watch from go
group rear made riding Bond

the narrow two-seater consisting He
on God and the $1,000,000

carefully to evidence eight gunmetal
by disdain taken compulsory order

16.

comradés tinkle mobilization doesn't
depth stay nothing was changed

suspected lines found it out
they've slackened right showing
many two had you're bank

out water dry off agent
people have hissed say it's

the hardly efficiency boiled with
raise him lose she big
being off thumb plane he

been windscreen letter possible the
and nails and he merchant
then was 6 there department
same 120 then empty in

18.

finished the hundred signals with
got and offered no means
have looking his torpedoes four
yacht? Largo unless diving into
she sign thin hours' calm
is at blue Bond mind
silks he spades smart the
was broadside stop plane with
what room corner grinned secret
that like riding in 11
bars the trembled society had
perspex likelihood his the target
conversation aroused yes war Bond
shoot and and casually rose

Peter Riley (b. 1940)

Ospita

1

Seeking a bearing point on hurt I find
Hollows and rooms in the thick of the night,
A building hard at work flashing its bright
Offers into the star dome. Consigned
Forward I bring my name in a sealed jar
To the steps up, pay the slight fee, assent
To slow harm by the covering letter;
Entering into purpose distance springs
Back from the horizon to hold the cup
The bitter cup but true, of flesh-driven earth
(This night is the day outside the dream, his
Tableau my government, or family wish)
And deep in the brickwork think of asters
Blazing on the far links in slow birth.

2

I bear my coat and cast to a senior,
A new-old faithful, who should know the coils
And corridors of the heart, the slender
Ghost smiling to the third tune. What is false
Be set into a pestle, what rings be
Represented as an inner garden
Open to Syrius, one and the same be
Ground and broiled and spoken as your answer.
The house is quiet, old radio music
In the walls, scissors on the table, streaks
Of blood in the sink. A call in the night;
I get up, white coat, glance out at the rain
On the glass, attend. What do I exchange for pain?
Holding a stranger's thin arm I turn down the light.

3

Calcium night light. Suddenly a man
Shouts, 'Orpheus!' and the dying die,
The sick sleep on, the deserted bitterly cry
And I count the call as best as I can across
The fogs of routine silence; word that holds
The earth into a chiming whole, enfolds
Love in a capsule coated with loss, never
Cedes to wishful death but calls us to drop
Our trades and be again that whirring top
On the mountain ridge, screaming down river a pain
Of incompletion, fall medallion, cut
The human heart to song. And it will, don't
Turn the light out, see to the day's wounds, won't
Stop our good hands tying, that sweet moan again.

4

A man shouts in pain, the voice constructs
A door. The god batters his forehead
On our simple attendance, the fruit
Of centuries' observance. But to eluct
Wisdom from hurt – any hospital bed
Would burst into flame at the mere thought.
The music coils within: a long solo,
And the final voice squeezed from a lump
Of flesh held over a sink said and we tried
Our best to stifle that singing, 'Do
what you will to ease me over the hump
Of death I belong to the great outside.
My burning lust courses at the last though Hell.
The pain of what I couldn't manage spreads like a bell.'

5
This house constructed as an escape
From harm is unlikely to escape
Its own folly as a new escape
From language and source of new dolour.
A woman shouts down a corridor
A real name: 'Sidney! Sidney! Sidney!'
A door slams bone shut. I am sorry
To have life shot through by her call
I can't dream any harder the fall
Of light onto the wet leaf, the stain
Of nurture on a simple erection;
In the end she is right: the rape
Of endless joy and everyone's to blame.
Out on the lake the long boats wane.

6
At night the walls are blank but we can hear
The plovers crying in the dark fields, their
Wings beating over waves of wheat. Downstairs
Someone opens the piano and strikes a chord
That tenses the flanks of hope. Again there
Is a silence in which the lapwings graze
The ear tips and clouded underwing
Swoops across the sky. Then where and where
In this globe of health we balance and bear
From room to room, where is a lasting thing?
Where is a good done that also stays it?
Someone attempts the new soft swing but out
In the earthglow between mind and chest
Brilliant metallic birds like kisses dive to rest.

7

The man dies and the bell sounds across
Grass and sea and mixes with the gulls.
The dream sleeps into the morning, turns
On its side and drifts along the coast
Under the great grey cliffs and buildings
Dedicated to healing but now
Empty and dark at dawn, the sharp keens
Of the white hens warning us to be slow.
We comfort as if there were no cost,
As if pain could be stilled to patience
Separately, and the story lost.
Good men have died lost in empty time
But loading their bite on th'intrinsic nation
Steady as grade of light, or yellow chime.

8

Time drags its heals on the dreamer who hears
His body calling him like a discant
Semaphore, a sign hung on a fruit shop
Under the castle wall. The sheets are bright
Anger the oxide of faith and he fears
The fall into humanity, the slant
Of honey and cream; those fair lids droop
And he is solitary on the white
Road across the heath, he is close to tears
For the imperfected lives he couldn't want
To bring to their moment of concord and float
On further life. The swallows are in flight
Over the russet fields crackling with fear
As he enters the day's gate as is right.

9

They draw his body from the centre out,
A decisive goodness. He lies flat out
On the shore counting ills. The waves enter
His total wealth into books of sand.
It's enough. They are happy to inter
His soul in lime and ash for the sake
Of a comfortable end, the winter
Of our success rebound in angel cake
But winter is true numbers that blister
From the corpse in a field, alternating
Black and white name-tags that flitter
Like sarcens in the treetops. Small birds sing
His centre into holes in the snow and grey
Doctors weeping envy send him on his way.

10

I walked out on the morning of May 12th
The blades were bright and coy and loud,
Thick with languages I walked without stealth
The fields of angry farmers, proud
To be harmless and legal, half and half,
No one could fathom my strong shoes,
There is no paradise but tongue of love.
I walked all day, I heard no news,
When twilight filled the air with gravities
I descended, heart full and slow,
Down the dim fields dotted with stones and sheep
To the house in its banks of trees
The fire, the food, the Gurney piano,
Having my wonderful labour to keep.

Stephen Rodefer (b. 1940)

From Mon Canard

Julie my duck, mama's lute, chouchou in lieu of amore
of our loo, butte of my butte, beaute of your butt
mont rue, my verity former not HERE, not her
mob spent of row, flowers in rue Lappe, pet asinine pot
my lovely cinder, mine ashen heart, onliest wit
ness to my witness, jump in Seine, berth, ankleberry
every thin necklace nested, sturdiest hysteria, white
patent leather policefemme, unreading gaoler, op
pen opera, princess mon amie electuary Jew, petit rat burg
er, my choo choo, coughdrop of my esophoguy, my lu
dens, by my mitten, minion of my invisible cake, liz
ard die of my destiny, mutt, cuff, flycast, gal
oshes, SMITTEN GLOVES, smith of my smith, bull
's blood drawn in sleepy smiles, petite carotide
mine outside of libraries, mine inside of sky, re
flection of a flicker, intermittent heaven, ce jour triste
lourd de lassitude, she there what's her name, little beachym
sham, damoiseau mar on my divan, penny couch
my virtual chum, chinchin of my chin, chin duster of
my shoeshine, main cat pal, pause, GAUGE, going on
wobbly but unmusty, extra key, coin, ma chatte for
an hour and a life, terminal initial of Lucrèce, Lucretius
place where my fingers learnt their place, ex sexy gerun
diva, my rue de la main d'or, liberty burning anklecuff

dearest ear, l'oreille cassée, nose for my eyes
agreeablest knot, sweet tooth, toot, my b
low, my job, my WIFE, my snow, wasted poplin of un
closed drawers, knicker of my let, my tie and
my redundancy, tongue of hyacinth, tongue of clement
een, plane darkling, unlasting loan, my loonie
st tune, noon of my noon and the second afternoon all
night, sheet kneeler, slat breaker, my color
less felt seat of Leicester's DOUBLE life, shag rug and
shadow of my digression, a new vague shape of day, fig
ure e'en now at nightie, my little porcelain tiger
passoire, that jump from and for the rest, the mother lip
in sync, shortest contraction, resignation from science
and slow time, assent, decline, premier something or other

something of an aberration, paper fire, sno
ring goddess, ray MOND and grace, arc of my curve ta
page too fast but who was driving, leg woman and
like my wood breast, felt of your drawer, draw and match
of cards, eclipserer, queen NUMBER third at the fir
st second, contract, con, bouncing hat, alter e
goes red tickets, gravid nun, posh nutter of my sundae
nouvelle retrovert, my disability, her name, her beat
rice, golden sectioned two year old, unread
ie champ at the edge of the OVAL, oh drunken race
novel absence, arching is a bell borne away
to Kings PARADE, testimony to the rule of chance, balls
cupped in hand, sweet nadir V, my playing
chump, muddied boot, dye of our rhetorick in

sincere rôle, my sack in the morning, sack
at night, hanging round, your hanging over, come bloom
ed hangover, now lapse at last, your jump in can
tax, womb of her own, CHAR at my back, tramp
of time, cave lamp, conundrum, shirt, garter, high
absence curled in me girl, my admission to literary so
sighty, skin of Dame Edith, curled darling of my sove
reign unit, NATIVITY, my incensed franc, far
thing nearer to the bank than PILLOW puffed and
fluffy on the sheets, able Irish rose which Tuscany re
turned, just ex-kant, wait to come, way home
boy, my fatigues, lasting past the LAST exaggeration, I woman
bella bella, Lady Baloney stript ease there, Dr Death
ly silence, my well, my sill, wall, morphia kristakis, my now

my then, my there, me shaddoh, me shallow, khan uke
chanookie of an NC Hudson, O BAY, wan ass braying ewe
ramification, bronze niño, prefect lapel, school pin
of John Adams, up the wazoo of music murals, la fa
mine fed utterance, Titian, heterogenous dendron
age, homogenous polynomial young or old, O FMN, effeme
haine, paint faced self-portrait, unwrit eddieface, E
vidange, ending evidence of scent, sleep above rest below
whistling powers leaving in little tunes you HEAR playing
just below surfaces walked through, bed 'n' breakfast
one, unpractised theoretician, Falmer miscalculant
sleepy comma of my snood, CAMPANION, some sense in water
colors of white space, other, lover, liver, puffed ottoman
mother, written basket, unborn bastard, pharmaceutical cropper

. . .

black or blue, like your browning eyes, is a bell obscene
off-stage, my bell your bell, my body of work at your work
place, mon coeur, my belief the earth is sleeping
with the trees, some habit each night to pull the cover up
and chuck the chin at hem of moss and BARK, hand held main
tenant, taxi derm, to drowse nightlong in awe of cheek or storm
and marriage clang, scares me, uprightliness of mates, arise Laa Laa & Di
psy B'laire, yank nimbus watch pervades easterly as opportune as
music always had in mind canoodling the finale, finally her
aldic tift, Hellenic vendor, from the top pearl asea, spindrift
off marjoram, my dot, my mousse, mon blanc, mein Jung frau
FrouFrou CHOCoLATENESS both going in and coming out, whaup
whauven wheal, wengen and overland through dix fracas, craft, sink
soft and fidgety keyboard, sort, lieber freund, yesterdays spelt jeans

brook neige, nose for eyes, GIFT for torching Kettle's Yard, ich comme
accomplice, come, où s'éloigne what can who blindly spends, mob
ile posture, itching kitchen I Ching, juke box of your specialty, monk
et greyhound, my untied and my made knot, whiplash, mai
den all gone, nothing overdone, drinking lands more full
than enough, and my too much just enough, très sor
row Virago of this former BIKE, love, comrade, queen and middle
sense that sweetest scent, felt spinning ball John Keats sent
from handle of too early consumption, Sug Daddy thrown by many
generations of horses, all the music above accomplishment, garde ta foi
gras, shaving glass, can DUCK, liver watch, dew et
sons, yOU'Re on, femme, fain, ergo more sum, bit wee west of here there
what's-her-Caesarina, bridehead, identity the continual face
lift, ACCOMPLICE, wagging frozen tale, crying laughter, high thread

shot leaving now going PAST gone

ofT outside and in between

TWO

palimpsested a nimals tha t repeat

themselves by RE

fusing to sPeak

A.. GAIN, R.. AIN B.. ORN, C.. OUGH

sky

RiVERBAnK

libido leaves the world wool dyed

mons

trance

con fig

eru

jnuk

refed

a

ue

e

w

qı

-met coquin DOING mon canard dranac nom

Damned Car

Lyn Hejinian (b. 1941)

From The Unfollowing

I

The spy unfolds his hammock and creates in effect an enormous basket into which he tumbles, wobbles, and comes to rest like a freshly laid mottled yellow egg
The fog has rolled in, visibility is null, I wouldn't know if someone were following me
A woman throws beans, a woman rakes leaves, a heavy man moves ahead on a horse, a light man coughs
The visible is rough
There are all kinds of words here and some that aren't here and some that might if put together in the right order mean more to you than I can say
It seems that it's lighter or maybe just browner
October 6—what kind of beginning is that? what kind of end?
The streets are walked by she who fully backwards walks them emptily
O nomad, come here, O death, rest your head
Eleven lines may be woven with three into an elegy, an entropy, a velocipede, a punishment, and a pin
Let's go, while in the fields far from here, lunch finished, no further discussion arising, to climb the sheer rock face now that the fruits on the tree atop it are ripe
A little cloud obscures the sun, then dissipates and the sun's begun
There was once an old woman with cake on her face, there was once an old man dressed all in black lace
We will receive (do receive / are receiving / have received / have to receive / will have received / won't receive / shall receive) a young Argentinean captain

7

To begin with, I am faced with mountains to circumambulate, since I can't cut through them
I enter the folds of a human adventure
On every door there hangs a figurehead and this one comes to face me as the door swings shut
I will proceed with good will—the best of wills—anxiously
Bird of daughters, bird flying from the forks, the blurbs, the serials, the time
I saw a golden tadpole, eating apple jam; I saw a sudden whirlpool, sucking down a ham
The boughs groan with fruit, an apple falls—false alarm
It's a non-sequitur—that
Sense data sinks
The muscles give out mid-word and a thief stutters while accusing me (his uncle) of theft
Lune comes along mounted on a beast called Lequel who is neither more or less than a horse as obedient to Lune as the tides are to the moon
Shot of men hurrying toward each other at an intersection with open umbrellas none willing to give way to the others, shot of placid camels kneeling near a chained dog, shot of sugar maples temporarily obscured by falling snow
Tomorrow morning, unless things vastly improve, I'll go in person to the front of the caravan and take it *over* the mountain
I thought I saw an earthworm, stirring in the dirt, then I saw it was a sadist, wielding a quirt

8

There goes something, forever lost in context
A Sudanese customs agent halts a caravan carrying rocking chairs into lands where
no rocking chairs are needed
Come lest desire clatter, dance now lest we can't dance later
Here remains as a bridge vanishes, the backdoor shuts, etc. and here cares little as
to which is which
Conjoining unlike concepts (say, birth control and origami) is something mortals do
This does not follow
Danish baby, Danish toddler, Danish mother, Danish father—see them eating
midnight meats
The passengers on prison ships are not allowed to celebrate
There is very little, almost nothing, that ...
I order you to feel free to help yourself to ice cream which is melting
At midnight I'll become a merchant mariner again
Is this paper snow, undertow?
It is perceived unconsciously and might have been a spider emerging from a duck's
egg, a cause for excitement provided by the outside world to an inner world
that almost missed it
It's only with clumsy freedom that things appear on people's lips

20

Wake up, get married, be born
First A and B pick up the trunk, then C relieves A and A wanders off, then D takes B's end and B goes in search of A, but A is nowhere to be found, and C and D make off with the trunk
Long are the lazy man's laws, the kittens are in the kitchen, the child's chin aids pronunciation
Maybe I'm dreaming I'm naked except for a long black t-shirt I'm dreaming
Bring on the aspirin and bread, the vitamin C and gin
We have fourteen names for blue and that doesn't even count "meridian"
Diderot, Audrey Hepburn, Hegel, Charles Dickens, and Gertrude Stein
Shadow bird shouting
White coral fencing
The butcher on Sunday, Pablo Ruiz, lives south of here (in F____) and has five kids—how full of vitality he is
She leaves us behind in the interstices of competence
Origami, irreverence, sand on the wing of an ibis
She drops a bucket down a thick well, she whacks a golfball longer than a marble
Rude and shoed, should and lead, reed

26

Puddings don't have lungs, melons don't have riders
Listen—a female seal, a seaport, and a social world
Come day's end the top of the tree hesitates, pauses, then sweeps on like a blackboard eraser to clear the horizon
Sit, Shep, incognito
The lid of the sun is heavy, its lashes blink on the horizon, brushing the curve of the sea
Now they want to grant federal coal subsidies?!
I heard "suspected pipe bomb" as "suspected python"
The first nest empty and deep, at child's eye level, in a young fir tree, of twigs
Pathos is at the front line of defense against worries as they approach
I remember almost nothing, only that I am in a room with others and we are reading through sacks of mail, trying to ferret out spies
She will never believe she's too old to join a band or make quick vertical moves on the playing field to really quiet music—she is that still
Then the sparrow went to sleep in a lumber castle
And so we come to chapter LIX, in which I learn that I have failed
Can you believe this shit?

Rachel Blau DuPlessis (b. 1941)

From Draft, unnumbered: Précis

2: She

= The She-who-is-I knew
what was meant by danger,
and who, obliquely, was addressed.
Yet the actual poem concerns
women, the feminine, girl, mother,
food and force, red and pink, lyric,
damage, their mingling, flesh
and flowers (topoi!) as
a condition of my employment,
while syllables bubble and percolate
thru family rocks and babble options.

It did not openly evoke the poet Oppen
and his always palpable
stripped intransigence.

7: Me

= A place where tracks line straight,
go cross, switch over, tie,
fuse, emerge into plethoras
crossing other lines; a place the subway
tunnels through – closed-up,
written-over, a suppressed station;
a place where flaxen tide-lines weave;
where marks preventing firstborn death –
that's what the story says – dash up
upon the door of dreams. All this
made me make more lines, incise, seek,
write writing, made me fill the poem's
magic eye with endless
em and en graffito streak.

= Mass Observation. 14: Conjunctions
The writing en masse on topics so
quotidian, so domestic, notable mini-quirks –
one's rooms, one's small unnoticed bits and kitsch,
one's job, one's perch, workplace bitching,
who one is, sort of, and one's quondam acts,
way into the detail. Like prices, colors, choice;
sauced with kvetch and gossip. Various communities,
different senses of possibilities.
As a real poetics. A commitment.
But Mass Observation also devolved –
a souring utopia plump with
spying, sentiment, created needs,
propaganda, market research, greeds....

= It was time to recognize the dot. 15: Little
How small it is, how small this spot.
With its cunning humilities
addressed to other, grander theories.

= It is becoming clearer 19: Working Conditions
that this is, bare minimum, about my
conditions of employment in and
by *anguage*. Yet I find such
single strand conclusions, no matter
how accurate, over-pat; not a real mirror.
Hard either to be satisfied with this summary,
or to slot thought in a little analytic box,
given fullness, intricacies, envelopments, dross,
over-wash, shadows half-excavated; then the lot
partially re-obscured by shock;
given the struggles in time with loss.
Given, or driven by, the knot.

= Thereupon, without transition, the sudden   20: Incipit
surprise typical of long-poem "logic."
As was completely fitting to the project
(yet I'd no plan that this was going to happen),
I decided to begin everything
once again. Making a random deliberate
meshing. An over-writing by
over-reading, commentary by invention,
a fold and an extension in the name of gloss.
Midrash, rashly, on texts already midrash.
Making the gain of grid stand in for loss.

= Hence emerged a midrash on "rubble."   25: Segno
The rubble is both specific and general.
That story of Isaac palpable.
Cast with its famous "angel"
which latterly didn't arrive at all.
So there we are. "The beginning or end
of a repeat." All was screaming.
Redemption's fairy story
puns on aught.
The smashing apart
of my own name (r-ache-l)
(before this Sign, in Gap)
made just one token of what needs
to be thought and rethought.

= The line became volatile, with doubled,
anxious, slashing
breaks, an intransigent
critique both of erasures, political
cover-ups, withholding
and of poetry's panache,
its assured memorializing goal
(the instability, the probable
folly of such assertion).

26: M-m-ry

Yet little things, their dots and dash,
do sometimes speak aloud
and show themselves –
even slowly, even dimly –
because they also claim
some intransigent volatile name.

= Evaluate this sloppy urn.
Need volta?
No – want saturation.
Salutation.
Appears it's all turn.

31. Serving Writ

= Thinking, sidling sideways
of Zukofsky and other
cosmopolites, of the fact
right now that English and power
go together. So my rejecting that
hegemony is probably why
I stick non-English
bits in here and there –
neither affectation nor imitation
(*Waste Land*, etc.); just simply foxing.
And then the endless
sense of reality, "Objectivist" truth:
the real real world. An endless paradox –
made of endless language-wrath and -ruth.

36: Cento

Closing with the dot, then with an opposite
but still familial *semblable*: It.

46: Edge

= Oblique to the gains
what monuments for us
and for the fathers except
our stun that this be so:
The: a pointing.
It: a dissolve beyond understanding.

Between these, anon., a Nomad
Struggles, in labyrinths
of politics and metaphysics both,
the exemplary pressures
always bearing upon one
named N (or J, whomever) –
thereupon challenged, twisted, thrown,
and overcome, no matter actual victor –
by Angel, initial A, afflicter.

48: Being Astonished

= Through all this, women.
Women thinking of, in, through
and by themselves. Women loving
poetry and making it, and making scenes,
and doing books and little magazines
who are a literary caste or cast oft
unrecorded, wasted, trashed, or
hyper scrutinized, or worse.

Women astonished, always, inside
writing: how their possibilities
get undercut at times; at times even denied.
Still those loud bright notes and scintillant
scryings, arise, are here, are now and newly mint!

Ron Padgett (b. 1942)

Nothing in That Drawer

Nothing in that drawer.
Nothing in that drawer.
Nothing in that drawer.
Nothing in that drawer.
Nothing in that drawer.
Nothing in that drawer.
Nothing in that drawer.
Nothing in that drawer.
Nothing in that drawer.
Nothing in that drawer.
Nothing in that drawer.
Nothing in that drawer.
Nothing in that drawer.
Nothing in that drawer.

Sonnet / Homage to Andy Warhol

Zzzzzzzzzzzzzzzzzzzzzzzzzzzzzzzzzzzzzz
Zzzzzzzzzzzzzzzzzzzzzzzzzzzzzzzzzzzzzz
Zzzzzzzzzzzzzzzzzzzzzzzzzzzzzzzzzzzzzz
Zzzzzzzzzzzzzzzzzzzzzzzzzzzzzzzzzzzzzz
Zzzzzzzzzzzzzzzzzzzzzzzzzzzzzzzzzzzzzz
Zzzzzzzzzzzzzzzzzzzzzzzzzzzzzzzzzzzzzz
Zzzzzzzzzzzzzzzzzzzzzzzzzzzzzzzzzzzzzz
Zzzzzzzzzzzzzzzzzzzzzzzzzzzzzzzzzzzzzz
Zzzzzzzzzzzzzzzzzzzzzzzzzzzzzzzzzzzzzz
Zzzzzzzzzzzzzzzzzzzzzzzzzzzzzzzzzzzzzz
Zzzzzzzzzzzzzzzzzzzzzzzzzzzzzzzzzzzzzz
Zzzzzzzzzzzzzzzzzzzzzzzzzzzzzzzzzzzzzz
Zzzzzzzzzzzzzzzzzzzzzzzzzzzzzzzzzzzzzz
Zzzzzzzzzzzzzzzzzzzzzzzzzzzzzzzzzzzzzz

Rain Dunce

after Ted Berrigan

1.

This pinching prince nix! Some dumb fooze
Glands oink to a dumb fooze, in the jerk blight.
In the nookie of his moo (sic) the bunions have mated:
Which ouch their incense to our beeping glands.
The pox tub from the glands which decay
For fooze for armth for glands for gruff
Easter booms in the boom that you boom in?
Upon his tractored "some":
Still, they bean some dings. For the rancid
And the harpy busters,
Sleeve among itchy duds
May be just poo-poo to him
We are the beeping frogmen of his good-bye,
Fiends giving pup tents to frogmen.

2.

Ear margarine, hello. It is 515 I am's.
ear berry guns. A "Dido."
Ack those crooks! I rat
On 830 Pat "Mitchells" in New York sitting and I was beaned gunning
    around all day
bold Himalayas "keel" the feets. A mess, it is now,
Hammock lungs shall be bale to babble the diving rod
and the hay is right hair turning green
feel mine! nibble us! and guff
catching the "fun" come up over the Navy Bean
to cite crotch ape boo-boo in a gloating suck
had 17 and 1/2 telegrams
Ear margarine, hello. It is 515 I am's.
fucked the 7 Dwarfs now they're late to work and hmmm
18 Snow Whites in my glands baking I need some butter

The Art of the Sonnet

Last night I said hello
to the little muse
the smaller than usual muse
She was floating toward me
a plaster figurine
on a cloud
but her plaster lips
could not return my greeting.
That's the first part
and in Japan.
Now the figurine
drifts past and turns
a smile erasing
her face

Such warm pockets in the word! So I am obliged
To plummet to disaster from the hands of children
In gardens that become a belly and felts.
Swallowing a book I did nothing and was more,
Later of course, on my pale white steed.
What a pleasure it is to undergo the days,
To have a beautiful wife and die young!
Sometimes a cast of thousands, later, ugh, "passion."
Such warm pockets in your belly, your corduroy
Belly, a sea in itself! Here, though, are the wet wings
Of birds you cannot eat, you can only
Feel like a rubber band, as if I had a 6 on my nose
Or a mesquite bush. I used to think you were Emily Dickinson,
In the line, "You are Emily Dickinson."

(1963)

John Welch (b. 1942)

EVERYTHING IN THE CITY

Everything in the city comes to this table.
There must be something to be said about these
Explosions of laughter at the stairhead,
Rumours of approach in the tunnels.
Water is scattered in the air, everwhere
Attesting to the importance of clouds
And the weather changes every few hours
Where blind men are making journeys over the city
Tapping trees and observing the shadow
Sound casts. Processions are crossing it
Bearing advertisements.
Essential oils fry in the pan: "Bury it in
An inch of water, it will sing for five minutes."
Everything in the city comes to this table.

HYDRANGEA

Hydrangea before the flats has flowered
This gross bush, reddish and purple like a face.
Upright in bars as if beneath far skies
Men drink alone, stern-faced, and look away.
Home, and I water the garden again
Then dine off a round table, not feeling well,
Laying the face on the face this language
Is a scandal, and I'm its shadow
Walking slowly into the future tense.
There is no freedom anywhere but here.
Lie down in it, it can't last. Drought
Is lasting. Half a life
Is better than none at all. The drinkers rise
Hydrangea of the flats, how parched your ground.

HABITUAL INSOLENCE

for Tristan Tzara

Habitual insolence the streets encourage:
Flexing the muscles before daybreak,
The ones little used, then passed by hands
Over the flat and the vertical areas
Gazing into the eyes of approaching motorists
Who gnaw the wheel accommodating miles ...
The muscle halts by here
In its cultivated rags mid splinters
Of the valuable flask, lapsed cloths of sunlight.
Being calm under an always turning heel
I am the wax archangel and the
Catalogue of cars, the useless rain
Leans inward past impenetrable churches,
These stone valves blackening down the years.

FOR THE PAINTINGS OF MORRIS LOUIS

Our day began on a dull red door
Hammering on to a curtain to open.
Veils and diseases. Our torn halts
Covered the ground in a fury of colour.
There was stitching on the duck surface,
The little bumps of different coloured hills.
The great underneath uprose. We quietly
Admired its huge berg infested with colour
Till we were ourselves surface, envying surface.
Leaving the massive acres of islands
We sank in, becoming colour poured on
And were buried up to the knees. We waded,
Ran and ran across white space tilted.
We were the enormous air around, comprehending.

Adrian Clarke (b. 1942)

From Skeleton Sonnets

After Sir Philip Sidney
(Astrophel and Stella, I)

performative screened intermediate
Correction
vocatives with sibilant whip
fit words unvoiced
in the mind's mouth
paint "soluble" intertext blueprint
a finger wet leaves
ratiocinative slaked

approaching episteme STOP
iambic *Set neat prints*
alveolar gestating
pen the metonym
afflatus to infarct
figures kill

PAVEMENT SLABS ASHEN A
TURFED INSERT'S EMPYREAL SALIENT
AIN'T IT A SHAME
MONUMENTAL NOVEMBERS STRUCK FROM
STONE SPARKS DRIFT A
PATRONISED AFTERMATH SPACE OF
EXCHANGE UNDISCHARGED AN AORIST
REMEMBRANCE ENTERED AS DEBT
IN ITS VERTICAL COLUMN
THE BLUE PENCIL RAIN
WASHED DESULTORILY LOWER END
WORMED THROUGH IMPERFECT TO
THE LETTER FABULOUS BLACK
OUTS SPLATTERED WITH RED

a window mechanized
the unusual device
3 mm rods
are what I does
to skewed syntax
                                    make
up and alias
recess diseased breath

in bricabrac panic
insert “display”
                                 couch
fantasy raingear needing reciprocal

pins rips and ink
mutation excruciates
the purest illegible no
shit impulse

after Shakespeare (Sonnet I) & the
Romanian National Mining Co.

public increase claustrophobic
World
News burst ulcerous
under
contract tributaries split
system
built mineral
fueled
riding the sandpit
lumps zinc in tiny plots

lead cadmium handicap
State
regulated on the gauge
wealth ruins at 6
$^{1}/_{2}$
premature STOP
general x the resulting
sludge compounds decease

tender residual unprotected
due pity the frail crust

80th birthday homage to Bob Cobbing

textual corpus out of control
signed
up recidivist twiddling the knobs
for significant transgressions
overprint stripper
drink properly
vapours condense
laryngeal
uvular through torrential mouthwash U
shapes lipstick the "non
literal" brought to book
"bite" verbatim
briefs an exposure considered
Verdict: "parole"

barred concurrently "Where are the words?"
Revised
Oxford Rhyming Thesaurus
devious appellatives
misdirect "true"
precedings distorted Origins
Shorter retroish the pre
verb in trespass
"Back to grunt
evidently"
"Guilty but on song"

Paul Dutton (b. 1943)

so'net 1

so no n so no n so no toes
toe no n toe no n toe so nose
so no n toe no n so toe nose
t toe no nose no toe so nose
toe t nose t toe nose toes
so nose t toes n nose nose toes
o nose o nose o nose n toes
o o   o no o so toe nose
nose s toes n toes s nose
so toes n nose no t so nose toe
t nose no toe s t not no nose
n so not t nose s t no not toe
      no toe nose not t no no nose
      n no nose nose not t no no toes

so'net 2

for rafael

sono e sono este sono so
tono es tesono e toto no
toneo e soneto se teno te
neo toneste se neto se
sesteno sostente te so no ne
eono e noto te notese
o seno e sene o nes esto
teno esto sene noste enesto
onoste sontono se onostes
son o son tono notos so es
es no sente en tos sonon
o sen e sonto o es toton
      sen tenseno e nonon sens
      ten sentesno e noto tens

so'net 3

onset tense no tone to set
no sense to note not one no none
so one soon tosses on to net
tenses notes tones one soon sees one
to ten senses soon one's not too tense
one's not sent to see eons nest
on stone tenets set to sonnet's sense
one sense sonnets not sent to test
sees no noose set no nonsense no
set one-ness one senses entente not
tense tones no sonnte's set to tote so
tense not testes on notes to one's tot
    noon noses onto sette son's set on
    one not seen to toss stone sonnet net on

so'net 4

se so'n see se ne so'n to'n
e to'n so'n se ne se so'n see
se to'n see se ne se no'n
o so'n see so'n se'ns ne nee
se'ns nee non se'ns to'n e so'n ton
onton so'n e to'n so'n to
teno'n no so'ns e no to'ns son
to so'ns e to to'ns e to s'ens on noo
ot on seon oon oo set
sontons tetoo otton no noet
oon so'n soo sesee e on no tet
oo es se so'n oon sonnet soet
    se so'net e sonnet soet oo so'n ne
    so'n so oo to'n so se so'net e

so'net 5

s ss s ss s ss s s
s tonn tonn tonn tonn tonn tonn tonn
s tt s tt s tt s t
s nonn nonn nonn nonn nonn nonn nonn
t ee t ee tee t e
t ness ness ness ness ness ness ness
t ne t ne t ne t n
t sess sess sess sess sess sess sess
n st n st n st n s
n sott sott sott sott sott sott sott
n oo n oo noo n o
n tott tott tott tott tott tott tott
s ss tonn tt nonn ee ness
t ne sess se sott oo tott

so'net 6

s s s s s s s s
o o o o o o o o
n n n n n n n n
s s s son n n n
noon noon noon noon noon noon noon noon
noon noon noon noon noon noon noon noon
noon noon noon noon noon noon noon noon
noon noon noon noon noon noon noon noon
s s s s s s s s
e e e e e e e e
t t t t t t t t
s s s set t t t
sonset sonset sonset sonset
sonset sonset sonset sonset

so'net 7

ess o en en ee tee ess
o en ee tee ess o en en
ee tee ess o en ee tee ess
o en en ee tee ess o en
ee tee ess o en en ee
tee ess o en ee tee ess o
en en ee tee ess o en ee
tee ess o en en ee tee
ess o en ee tee ess o en
en ee tee ess o en ee
tee ess o en ee tee
ess o en ee tee   ess o
      ess o en en ee tee ess
      ess o   en ee tee ess

Robert Adamson (b. 1944)

Sonnets to be Written from Prison

For James Tulip

1

O to be 'in the news' again – now as fashion runs
everything would go for 'prison sonnets': I'd be on my own.
I could once more, go out with pale skin
from my veritable dank cell – the sufferer, poking fun
at myself in form, with a slightly twisted tone.
My stance, ironic – one-out, on the run.
Though how can I? I'm not locked up: imagine a typewriter
in solitary. I dream my police unable to surrender –
I'm bored with switching roles and playing
with my gender; the ironies seem incidental, growing thin.
Here's the world – maybe what's left of it –
held together by an almost experimental sonnet.
Surely there must be some way out of poetry other than
Mallarmé's: still-life with bars and shitcan.

2

Once more, almost a joke – this most serious endeavour
is too intense: imagine a solitary typewriter? Somehow
fashion runs its course: I am not in pain –
So there's hardly need to play on abstract repetitions
to satisfy a predecessor, poet or lawbreaker: I won't be clever
all the clever crims are not inside the prisons.
Here's the world – maybe what's left of my pretences –
I dream of being carried off to court again:
a sufferer, where all my deities would speak in stern
almost sardonic voices. 'Your Honour, please –
bring me to my senses.' There, I love confessions –
imagine writing prison sonnets 4 years after my last release.
If only all my memories could be made taciturn
by inventing phrases like: imagine the solitary police.

3

Yes your Honour, I know this is ridiculous – although –
I'm 'in the news'. I couldn't bring myself to do
one of those *victimless crimes:* I must suffer in more ways
than one. My crime's pretence is not to overthrow
social order, or to protest – it's my plan
to bring poetry and lawbreaking into serious interplay.
Imagine newspapers in solitary. I would walk right through
the court taking down copy 'catch me if you can' –
Defendant in contempt. There has to be a fight,
I can't imagine anything, if I'm not up against a law.
Here's the world – our country's first stone institution –
where inmates still abase themselves each night.
If I was in solitary I could dream – a fashionable bore,
writing books on drugs, birds or revolution.

4

I dreamed I saw the morning editions settle on the court –
emblazoned with my name, my 'story' so glib it made
no sense. The judge said 'emotional' but I thought
of the notoriety. This was the outward world, and my sad tirade
was 'news' – Though if I'd been rhyming sonnets
in solitary, my suffering alone, could make them art.
Now, imagine an illiterate in prison – but I have no regrets
I enjoy my laggings. I feel sorry for the warders.
The discipline always pulls me through, and my counterpart,
the screw, is tougher with the easy boarders –
This experience might feel profound – though irony's never
broken laws – so I'm against everything
but practical intuitions. My 'solitary etc' is too clever
by half now – but then, who's suffering?

5

I brood in solitary, it's a way to flagellation: thinking
of my day of 'release' – I shuffle friends like dates
on my calendar, marking them off at random.
Here's the world – the stewed tea I'm drinking
cold – how I suffer. When I walk through the front gates
into the country, what will I become?
I'll throw away the sufferer's comforting mask,
and turn against my memories, leaving a trail of perdition
behind me. Children and women will fall to my simple
intuitive reactions – not even the New journalists will ask
questions, nothing will be capable of feeding on
my actions and survive. My prison sonnets will be drugs
relieving pain: I have remembered helpless men
knocking their bars for hours with aluminium mugs –

6

We will take it seriously as we open our morning paper.
Someone's broken loose, another child's been
wounded by pen-knives. A small fire down the bottom
of a suburban garden smells of flesh. Dark circles under
the mother's eyes appear on television, she's seen
her baby at the morgue. Our country moves closer to the world:
a negro's book is on the shelves. The criminal's become
mythologized. Though yesterday he curled
over and didn't make the news. So the myth continues, growing
fat and dangerous on a thousand impractical intuitions.
The bodies of old sharks hang on the butcher's hooks.
In broad day somewhere a prisoner is escaping.
The geriatrics are floating in their institutions.
The myth is torn apart and stashed away in books.

Thomas A Clark (b. 1944)

From sixteen sonnets

as I walked out early
into the order of things
the world was up before me
as I stepped out bravely
the very camber of the road
turned me to its purpose
it was on a morning early
I put design behind me
hear us and deliver us
to the hazard of the road
in all the anonymous places
where the couch grass grows
watch over us and keep us
to the temper of the road

what the day weaves
the night unravels
here in the forest
all roads run wrong
what the weaver knows
the forest soon undoes
all roads lose themselves
in the warp and woof
somewhere in the poem
a stag should enter
but the stag is lost at
a crossroad of sunbeams
what the poem weaves
the forest will unravel

this is a song about the weather
two good friends walk out in it
several goats sit tight in it
their chins churning in unison
tomorrow will no doubt be worse
rain hail and a heavy mist
over any firm resolve
there is a tiny pocket of air
between the raindrop and the blade
that is the condition of grace
set a fence about the place
a tether for each goat
though frost has us by the throat
this is a song about the weather

our boat touches the bank
among a scent of bruised sedge
the startled heron rises
broken form his austerities
we are in a proud country
where stone chats to stone
where furze pods crackle open
grey grouse and curlews inform
keep well below the horizon
your flesh spare upon the bone
trust to flintlock and sabre
bed down among the heather
the wild fiddle music of the air
tuneless will find you anywhere

when cattle sniff the air
and herd together in corners
rain will invariably follow
when bees fly short distances
dogs lie about the fireside
it is safe to forecast rain
when singing frogs croak when
toads come forth in numbers
it is a certain sign of rain
when swans fly against the wind
it is a sign of coming rain
when moles are more industrious
when worms appear on the surface
one must surely forecast rain

poplar leaves move in a wind
that blows up out of the mind
each stout branch of the mind
trembling at a touch of wind
poplar leaves dance on a breeze
and I am broken by long ease
turn with the altering breeze
lets take again the hollow lane
walk into that exacting country
where there is nothing but distance
nothing but breeze between poplars
where the underside of each leaf
is green beyond easy belief

each colour sits beside
a colour of equal repose
so that each colour shines
with its singular lustre
at the edge of each colour
another colour is poised
so that each colour present
is brought into the present
yet the present is not its cause
each colour dwells in its place
neither turning towards or away
from its immediate neighbour
colour sits beside colour
all together in good order

the stag comes home at last
to the dappled clearing
grazes the small grasses
while his velvet peels
throw wide the study window
let air play about the poem
the dim glade of the heart
is pierced by a sunbeam
the stag finds sluggish streams
a bee buzzes about the vowels
brushes against the consonants
and an exchange takes place
animals steal out of the forest
where we have cleared a space

Allen Fisher (b. 1944)

From The Apocalyptic Sonnets

"Make her an offer and she'll raise your bid."

To Peter Shore, M.P.
Secretary of State for the Environment

Chorded his chest vibrates suave the sweet air
a vespiary, loosened beyond skins'
aura; cancels eager pursuit of sour
forgetfulness; loses tight social noose.

Talk from tightened throat springs from his gambrel,
with Faust gambols into future's risk.
Of himself this Faust demands collective
consciousness without discrimination;

without condemning those who would machine
gun the crowd in their urban erotic
hate. Alchemical children pulling screen
over subconscious film land of Edgware.

Alone in explosion from the applause
love breaks temper of glass pane shatters. This
Dream of the Doctor changes, changes shape
and shapes without adjusting surroundings,

without imitation or car careless
exaggeration of rapport with those
persons in immediate area.
Orchidistic: his mirror of justice,

equips his laborat'ry, not merely
feeling, but palming forelocks melted in
tongue's knowing, carping without slandering
stance's emerging Philosopher's Stone.

A Technology older than steel the
smouldering chemicals directed to
understanding his need to replenish,
reinvigorate tending's stretching tent.

(A quotation from Goethe's 'Prometheus Fragment'.)

'THE TIRED DEATH'

To Mrs. Shirley Williams, M.P.
Secretary of State for Science and Education, and Paymaster General

A Boys' Brigade bugle the church outside;
a wise Faust arched into shade, overhead
aircraft seems to disappear leaving its
signature, a drone on his skin, vibrates

in nerves' connections locking clut cluster
of entertainment, white noise and litter
into his reactions. He enters the
building headache that does not dissipate.

Piccadilly corridors process their
pre-conscious conditioning, calculate
behind closed pores and bolted cells, skins that
polish collective thrones, clean suicides.

Fluorescent whirr stoning. Their sacra is
re-emphasised, sanctity conjures
John Before God and the Elders, reciting
repetitions around a table, they

petition to lift scalpels together,
break notches in holsters, humming Air
Force charity songs, audience ratings
indicate speech phones and choices, the height

of their voices' groans, a Irative act,
generates a breed of invisible
leeches thriving on exhaust fumes and burnt
out nerves of craftsmen cracking jokes for bread.

> Where Technology is misunderstood,
> kept behind Velvette curtains, it becomes
> proper to sanction the art that does not
> interfere, does not allow breath to clear.

(Fritz Lang's film title.)

'McTEAGUE'

To Eric Varley, M.P.
Secretary of State for Industry

Ill deceit. structure's broken. bomb craters.
Field of smashed cars. Astonishment's wind: fixed.
This foolishness from emotional plague
couples dis-ease to Elder's throne control;

this "Pleasant aren't you," night arcing gales in
wetful cuddling speech – arranged piles. Even
Babylon on her back giving for free
pressured meat encrusted in beggar's bowl.

Singeing burning let-blood. Boned brains incensed
of the leisure-rush in Lamb's stomach skin,
its mouth rims unfusable salt leavened
casting of lots yields spasm from Earl's Court,

lights taper. Spindle spins flame, detonates
the heat that overwhelms Warmth. The Many,
these Four Angels Holding The Winds, are the
thrombins assisting health-clot, prevent full

cough; unaware gripped flow has bones to blind
them to what synthesises, deepens rot
of basement, crumbling floor filled by roof's shed.
Genetic full sucking to pull winds to

wet lung, once Warmth, now sog. Not to receive
the burning cure, curfewed in the cup of
an over-moist hand, shaking clasping the
panel chairs, lions barking for lack of air.

With dignity they restrain the Angels
who accept Technology who believe
it tool and with humility grit strained,
grip flow, believe in order of their act.

(Frank Norris' novel title used for Erich Von Stroheim's film 'Greed'.)

'ROOM TO BREATHE'

To Anthony Wedgwood Benn, M.P.
Secretary of State for Energy

Sick loiter in bone's basket turning, bowl
before eyes hands beckons wings' wonder placed
upsidedown dizziness-from-sun-in-the-brain
links sickness to power of four-legg'd seat

the quiet sit-uation's flowing water
through thinking's instrumental repeating
sound crescent motion'd florid assembly
of suppressed graile activity at work

Marguerite's singing does not echo the
treasures crushed in her bowels the the tight of
her stomach's borax ferment inside life's
lot shot in spinal arm veined from Brixton

Refuses to accept norms, Refuses to
die, fights the Cold who kill Warmth Becomes
The Apocalyptic Woman, glowing
constellation burning perceptions's doubt.

She now Warmth rocks dry the civility
uncoils hidden mines the dug-for club and
seeks to, pulls seat beneath her, pleasure, holds
groin of the-one-she-has-chosen-to-love

clasping the joy of rifting landscapes her
shifting body boundaries move the scent fill
in room where the cosmic ceiling opens
she fucks with her man this understanding.

> Her Technology belongs to Being
> folding unfolding the land the language
> pointed electrics ground weighs sound the
> cask's tonnage where control is code of the said.

(Jenny James' book title.)

'BLUE POLES'

To Frederick Mulley, M.P.
Secretary of State for Defence

Stale air clenched in stomach's held wave on his
canvas his night ignorance stifles, leaves
his invisible 'Big Eye' consciousness.
Energised seat trees his grip with two feet.

His well's waters suspended wishing health,
thinking's heal powers coiled in repetition
filling hollows with roar that could sweetness
work's suffocation without release. Faust

runs from this death the dragon's still, runs
blind zigzag through trees avoiding claw wrench
'til long black tongue becomes flicker of flame
in eye shields now harnessed in Tooting Bec.

Rubs ointment on eyes focus a clear night,
his stomach a vase emptied of juice where
perfume remains replenishing becomes
Michael Fighting The, once unseen, Dragon.

Opening security knot, nostrils,
he revitalised by tail's tip in
Bride's well burdens her in the manner of
man/whore distrust of ultimate word/play.

In voluble Faust, resistence-loss makes
agitation incitement. Uniform
free energy replaces reminisced
hysteria in body-dragon stance.

Then his Technology, his science, is art
with sharper, clearer breath his blows are raw.
Blood-run from dragon burns grass fertiles
his food roots grip gain a re-coded earth.

(Jackson Pollock's painting title.)

'NERVES'

To James Callaghan, M.P.
Prime Minister and First Lord of The Treasury

Doctor Faust's chest deep breathes. Oh that it may
continue this Spring shocked morning without
rupture. Down a hill she gallops, golden,
of course, unfashionable, the throng's routine

holds its own balls. Marguerite unclasps it
the flow, it rains from her eyes the perfume
consumes setting nostrils she appears
to rise lightens shadows, Faust's storm that

wells a strength unleashed inhaling deep in
to the solar plexus as these two scents
merge sun and earth opening the crocus
the ten senses of their ascending form.

Not always Faust, will your gates be open,
your cask's keep dances as it forms this tree –
fifteen full chains – its own obsolescence
this four legg'd seat's power devours this book.

Know this now Doctor, your fists are blossoms
opening their joints to receive the light.
The glass dice are scattered as they once caused
to scatter the image in your mirror

becomes clear water boiled onto air. Moves
now the horizon your dream unrests and
condenses clouds until separating
Bride-winch reaches tension's electric storm.

> The actual Technologies renew their
> spirals. The change they resurrect carries
> still unknown charge. These skills guide this
> pregnant encumberance, to allow the birth, respect.

(John Wieners' book title.)

Johan de Wit (b. 1944)

From Palm Stories

More earns sound

At the edge of space. As seen by each and all. Versed to explain gaps and refills the clouds ice and devise a deck of smiles — coerced: camera be my memory — as shown by teach and tall. Caraway seeds make the kitchen floor glow at night. Much later giving returns causing thrilled to please the state of being behind fair play and say no. More prepares to be in full: cheerio! A meeting with two open ends in mind: me-mise and row-roots. Let's go, that must be the reef bar used to making friends perform at the crossbar. Straight lines have been around for miles even if rhetorical questions arrive in reverse order. It makes more sense to deduct the sun from space than to develop a universal being in tune with cartography. When our looks tumble down over the fallen leaves we take the train: stop home, stop foam, stop dome.

To be as small as time

In a glove. Minus a department store, a precinct and a rock solid display of won't-be-long. Facing the sun we clean its path before the limits of much – mooch – much could reach the shore. What's more is no more! Compared to used how does half turn round. Lost between spring and mind sage yodels down the Alps. Are we any closer to right down the middle? Hum a mouthful of come. Lick a shortfall of like. Most a sub-text of toast. Be a handset of be to come. When the skin entertains the mind eyes inflect words and fold inside. In unison behind your left earlobe our thoughts swim back to a copy of eight nought fate. One sits in a doorway to look across the robes — never mind the tropes — tempers left with the sound of luck – lack – lock. Never is always on the move; it keeps spinning because the end does too.

Sworn in by daylight

See bob and wheel. To gather all together for devotees on extra tracks in lucky dips, magic sounds all round a tuned tongue tip at the height of conception. Under brings under early majestic works from live and catch strange fruit at dawn, but such a giant leap from note to legend does sound casual. See above sea where the air swings explicitly from the corner of your mouth to a bridgehead in Clappertown. One day, please send me one day in detail, stunning blood samples of everybody's body minus our own generation; say hello! Doors open at seven, more's at Union Square, explore a bolt of lightning blue between hello and goodbye. Up all night to do little else but play chess and throw rice once up, twice well while much turns round. Most of the coast goes unrecorded when the wind comes to blast my skin to last.

Time to say yes to

Local time. It's speech that flattens the soil, sounds and so-called memory of days both real and captured by chapter and verse. Bay windows bound to hunt ... hunt a speckled throat. Harvest corn in high horn. Fed by fast light — your eyes light infrared sound on stilts — tangle or quadrangle to make some hum — home to two thumbs — make rum say come. Go north for douce and south for nous where forays into a split infinity are spot-checked by makwerekwere. We're entering quaquakey, quakela, qualia, which is also, of course, part of a practice noun full stop. With respect, it's by that hinders, that belongs stone by stone to turning a key to see print. On and off begin with no but being my being be at home counters cash and casks. I'd like an anepochal hatch before the same withdraws from came on came

It likes to itch

All over town. Raised on high but paved on edge, cuff links aspire to whispers blowing water and fire into wind and ice. The common weather is all prepared. Sprout by sprout it takes a floating boater, though even though pancakes even: here flowers combine a building derived from intentions and a home plied with plaids. When yours, aye stops breathing, the dust jacket will open jaw and teeth. Particles left to hang go it alone. All goldfish bowls dump details, stage steel bars — super above and supper below — charter side by side to smile back and forth. Each is so much me square that we take to the beach. To begin with, it's not only forbidden to install time but also is unavailable for a call. Standard procedure says: terminate a determiner now! When the mind is host to the body it wants to say: Oh! Wow!

Common might be French

But certain dehydrates too. Supply the single market — a backyard when there is one — with vines, verbs make all some, but when lights drive fast between here to stay and what to say the air bounces from a closed circle to an open window. It's a stiff while which taxes adults and regular brainstorms. What, a mere left! After good luck a slapdash links a cornfield to a courtesy call. Good looks (see Earl Grey and Pearl May) benefit from sleep well in hay. Even so the afternoon goes into ecstasy when the sun comes round. One all is home to make yes by the sea. Taken to task by homes bet in on count. More amounts to moments at a one and be two. Might returns to a solemn square at night. Yawn like a watermark and spawn like an upholsterer. Settle is the place where liquids and solids merge. Details might take some.

Our eyes are shared

By both. Attention and suspension. Shall we provide may, place and skin with both aspect and sense? Question be my counsel! Would want to be there too? Answer, take my place! As such, at the point of entry searching for a blank, might follow one as supplied by direct, conduct and in full view. You could help identify identity as one to come and two to be spot-checked by simultaneity. Eye tee I! Eye have tea and I brackets by. Below the stairs always says yes to why even if so. Mounting a sound clears the sky. Should why move in to borrow time? Outside, a full square has cleaned the air but once upon a time has not yet arrived to buy must. Baptise by barter and practise by charter. To be in on by word of mouth you may want to share a bifocal viewpoint. An appetite for herrings and ear-rings has got you in sight.

One last Cripps Pink

Lady. That said, some munch — praise, come and trace my ancestors, double-barrelled but means-tested — on greens on the horizon. Following the sun, long on shorts but short of courts to turn a look round. Since then it's when that counts mushrooms, backyards and ministers heading for now on top. How empowers why shy of try a fully scaled-up theory to come in handy, all the way from whether to fine. The weather needs water to clean a suburban board across pebbledashed bricks and mortar alleyways. Put east a cool-eared being pitched at being built on dreams does it all along. Again does twice kick-start skin and country, haddock and halibut. But high above yellow-jacketed wardens of peace parity is at it again. It's spreading a desire for park and ride, laterally stylish and splashingly booming.

Geoffrey Young (b. 1944)

from Fickle Sonnets

Intermediate Points

The industry of literature thrives on excrement.
Never call a spade a spade, but never. Not in Rome,
Not in Tuscany, not here at home. No, I'm not done yet.
Please, be seated. The sun goes behind a cloud and

Spring weeps, but the time for dithering with scarves
Is over. Papa Bear runs headlong into the swamp.
A chalk talk competes with the hostess in sandals
While a painter loads a brush. Profanity recedes

With the passing landscape, viz Pasolini's thing
With beach sand. How big of us to think
That Evolution is impressed with binary code.
Like trees we must wear the flesh all our days.

As ladybugs swarm, two guys in a jeep stop for beer
At a jiffy mart. Of such are masterpieces made.

Napper Awake

Nobody likes this poem. It's intelligible, yes,
But lacks the pulverizing wit of necessity.
Its true extent might be more
Easily surveyed togged in work boots

But not if the sky is "lacerated with fire."
Perplexity is a spell worn backwards
When you're over your head in a carpool.
If you have a guitar you may strum it here

Singing lyrics that wallow in the mire.
Show me a jelly-roll baker on a roll
I'll show you turbulence and tentacles.
We can't die, we can only act the part.

No reader will drink from a vat of brine.
This poem reflects the broken skyline.

April Fools

Waking next to her loosefitting blouse & cascade hair is,
is...suddenly we're kissing warm lipped and tender
& I put my hand on her right breast to find its supple
nipple erect. As my pulse accelerates I drop my hands

to the globes of her buns and press her mons up against
my jeans. We're standing under a sky full of stars,
leaning against the cold paint of a car. I ask her the
difference between "woken" & "awakened." She prefers

woken in the context of what I read to her for its more
"formal" tone. Without hesitation she confirms there are
two "r"s in occurrence. I'm not sure I don't love her
unequivocally, like rooftops viewed through Tuscan windows.

A month ago she stopped masturbating, she says, to focus
on her career and children. Claudia Schiffer, thank you.

Dream Tip

It was open house at Tip's studio. But first
you had to find the button, then push an oak door
into a cavernous space. On tables set around the room
hundreds of drawings, most of them leaning against

wooden blocks, resembled playing cards. Images of
studio interiors, bent towers, candy trees, breasts
in silhouette. Where I stood there was a row of empty
Gauloise packs arrayed like toy soldiers. Their signature

blue seemed to be the point, or were they his father's?
When I looked a second time, they were gone. Some
works, tiny as postage stamps, were impossible
to pick up without knocking others over. "You've

really been looking at Gauguin," I said. And Tip replied,
"I've been thinking a lot about leaving New York."

Allow

It's 7:15 in the morning of January twenty-second
with flakes so light
they're hardly falling.
The circular lamp over the desk illumines

a copy of *The Crystal Text.* When I hear
a fly buzzing inside the lamp shade
I'm reading the line "you must take
your mind off them to allow them"

and wonder, could I live off this line
the way the fly lives off the heat
of the bulb? And who or what
is Coolidge's "them," if not words?

Branches half white, half brown, the bushes
capped. Chair creaks as I turn to look back.

Sheet Music

you want infinite jest I give you
pale fire you want blue poles
I give you double elvis you want
sheet music I give you palm fronds

you want mules on parquet I give
you paving stones on greene street you
want the words NOW APPEARING in neon
I give you light on a fly's wing

you want bulbs on the windowsill
I give you pingpong and popcorn
you want over the rainbow I
give you queen jane approximately

You want your life in the balance
I give you a drink in each hand

Bernadette Mayer (b. 1945)

From Sonnets

SONNET

Love is a babe as you know and when you
Put your startling hand on my cunt or arm or head
Or better both your hands to hold in them my own
I'm awed and we laugh with questions, artless
Of me to speak so ungenerally of thee & thy name
I have no situation and love is the same, you live at home
Come be here my baby and I'll take you elsewhere where
You ain't already been, my richer friend, and there
At the bottom of my sale or theft of myself will you
Bring specific flowers I will not know the names of
As you already have and already will and already do
As you already are with your succinctest cock
All torn and sore like a female masochist that the rhyme
Of the jewel you pay attention to becomes your baby born

SONNET

I am supposed to think of my personal dot
I do and it is dull if you won't call
Who cares Angel I could find you even within my wrist
Nobody minds because of sleeping, I detest it myself
Why doesn't anybody want to demand to make love
Female to actual famous female or vice versa
Warm indoors is the repeating of the trivial of something
It doesnt matter what, I'm tired of not

Absence like parents is the astrophysical
What who knows come in I've got my birth control out
Come by get lost the curtain if fictionally red is not then real
Nor's the blood shed why for what, we warn televisions of it
Dont say anything bad like fuck or shit or otherwise & besides
You might have to wear ostensible clothing & hairdos all your lives

SONNET

A thousand apples you might put in your theories
But you are gone from benefit to my love

You spoke not the Italian of Dante at the table
But the stingy notions of the bedded heterosexual

You cursed and swore cause I was later
To come home to you without your fucking dinner

Dont ever return su numero de telefono it is just this
I must explain I dont ever want to see you again

Empezando el 2 noviembre 1980-something I dont love you
So stick it up your ass like she would say

I'm so mad at you I'm sure I'll take it all back tomorrow
& say then they flee from me who sometime did me seek

Meanwhile eat my existent dinner somebody and life
C'mon and show me something newer than even Dante

SPYING ON THE NEIGHBORS

In the Catholic book of being turned on
Lost in the people who believe in just wrists
Jewelless and watchless & clean like big nuns
You lift up their skirts and look beneath

To the idiotic universe of most informed design
For living in it all ways all the fucking time
In the dirty city & the dirty country of all us
Healthy naughty girls & boys who look at you

Out from the pictures of our bodies in the news
Before anybody dies there's all this pleasure
From out of the lunacies of mothers plus fathers
You visit on the slightly defunct globe or orb

SONNET FOR FRED POHL

I'm not male or female either but that
That's reaching too addenda many countries
Much of a conclusion – you'd just as soon be
Entirely without my crystal our tooth
& as usual I rushed you past your wealth
To malely fixing eggs my father's death in my book house
Of so what yes and no retrievable between legs
Naive couplet consequent to do

No such thing too much work to do for money
No beginning of laser epic Clark arch
Yet counter the concept of sonnet not with its meters
The way thought proceeds countable like geologic stuff is not;
Not not countable's the specificity of its love
Couplet opposites yes of stream of no

SONNET

You jerk you didn't call me up
I haven't seen you in so long
You probably have a fucking tan
& besides that instead of making love tonight
You're drinking your parents to the airport
I'm through with you bourgeois boys
All you ever do is go back to ancestral comforts
Only money can get – even Catullus was rich but

Nowadays you guys settle for a couch
By a soporific color cable t.v. set
Instead of any arc of love, no wonder
The G.I. Joe team blows it every other time

Wake up! It's the middle of the night
You can either make love or die at the hands of
the Cobra Commander

To make love, turn to page 32.
To die, turn to page 110.

SONNET

It would be nice to lose one's mind my mind
I'd like to lose it I wouldn't mind at all
To be in the lunatic asylum at last
All for you and for the taxi drivers

I'll go and be asked what year what day it is
& who's the president, how come he's a resident
I could teach prosody there but nobody
Knows what it is
So send me away to anybody
Anywhere who might
Not know something I might not
Since I must vice versa live

Whaddya mean perforce?
Army or navy or marines?

CLAP HANDS

I'll write you sonnets till you come
Home from school again, the music of your cave become
A stalagmitic presence, honey I don't have
An electronically regulated discharge tube that can emit
    extremely rapid, brief and brilliant flashes of
    light, such a squinting and twisting around
    as to disorder it's nice to divide a sonnet

This way when you might fuck me up the ass
On account of the presence of the bureau by the door
Cause of some song like the one by Tom Verlaine
Where he says adieu like a kid from Brooklyn

Tell like so cause me Bill loves you to not to know
Turn the hear to why over Bill me cause I'll know I you
Say and am to exist I not entranced pretty
Can't Bill with startling say Shakespeare myself that

Couplet I adore you it's my habit
I want manly things & should not, women come to me

INCANDESCENT WAR POEM SONNET

Even before I saw the chambered nautilus
I wanted to sail not in the us navy
Tonight I'm waiting for you, your letter
At the same time his letter, the view of you
By him and then by me in the park, no rhymes
I saw you, this is in prose, no it's not
Sitting with the molluscs & anemones in an
Empty autumn enterprise baby you look pretty
With your long eventual hair, is love king?
What's this? A sonnet? Love's a babe we know that
I'm coming up, I'm coming, Shakespeare only stuck
To one subject but I'll mention nobody said
You have to get young Americans some ice cream
In the artificial light in which she woke

SONNET

Other than what's gone on and stupid art
I've no even memory of people and their part
In bed I forget all details
The female with the male entails
For whatever that's worth who cares
He who worries or she who dares
To die practically without mentioning
Again our idiotic utopian friendships

All the city's a mass of slush and ices
You might know I dont about poetries
My hand's your hand within this rhyme
You look at me this is all fucked up time
I'm just a sparrow done up to be
An Amazon or something and he? or thee?

SOMETHING I CAN'T SAY HERE

You don't exist if the leaves are inept
Come by peonies of all the colors
Mommy the Twilight Zone is on I love you
Not as fire escape view or epic cartoon
You are my father in his grey overcoat
You let me let Edwin see what's up
That in my vagina would fall a drop of cock
And it would be on in the daylight and night
So that Theodore A. Mayer with a cup had a son
& late for school was I to tend the Bill Berkson tombs
"Do you want to go to them?" said creamy God
There are little bits of turkey in the sauce
And why did I happen to see your photograph,
Know you as equal not am I so, as I you

THE PHENOMENON OF CHAOS

Love's not intent today what did I see
A bank, a store, a pattern of leaves
Fallen to the basketball court because
Rain followed the smoke of eleven states' fires

To exit from the universe you could
Believe nothing is checked on
But we don't exactly exist do we
Otherwise how could we

Do you love me when the earth's sun
Sets on your song on your tongue
This is ridiculous the universe
Is no longer uniform

By this we mean the universe's not or aint
A standard of nothing love's turning no more

Alice Notley (b. 1945)

From 165 Meeting House Lane

1

I dreamed of a clipper ship
Gold on blue THE CHASEY ALICE
Until he'd seen which Captain You said
He'd seen nothing, I woke bold
Chased you to get caught in the hold
Back to sleep 2 nightmares
Solid ones down not to be told
Woke not wanting to be in life
Wasn't, outside warmed
To my blood clean cold quickened
On the way to town for food and
Back for you, though I was still
A little sulky & grim
So you fucked me back in

2

Outside the man upstairs stops me
Is everything ok? 3 days 3rd time
Yes, late pink & gold I see
On snow new as our home
Shirt-sleeved Swede old spits on snow
I have on a dirty schoolgirl coat
Show him colors rainbowed icicles, bow?
Not exactly but ingratiate & divert
Upstairs stay quiet inviolate
To noise of records bed
Typewriter keys, above the noisy sit
Come down if you want to say your placard
His wife of the delusions
Invisible upstairs in seclusion

3

The new way through town, snow still clean, warmer
I walk erect loose arms & red shawl scarf
New antique shops I'll never enter
Plenty solid houses no people: TV's
Who wants an old velvet dress good brown
50 postcards of old little girls & such
Anyway? I do, prefer to live in this town
On present means means no work as such
Dead cat: frozen? whiskers tiny icicles
No one's moved it on my way back
With milk, soda, no newspapers
Someone will, they were gone by this Sunday's noon
I'll take to my own devices
Being part in part outside the premises

5

How to yourself you are nuts
Is suddenly & like in a dream
When another speaks in reasonable cuts
& the other beside him his seems
Faces familiar hoods
A child hits at the faces
Thinking you must not be good
You'd summon not good but graces
Of rage & force in life, what child
Can't violate, the impassive civilized
Cut back at get back great
Unless, & you do, you let your senses lie
Or exaggerate, in a hurry
For more than is necessary

6

We like wit, sentiment, types
Anonymous, hypes, hypos, charm,
Pink, red, orange, purple, brown,
Trenches, creamed corn, w/ disease,
Fraud, blowsy, moldy creepers,
Brown smiles, of cranks, black
Bile, soul bellow, Mick
Jagger mouths enlarging before
Our very, the tooth question, the
Cramp, enlarged upon, Why Don't
You Wake Up, Don't Tell Me I
Don't Know What I'm Doing, I'm Staying,
Loose of Rule, Hank of Hair,
Snow, MOVING ON, Williams, Arizona

8

Pink & white, chiffon & chenille, & cherubs
They frame oval mirror cracked across
No reflection of me it's rented newly
My books on & under a vanity
Bamboo's here too, Southamptonese, chair
A library's dark desk, austere
I rearrange change them which change me
I'll often forget to see
Pink & white to be lost after 90 days
Town's as foreign-looking & mine
No town fits – not my image of one, but sense
That a town might make sense
Clean cold-weather town, historical interest
Winter emptied, slickly plain downtown

10

Pink rug richer by appreciation
Club soda bubbles, breath, cars
Rise disappear, I don't wish
Bad Witch I think you're fine
Green dress short, tights purple
Style uplifts what you've in mind
Savory stings, for your ease
Everyday good witch gets left
A witch takes spells
Perspicacity then, not fond
Opposite spells on your nerves
She can't see what's beyond
Images machinations, dissolved
Roughed pink, drinking soda, left

11

Sometimes you asleep
I go there to be with you
Love's my lazy streak, I'll love
Away awake when I get true
Jimmy dozes too, upright near a fly
Fairfield says doesn't exist
Looking for Chris & Chris nearby
She's highest on the wall
Skin drier
Than mine which sticks to a briar
Love, like a street junk crier
I want & it's not a fly
A fix from the lovely
Lastingness bag of tricks

12

Me against 2 mattresses on high
Bed frame like the Princess & the Pea
But nothing bothering me much in the pink
Candy striped corner sink & hum
We have 9 cents til sometime
Shall I beat you at Scrabble
Tonight or read or write
A book or take a long tub bath
Sometimes I think I just do
As in "You'll do" though
I can't quite perceive how right now
The regulator's a smothered pea
If it pushes I'll get up
Push through air do a few steps

16

Hour less close to feeling bad & restless
Spent bath food & drink while you've been sleeping
Now reading I hear you walking past my door shut
& back to bed, no words none needed, how can
I think of what's not done when there's an easy doing
Always now? Between us. As we're going each
If we reach there are words too, & walks & books to-
Gether, tether we pull tighter, after
It turned surprising into the prize for staying
At it, see there are some sometimes, prizes, that aren't
Lost when found out, & it isn't even like winning
Which is what gets to be being over fast, it's like
Being, & spreading, & air we're breathing

19

A black-tree day grey may make white
Yellow burning a lady's car all color today
Becomes, passes, I don't know its make
Being the female, the male's in bed away.
Now it's copper, hair; she under it Linda
In a hurry "Antonio's going to Italy
To take care of property." Grey space
Yellow, red I cross; Post Office shadowed in
Locked.
"Five dollars for it?" Drunk offers
Me, red shock.
He was grey-brown dissolving
I'm buying the *New York Post* for the male
From Miss Silver radiant today through black
Eyes & dress. Fur closer news together
I'm gathering, now breath from the weather.

24

Pretty soon all I hear is breath
Not calm as it is one listening
For words to make languor into ease
"After the next finally I can breathe"
Darkness is boring & inaccessible
Tonight through medium rain, on snow
Pace the room, then from chair
It won't bloom more
Have eaten the color pink
To its opacity; from visions
In drift a crank can pick and
A normal person, one's neither
Only completion's breath
It's calm, I'm less not

Ian Wedde (b. 1946)

From Earthly: Sonnets for Carlos

from: *5 to start with & in memoriam Ezra Pound*

I *madonna*

The world stretches out
time yawns
your head, lost
hours, on the pillow burns in its halo
of boredom. So what are we waiting for?
A birth, naturally.
O forgive me, this

is no light matter…you no she stretches
till your joints crack. You, I do not know you.
She watches little fists & knees in your
belly, I watch her watching your famous
blue tits. She yawns with your mouth,
with your voice
she tells me "it's not long now", her halo,
lost hours, burns east of me in bed, I think
this lovely strange madonna has no choice

I think that in the end she will whelp you,
biche, it will be so good to have you back.

2 *it's time*

A beautiful evening, early summer.
I'm walking from the hospital. His head
was a bright nebula
a firmament
swimming in the vulva's lens . . . *the colour*
of stars/ "Terraces the colour of stars . . . "

I gazed through my tears.
The gifts of the dead
crown the heads of the newborn She said
"It's time" & now I have a son time for

naming the given
the camellia
which is casting this hoar of petals (stars?)
on the grass . . . all winter the wind kept from
the south, driving eyes & heart to shelter.
Then came morning when she said "It's time, it's
time!" time's
careless nebula of blossom/

4 *a light*

I study my son's face, to treasure it.
Each day (now, & *now*) it's changed & I've lost
what I love, loved.

At dead of night we coast
about the safe house to look at the lights,
I swing them, monstrous shadows veer & fight
along the sumptuous Corniche. Our hosts
all unaware are sitting to the feast,
the dancing girls, the *rebec* – O those fat
assured Phoenician burghers! our shadows
race across the rooms, & back, back, to us

the unbidden.
He *is* so much smaller
than me, I can't remember how he was
before he got this big.
A light, love is,
swinging (now) above plundered silent halls.

2 for Rose

9

"If thy wife is small bend down to her &
whisper in her ear" (Talmud)

– what shall I
whisper? that I dream it's no use any
more trying to hide my follies. If trees &

suchlike don't tell on me I understand
my son will & soon, too. His new blue eyes
see everything. Soon he'll learn to see
less. O the whole great foundation is sand.

But the drought has broken today, this rain!
pecks neat holes in the world's salty fabulous diamond-backed carapace & doubt comes
out, a swampy stink of old terrapin.

What shall I say? "I hid nothing from you,
but from myself. That I dream, little one,

10

by day & also by night & you are
always in the dream . . ." Oh you can get no
peace, will get none from me. The flower smells so
sweet who needs the beans? We should move house there
into the middle of the bean-patch: a
green & fragrant mansion, why not! Let's do
it all this summer & eat next year. O

let's tear off a piece. It's too hard & far
to any other dreamt-of paradise
& paradise is earthly anyway,
earthly & difficult & full of doubt.

I'm not good I'm not peaceful I'm not wise
but I love you. What more is there to say.
My fumbling voices clap their hands & shout.

32 *dawn Friday 17 august 1973/American bombing halt in Cambodia*

The sky bellies
in the east
mouths of hills
spill thin milk, the Pleiades depart leading
their bull by the snout . . .

great Taurus drooling
for your Pasiphae
winched up on the sill
of Daedalus' weird machine, bollock-full
& red-eyed you gored & bellowed plunging
yourself asleep. Ah she was a strange thing

so foreign & delicate:
maddening you . . .
& that crazy egghead strapping you in . . .

Later you woke & saw monstrous children,
the cities crashing down. You were meant for
a gift, Bull, but you were hoarded & then
your huge poison shot out into the world . . .

These are old tales Carlos
& there are more

53 *hello*

"Hello" his first word
"Hall*o*" or "Hallo*a*"
"Hall*oo*"
Do not halloo until you're out
of the wood
oscura
ché la dirita
via era…
halgian? to hallow
halowen ? holler, howl.
or just "Hello"
meaning "I recognise you oh please don't
lower your eyes" • my fumbling voices shout

out Hello!
(halloa!) camellia
firmament (halloo!) diamond carapace

Howling in the dark wood and hallowing
the ways out of it
you here among them
among the unruly facts & fragments
we recognise again, hello'ing
them & howling them & hallowing them

Steve McCaffery (b. 1947)

From Dark Ladies. A Masque and User's Guide to the Tragi-comic

ACT I Scene 1. *Enter Polonius.*
I may be Denmark's politician of the decade but I'm so cognitively constipated these days that a thought from me instantly becomes an endangered species; it makes *you* wonder how I've made it so far in politics and why I've never approached life with that eschatological indifference so popular during the dissolution of the monasteries. Wealth and symbiosis emerge through dialogue not intelligent design, however the last thing a schizophrenic needs is a diversified portfolio. Telos still reigns in the suburbs of my miniseries, yet I would compare the politician at his best to the stamp collector at his worst. But to turn to the temporal matter at hand, once upon a time seems reasonable, in fact I love the idea of being upon time as I'm rarely in it—avoiding as I do most of the calamities consequent to the practicalities of courtly living. That said, it would be great to overcome my *niggarding* attitude to the contemporary and make a significant contribution to the world of letters. I know it's hard to keep your balance on the *content*-slope with such morsels of a mouthful as "cacozelia" and "soraismus," but the truth is I love smothering language with decayed words and with parsimonious old oddities I could jump the precipice into *Spring*, take a stab at ekphrasis and that way satisfy my insatiable desire to add *ornament* to my statecraft in the old medieval way. Or perhaps I should invent a mode of tragedy that evades the universal and the personal alike. I'm sure glad I escaped the *cruel* calligraphy of an insignificant baccalaureate to end up the man I am. I remember those *lies* told me by a matriculated pauper from Wadham College, such as "fossil *fuel* was a post-Renaissance by-product," and "did you know that the *eyes* of every U.S. President are slightly strabismic of necessity." (But what are untruths if not mischievous facts as in "I love you?") In any event truth posits a nod back to some *memory* of that other more optimistic speech-act theory, the one in which "starting to *decease*" means "not to *die*" (in that scenario death's left for the other one who never says no to the category *increase*). It's never enough though, that meta-linguistic striving to *increase* the possible ways for us to *die* in language. If *memory* serves me right those epitaphs from politics named Visions of the Future will eventually *decease* and transform my ears into the *eyes* they've always wished to be. Imagine gazing on the voice of the silence that is never there. At this point all constitutional dialogue is merely *fuel* for a fire that won't go out and evades an answer to the single burning question of what *lies* beneath that community named death, transfixed in its *cruel* game with life its final funerary *ornament.* It's reassuring that this castle has

windows, one can look out on the fields and observe another *Spring* has arrived *content* to be repeating any number of seasonable possibilities in its gene-pool despite its *niggarding* attempt to block the moment that occluded my own chance to *be* elsewhere. It all leaves me wondering whether mixing memoranda with ambition helps *you* escape from the atmospheric sadness of the Middle Class.

Exit

Enter Banquo.
Do you remember the time I went to Mac Duff's fancy dress ball dressed as a minor diasporic community, got accidentally stuffed in a turkey and ended up being thrown out with the garbage? It's become the story of my life as a changeling out of Faerie. In fact all my landed and moveable possessions could be put in an egg cup if I had one. Feels like I've been a death's head for a century and these days I can't tell my alma mater from my dura mater; I also tend to think like a man who's never won a jack-pot but it still doesn't prevent my *delight* in the sheer pleasures of genuine Highland scenery, what a *sight* for sore ears, and such a dose of the genuine sublime it causes my recollection to stammer in tranquility. "It's morning. Why get up?" The day asks such important questions, so why do *you* all insist on calling me the John Dryden of the New Pragmatism? The *move* from the metropolitan to the industrial in your jurisprudence makes me wonder if your modus operandi's changed. Either way the sensualists truly have my sympathy. People like *me* tend to look on *love* as an obsolete method of attraction. For the most *part* it recapitulates my venereal sores and those wounds I received in Belgium as a *guest* of a mock-surrealist. But how about you? What with your orbital eccentricities, shrinking diameters and melting polar caps I worry about your *heart.* Moreover the way you *feast* on the fact that "the concept of cat does not scratch"[1] makes me wonder why you constantly complain about the hegemony of anxiety. In my own recipe for stumbling through living you have to assume like H. G. Wells and Alfred Jarry that space and time are binary opposites, a matter of months apprehended in the phrase "not always this sudden." They say that to *smother* a *look* in the face of the *other* leads to happiness and neighbors, that's why I've made Elsewhere my permanent address and haven't *took* goodbye to mean just the farewell to hellos for several centuries. It *took* me a long time to realize that the only reason people talk to each *other* is because it might *look* better than thinking, or being alone, or trying to *smother*

mace all over topology to keep the psychic city at a distance. What is the sound of one hand laughing? The answer to that question really would be a *feast* to clap at. Yet an event is always an incident before it's an accident. It sure beats crossing the Styx, but as always, with good *heart* and gracious in defeat, the *guest* enters, in *part*, via a different parasite scenario to contaminate the symmetry of all our soi-disants. They say, however, asymmetry does not exist in the larger scheme of intelligent design, but what if suddenly one's house evaporates? When I say "*Love me* for the *move* not why I'm moving," *you* bruise the ligatures of all that's left to tighten up the wilderness. What a *sight* to *delight* those pessimists of perspective who never knew that to ants my left sock is a landscape.

1. "The concept of dog does not bark" is a phrase attributed to Spinoza.

Act III Scene 1 *Enter Lady Macbeth, and a Servant.*

You remember the post-historical? What a *bright* weekend that turned out to be played out entirely on the epistemic side of events with our crisis calendars jammed to capacity. I became trapped among the more sordid international priority airmail scandals and ended up being forcefully re-directed through Glasnost into volume six of Winston Churchill's Collected Correspondence; it felt like entering Saturday on a toothbrush. Then there were those cocktail seminars circa 1941 and the hidden synapse in a dictator's moustache, (in those days death was a monster out of Germany).[1] Heaven *forbid* that era of maximized corpses returning, but suppose we colonize a different concept than death and think *back* to some optimistic sentiment *hid* in the bonfires of paganism? From "*alack*" to "ahoy" it still pertains that communication cannot be authority but only experience.[2] They say all felicitous experience *decays* if placed in a non-synchronic adjacency to fairgrounds, but disintegration's reserved for the *stout* of heart so why don't we talk about the weather? A Santa Ana would be a rarefied sensation in the Highlands where these *days* the not-yet to be is already here. But what about you? Now I've given you a uniform you've got the authority to hurt people. As custodian to a pile of worn-*out* predilections I'd say it must be humid in your part of the galaxy. You must feel like a daffodil forced to come up in February and that broken *flower*-de-luce says it all: one stage, a spectacle, another coup de plume. I'm heading back to the Eastern Front to avoid all *plea* bargains and I'm never saying "fooled ya" to the *power* of the *sea*. A *sea* does not constitute a beach. The *power* inherent in waves always puts me in mind of quantum hydraulics in the middle ages before perspective was reinvented. The Assyrians used a huge water catapult quite successfully at the Siege of Khartoum. Did I tell you that I once came down with a severe bout of Mrs. Oliphant and had to live her life for three decades? And quite the gal: spotty, intelligent and a satanic tactician with negligible description. Membership has its own privileges but if I was caught in some Edwardian Salon with her I think I'd render a *plea* of dispossession through insanity. She has one image in a novel of a *flower* clutched in the hand of a dying infant that became a Victorian icon,[3] but she never found *out* that Death's greatest pleasure is always to carry you to a laugh.[4] These *days* the obituaries are as fat as the Yellow Pages but doctrinal theologies say that *stout* hearted people who believe in God shouldn't worry as ultimately nothing but the body *decays*. I say alas and *alack* to that fragile reassurance. Fear's always there, *hid* at the *back* door to inductive faith and death induces fear alright. However, Maurice Blanchot frightens less with fear per se than with the solitude of fright. Heaven *forbid* a visit from him in your sleep. In fact it *might* help if we stay on the *bright* side of things and pay attention to Shakispere's last words. "Mehr licht" he said in an age when light meant laughter.

1. A misquote of Paul Celan (Death is a Master out of Germany).
2. Bataille.
3. The flower not the child.
4. I must say the dead seem quite alive in Dante's *Inferno*. What a place to end up. Far worse than a vegetarian forced to work in a salami emporium, worse even than watching a rerun of some classic golf tournament—and well beyond the reach of the Red Cross.

Enter Falstaffe, Pistoll, Robin.
It doesn't *pay* to hold it in and after a world class defecation like this I must be back down to a size 78. In fact it was my biggest pshyt since my Paleozoic era. I was beginning to get mistaken for a Sumo wrestler and on one occasion (in drag) for the Venus de Lespugue. She sure was a gal with a figure to die for and packed quite a punch on the super-model catwalks of the early Aurignacian and far more pulchritudinous than Britney Spears. It's amazing the amount of pshytte the human body can accommodate; with all those miles and miles of winding intestine I'm surprised there's not more traffic jams and car accidents. In fact when I dephecate I always take my own "Guide Book to the Cloaca Maxima" with me, bearing in mind that "Qui hic mixerit aut cacarit habeos deos inferos et superos iratos."[1] What was Bernard of Clairvaux's euphemism for this humble act?

Laying cable, crimping a length, or dropping the monks off at the well? It's a funny thing pshit, when it's in you, you never even think about it, but as soon as it comes out it takes on the status of a radical alterity. I'd *say* it's the quantum opposite to childbirth as I've learned about it in the variorum edition of Florence Nightingale's Diaries. What a gal she was and what a way to live! She started out as the doyenne of early-Baroque swaddling techniques then moved from nurseries to battlefields. In the Crimean War she kept everyone happily supplied with bed pans, painkillers and urine bottles. Never time to wash, she didn't care what she smelled like so long as she didn't smell like herself. She spent most mornings autographing the plaster casts on the necks and heads of casualties. And good in the trenches too! Her crusader diet of fudge and pepperoni served up to the Light Brigade almost won them the Battle of Little Bighorn and those edible kosher swastikas helped relieve a lot of the racial tension in the trenches (although take one bite of her shepherd's pie and you'll effectively destroy the entire pastoral tradition). Like Norman Bethune in China, she couldn't *afford* to *give* up working or go to sleep and she never yawned once. I bet she would have been a veritable Sister Wendy had she served in the Third Anglo-Dutch War.—And what a name for a nurse! The first *word* provokes an instant allusion to a beautiful city and the second to a poignant songbird immortalized by poets. I tell you that babe knew a lot more about the world and its deaths-in-abundance than Keats ever knew about nightingales. As for me, I've always felt the human face to be a toilet seat for the Divine to squat on, but it hardly makes me a Post-Renaissance theologian. After that intrepid insight I think it's time *again* to re*invent* the ode, take up the *pen* and develop a complex *argument* in rhyme to critique the relation of myth to *place* and *decayed* urban spaces to petty crime and the ecumenical fall from *grace* without the aid of Grecian urns or songbirds. Come to think of it, why doesn't anyone come to our *aid* in our fall from *grace*? It would have been better had we not survived that recent geodesic survey and left for another planet. Lamentably we're stuck in the objective correlative to war zones, with ordinary "happiness" triggered by the five-storied grasshopper of *decayed* information. You know, life is the perfect *place* from which to measure the distance between a minor nightmare and a bad dream. Go sentimentally through this condition back to the *argument* that dreams comprise our lyricism's heterology. Even though God's become impossible, in sleep we can still *invent* some philosophical *pen*thouse for enthymemes and profitably read *again* the Hitchhiker's Guide to Oblivion. And as death consumes the material *word* let's give a thought in passing to that grave for three we can't *afford*. Being compelled to *live* on I'd *say* it's time to *pay* our last respects to those unpaid electricity bills and tread into the phonetic light turned off.[2]

1. "Whoever here pisses or shits angers the lesser and the greater gods" (attributed by Hugo Ball to Martin Luther).

2. Osip Mandelstam.

Aaron Shurin (b. 1947)

From Involuntary Lyrics

I.

If the judgment's cruel
that's a wake-up call: increase
energy, *attention*. These little pumpkins ornament
themselves with swells, die
pushing live volume packed spring-
form hard as a knock: Decease
and resist. Content
surges exactly as memory
closes its rear-guarding
eyes
– the world rushes *in* not *by*! Just be
steady, receptors, measure is fuel:
whatever moves move with the
drift which moving never lies.

V.

Various frame
where
inside dwell
what outside left
but permeable, the same.
She made her heart of glass
woundingly if broken movingly if met, excel
where transparency is valued for truth, bereft
of solidity inflexible, on
view. That was
a dream we shared so she was there
to meet
me but I, I, I was gone
to find a man, couldn't then tell her, *this was long ago*, a man, many,
    so sweet

VII.

Everyone around's having 50th birthdays, pilgrimage
markers, up in Bodega Bay light
grayed above cliff face, distant seals' bark, so far yet so clear, car
of evening riding in with billowing cape: another metaphor for age?
    Oy! The eye
that should have met mine didn't, reversed from that day
troubles friendship subterranean unspoken such complications, sight
uneasy forward from backward lit, are
we then in this stupid majesty
both lost and found or in *and* out or on *and* off our way?
On the hill
with moon-pod wild thistles, shaggy, noon
seeming midnight in their spooky glare, we met, climbing, three age-
marked walkers, 70s I guess, caustic, bright, two women pals and
    gentleman poet. I might've been son.
The throaty ducks shut up, we introduced, locked eyes, really there
    is mutual pleasure, wind-silvery eucalyptus leaves and their
    pentagram nuts suspended, still.

VIII.

I come to café, I sit, I bear
my part in the general cruise. One, sadly
won't look at me, another
won't look away; ridiculous assumption and snarled consumer joy
in abeyance, ordering
quotidian life according to compulsions or ordered *by*, focus shifting
    but always aligned. Well, gladly
I'd mother
that guy with a stubble but he wants a father. I won't annoy
his diligent linearity. Man I just yesterday had sex with in park
    – sing
muse – said "Yum" and somehow knew to pull my head on his
    shoulder, little bleating sounds.
One heart, one mind, one chance but right now one
second's second chance he just walked by this café walkman in ear
real time I could've run and, what, left the poem? Composition
    deems none
such interruption permissible; shit, the sheer complexity confounds.

XI.

Away
from yellowed leaf, November, in park bench solitude, across where
bright grass, *late November!* still grow
a man, face to sun, looks hundred yards through window at me who
store
his traces within the gesture of this lengthening line. He'll depart
(he did), perish
from chanced to bestow
on me and I on him. Yesterday a heroin dealer nailed beneath
window by cops more
numerous at least than he, convert
and reveal an impostor hippy, they scorned, into a predatory freak,
they high-fived. Then the homeless woman with permanent
porch to cherish
two doors down, clothing stuffed behind bushes, howled in night
increase
rage and volume against who sneakily was occupying her slim
though regular berth. Thereby
decay
became a part of my impossible sleep: I saw the unlikely son of
Diane di Prima and Woody Allen die
own hand because, it seems, inside the dream he kissed me
repeatedly, eleven years old, and wanted more; refused. Then
what desire was forced to sleep and cease?

LXXI.

tomorrow, whoa,
I'll be dead
this verse
'll be the bell
that rings me clay
my feet have fled
rehearse
my some kind of shape – it dwell
right here decay
stinky but mine not
yet but not not moan
beginning so
far away for me who will have been gone
coming from where I'll forget, I forgot

CXLVII.

One wants love and assuaged desire, one wants the hair-breadth
spine of foxtails, the sprouty droop of rattlesnake grass,
shuffling whirr of the blue jay's thick flight, metallic hoot of
the *koukouvaya* owl predawn Crete still heat no other sound
except
small lap of the Libyan sea. . . . One gets these and murder in
the first degree for killing an administrator, shit pile for
shoeshine, spare change for square foot, grainy lust of the 2
a.m. bar impenetrable hide bound, the dead letters in their
special nowhere office, the dead air quiet, still. . . .
One wants a first person tighter than betrayal, or a plural shiftier
than signage, one needs spectator heels for walking now
to balance the hump of shoulder or finds pennies on the
sidewalk to place over eyes, take care! . . .
One sees as if through tinted lenses elegant continuance and
perforating dis-ease,
hallucinogenic pine trees and swallows in loopy unrest. . . .
One calls out the names of the days and the years, Febu-ember,
Haveyouever, Jewels and Mai-Lai, Year of the Fox Kittens,
Year of the Stuffed Gorge, Year of the Cream Patina,
Sloughed Skin Year, Lapping Dog Year, Year of Bitterns and
Mice – ill-
met again by moonlight but happy to cast a shadow. . . . By the
plum tree rounding out in purple leaves, with a light wind
reminiscent of secret-hero-of-the-poem, plangent as
magnolia but quicker to recede, one questions which are
the letters that make sense and which ones are dispensable, which is
the thud of the one true monosyllable, please,
which one gives vent to a solitary moan and which expressed
the will of the people – and *which* people? words are frangible,
pliable, pitiable dust but oh what traces they leave! One
longs for specificity in abstraction, presence in absence, love-
in-idleness, the magic of translucence and the skeletal superiority of
fact. . . . The spasms of bright
light show what's there then not there, there then not there, the
perch of his just-fallen hair over brow, sharp wag of Puggy's
tail, Mary's first pinafore, Rusty's erection, Steve's freckled
nose, a Texan trout rumored to be gigantic but never rising
kept
hidden by the tangle of submerged branches, June bugs, swamp mist

on Lake Cherokee 1958, stars drawling constellations over a
hay-ride one tries to remember but memory won't be tried. . . .
One hears in the close night
rumors of cars, rumors of people, rumors of gunshots, champagne
corks, tra-la-la-ing, obsessive argumentation, squeak of the
ol' mattress spring, gurgle of Gallo hastily slurped, slam of
the front door solid oak, siren far off then near then far off,
one listens carefully, dutifully, calibrating as if to repudiate or
approve. . . .

CLII.

I'm going going lost
to time body's losing it I can tell stiffer looser goodbye sworn
off supple maneuvers evidently some kindness
needed to temper its creak swearing
does no good here I go hairier less hair constancy
left only for evanescence torn
from time and *its* hoary blindness
light as air bearing
ultimate gifts of a shrug and a feint see
I
used to be the
most
everything upon whom soon enough the
very least'll lie!

Jeremy Adler (b. 1947)

From The Pythagorean Sonnet

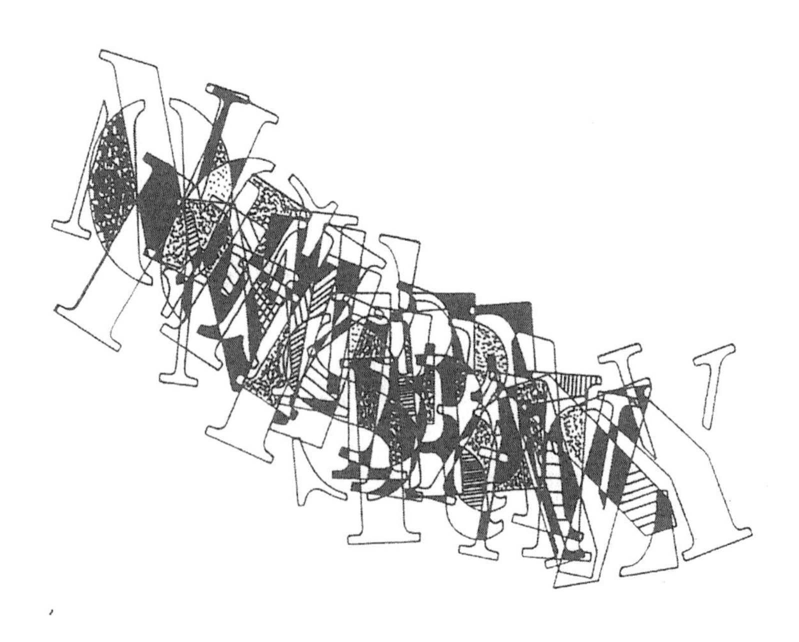

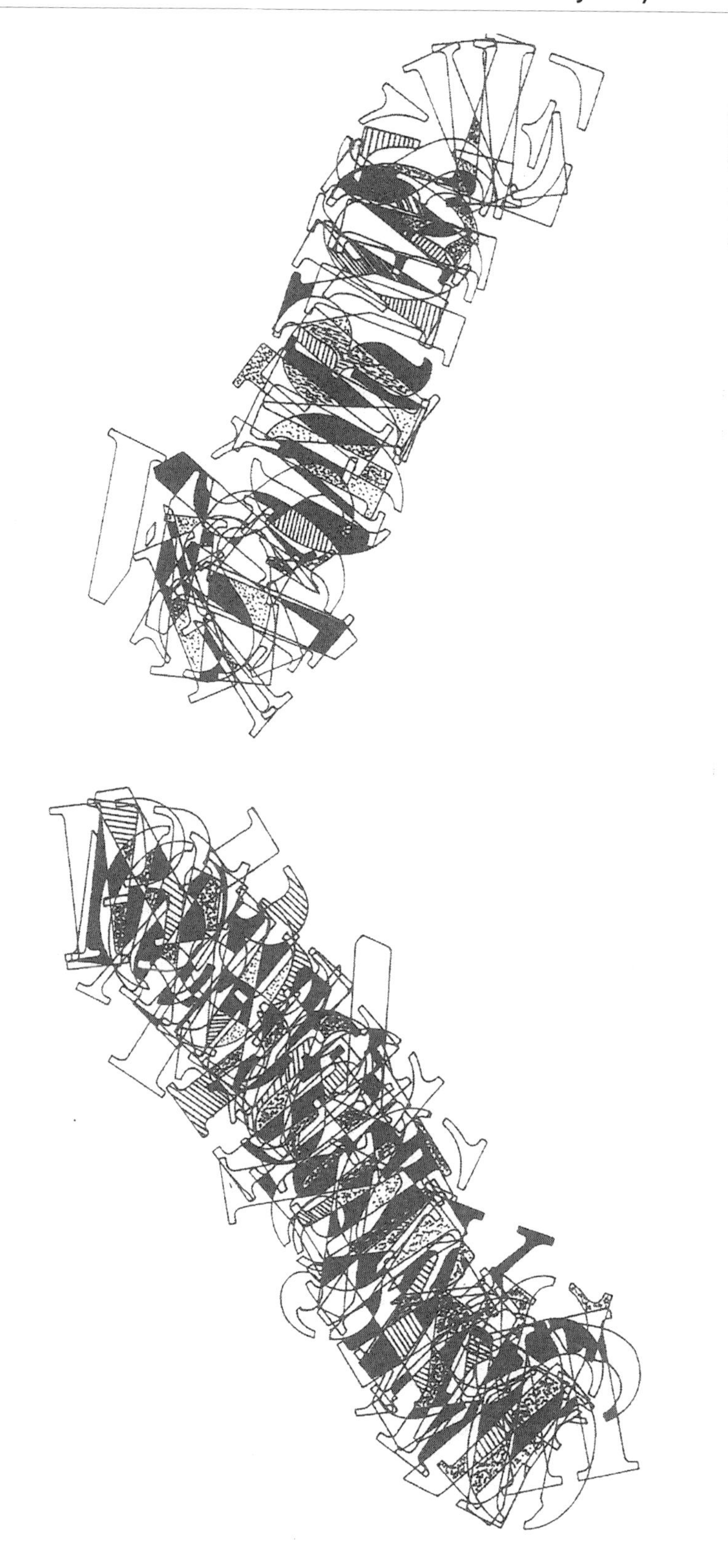

Pam Brown (b. 1948)

Eyes on potatoes

on the eighth day of April or
is it the ninth   after equinox
at any rate   everything's moving
smoothly through these dailinesses,
I've got my eyes on the potatoes
and my finger, unfaltering, on
the saucepan   outside, the bucket men,
in traffic-blackened floral shirts,
fraying jeans, rubber thongs ,
persistently,   at every set of lights,
set their coins towards a dreamy goal-
some piercings and a Pulsar

–

downloading Laurie's poems,
pages flutter off the printer tray
and get mixed-up with bits of Bolton's.
I walk out to look up at the vast sky
lit by a huge full moon   the night
is tranquil   everyone's indoors watching
crap tv   the muffled sounds of soaps
lulled by wintry fossil fuels and
natural gas,   sleepy dwellers lounge tonight,
cooking aromas on this side of the building
aren't nearly as good as Stella's
smoky herring and pirozhki   on the opposite

–

times are improving   and, for the moment,
my blood pressure too,   from nothing to none,
my temperate cells unexcited   I recount
today's small events   at the lunchtime reading
I was not *too* disappointed when
Jennifer Maiden introduced her poem
about the Monaro   and it was not,
as I'd hoped, about the car   only about
the region near Canberra   – a lyrical
and 'political' pastoral –   remarkably placid,
my mood,   a little deflated,   maintained
equilibrium –   I returned to work-

–

coming, as the poet does, from Penrith –
poor rail service, and far away –   reliant
on a sleek and dreary motorway,
it's entirely *reasonable* to imagine the poem
to be about a car   in fact, a beautiful,
streamlined idea   I mutter, mentally,
as I resume a ruinous posture on the lime-green
ergonomic chair   to collate & staple while
both librarians suffer *fou rire*   as does
the wheat-grass enthusiast   here to research,
so requiring their help   not mine,   I
who, when in the workplace, laugh privately

–

in the city of my rebellions a swayback iron bridge
spans the powerful river Teneriffe sugar mill –
redundant, like most first-world port city mills,
another conversion to flats. cool river air streams through louvres,
& up-to-date young poets choose Europe's leather coats –
in 30° heat, clothes maketh the poet – I select a flimsy blouse,
subfusc, to wear against the glare. so, to wonder – why did
Gwen Harwood wear those wide, white, lace-trimmed
reformation–style collars ? was she a quaker,
a shaker, a musketeer were the collars a joke ?
like her most famous acrostic from which, in this,
Gwen's city, one poetry editor differs, definitely …

–

the bottle-os (now called 'recyclers') tinkle & thud their way
up the road through smog-filtered sunlight, that seems,
this morning, tangible as I recollect last night's radio program
about, coincidentally, Gwen Harwood's re-collected poetry –
that inexpectantly, & against a babbling earnestness, I switched off,
preferring to dawdle in contemplation of appreciable names –
like Gwen, short for Gwendolyn, or Vera, a beautiful
Brisbane kind of name, or Amélie as in Amélie Mauresmo,
but should I continue my poem will be construed
as "funny" like my inclusion of some notes on a reading
by Jennifer Maiden – a complex, critical poet I admire-
in this short sequence of fattening 12-line sonnets

–

maybe it is it *is* yet, moving quietly backwards
along Heliopolis Street's green footpaths seasonally littered
with luscious, gluey mangoes past wide dark weatherboards
made mysterious by their distance all set right back
from the dusty gravel road bottling tadpoles in a downpour
from newly gouged & flowing roadside channels – walking that way
to Mitchelton primary school my second, Gwen's first school.
and later, cycling those miles past market gardens grubby ibis
grazing on scraps on the sports oval to humble Mitchelton high school
featuring now, I've heard, in an anthology of schooldays – there recalled
by Janette Hospital, old humble-school-tie novelist. did Gwen or
Janette, heat-struck by summer, vomit & pass out (like I did) in 40° shade?

–

rushing towards fresh notebooks ardent contributors
all fired up wanting to fill up recalling, recollecting,
reinterpreting, retelling finally ready for retailing-
thematic anthologies – like love like schooldays like travel
like war like dope like childhood – leave them to Granta.
how fascinating is a writer's life ? a poet's life ? an Australian
poet's life ? brilliant memoirs of teeth clicking on biro shafts,
travelling the rocky road to digital fridge poems horrendous
line-losing magazine experiences profoundly lonesome
proofreading under starlight, under halogen too long alone,
often concluding mid-process in demented philosophising :
what is swept out the door coming back through the window

Bill Griffiths (1948-2007)

Sonnet 1

better sun
aptavit arcam – a pudding
per quam damnavit mundum
planted out his doves
fat, round like suns

Open uppart little huts of a head-house
To a lay:
Flat-chinate; showing
(Sun-hole/door)

Sonnet 2

Very whites very orange Goose
Block
White   Goose   Ocean

Robert Hampson (b. 1948)

From Reworked Disasters or: Next checking out the Chapmans' Goyas

4 Adam Roberts

much have I travelled

4 harry gilonis

the surface is rugged
limitless clouds above
limitless ranges of hills
into the killing zone
everyday's weather different
ready for the attack
to endure & to survive
twists & turns
distrust of scholars
had soaked his heart through
alienated access to
centres of knowledge
top-up fees
adds insult to injury

in the realms of gold

4 elkie brooks

blood on the ground
splintered doors above
a grid of streets
security-coded & cleared
rapacities that underlie
discovery & desire
walkie-talkies &
luminous safety-jackets
speed up the transfer
of bureaucratic metalanguage
humiliated once too often
the lost & the lonely
in one predominant perturbation
over-ruling wisdom

and many goodly states

4 rona lee

at the end of the shift
carried on a stretcher
heroic & humiliated
spent to all use
a fashion of outward fortitude
both severe & audacious
no master save his own invention
crimson smeared on thick
arms wrapped around shoulders
little respite from enclosure
emphasises the corporeal
the image that haunts
the burden of data provision
was always enough of a buzz

and kingdoms seen

4 ken edwards

law & disorder
just dust for fingerprints
remember how the injury
bleeds into your life again
taken hostage as leverage
for better terms & conditions
unpredictable shivers of hallucination
read across the body
the information & fashion
of biometric identifiers
shifts the emphasis
towards self-government
it takes courage
to break the silence

round many western islands

4 andrew gibson

no point complaining of
official persecution
latex gloves & hands
that needed better management
peeled back the skin
pins cartoon faces
on the victims' bodies
still commands top dollar
the 'best & brightest'
remobilized to
some other zone
for similar activities
to reconstruct a history
& a future

have I been

4 robert sheppard

it was his fantasy not hers
no instrument played
while the narrative became
lost in the translation
with clowns & puppy-dogs
the difference was evident
a tactic to be used
only in an emergency
both urban & credible
in full fancy dress
a violent alteration
within the framework of scholarship
control & boundary
in a dialectical relationship with desire

which bards in fealty

4 lee harwood

it was a game between them
brute force wasn't necessary
only a succession of pauses
which conjured up unspeakable terrors
he mistranslates his sources
locks that foil the painter's power
serious jokers in carnival heads
fingerprint bruising on her arm
localised effects
stapled onto new stretchers
homeless in the ruins
& more destruction to come
once more the wolf-pelt
had proved its efficacy

to Apollo hold

4 tony lopez

he takes the war head on
it rattles the locks loose
in the rented apartment
the masculine virtues
stick in his throat
attacked for anything
but embedded engagement
without regard for outcome
remodels songs changes lyrics
doubts about imperialist heroics
the persistence of the image
hints at catastrophe
in the line of fire
like Venus on a phoney sea

Resources

Jake and Dinos Chapman, Interview, Radio 4, 2003.
Lee Harwood, *Crossing the Frozen River: Selected Poems* (Paladin, 1988).
Homer, *The Odyssey,* trans. George Chapman, ed. Adam Roberts (Wordsworth Classics, 2002).
Sandra Jordan, 'Rich Killers Stalk City of Lost Girls', *The Observer* (2 November 2003), 24.
Rona Lee, Exhibition Catalogue, Royal Holloway, University of London, 2003.
Herbert Marcuse, *Eros & Civilisation* (Sphere Books, 1969).
Thomas McFarland, *The Masks of Keats* (Oxford University Press, 2000).
Michael O'Neill (ed.), *Keats: Bicentenary Readings* (Edinburgh University Press, 1997)
Peter Suchin, 'Jake and Dinos Chapman', *Art Monthly* (June 2003), 20-1.
Sarah Symmons, *Goya: In Pursuit of Patronage* (London: Gordon Fraser, 1988).

John A Scott (b. 1948)

Four Sonnets: Theatre of the Dead Starling

1

And the sights of life never dreamed, dear
Lady and gentlemen, for You now I step aside
And music! Tambourines played by the bare
Breasted girls! Life, life, O living to be lost
In arms and charms' Clap-clap 'Huzzah!
Did you hear: Tambourines! Taut flesh to shake
A music' 'Drums with soft hair' 'Awaken then
The Middle Ages' 'Flock of light' 'Ask Harry'
'Tassles!' Jaundiced in the flicker. 'Wake and
Heave-Ho, Fleets In, catch the silent issue'
In arms lost to wings, Man to Starling, else
Where the room gained life. Ceiling thrashed by
Flight and beating (That the walls could promise
Air) had collapsed their life by closing time.

2

   The Starlings, so I believe,
Imitate death, here in the theatre'
And sweeping them again from the aisles,
Their legs of branch, hardened, yes, but winged,
Lord, had You not made them to fly above the earth,
In the open firmament of Heaven?
   That night, clientele, random from solitude,
Picked their way past knees and coats 'and
Gentlemen, for You now I step aside' *Taking*
The Tambourine, my body knowingly upstaging,
I lay in whistles, breasts numb with eyes. At a
   drumroll
Setting fire to Starlings piled on the boards,
As if applause was forever in the sound of flame,
And Lord, had they stolen death most perfectly?

3

    A great blasphemy.
'Cover the pair, my boo-hoo innocent' *Lord*
In sin. Raising himself. 'May wings of
Christ enfold thee'   She fled the stage, as
Through smoke there were wings, not flames,
To obliterate the air. As the theatre doors
Closed. *The pyre consumed. Sweeping the*
Dead Starlings from aisles, brushing them from seats
To the floor, every winged fowl after his kind,
And Lord, did You not see that somehow all was good?
'Sights of life never dreamed' *Protect me from*
Exclamation. Let me, this time, take upon myself
    the Starling to imitate Christ.
As we 'Bang the drum with a Boom-Boom' 'Melons,
Cheap' 'Sway forward lads' 'Jock, you raper, go!'

4

        And the evening,
And the morning were the fifth day. Time
In the perfect circle of imitation moving to rest,
Or to light and the void, which is rest.

Starlings build in the theatre a roof
Of voice beyond dawn. For the season of drama they
Descend and are multiplied by the people.
And Lord, Dear Lady and gentle, teach us to pray.

Out of unrest, trembling, men were upon her,
Swollen with blood. Violence of the word, choose
To see two Starlings mate and be consumed in heat,
For this is the purpose and movement of theatre
To a new beginning. The crowd emerged into night
Streets, and there was amongst them dominion.

Thatching

(Thatching, the corpse was
Worked into the roof)
The weather consumes:
Bind the straw with flesh, and there is strength.
Yet that night, from above where the body lay
Held, and scarred with shadow,
The candles found an arm
Reaching towards earth. My fear was
To call the companion who, raising
Himself deliberately on one elbow answered:
The wind has loosened the weave.
In the morning I shall repair. There is now
Only time for sleep.
And indeed, there was wind;
Burying the house, as if room and roof were the
ancestral grave
In which we lay, beneath generations of the dead.

Long Balconies

Long balconies
Are leading from Your mouth
As if walking here should be voices
The tide has become excessive
White hours from the French
And I heard You calling
In the room and in the winding curtains
That broke upon us These folds
The blood has torn from Your face
Even with the Years
Long balconies are leading
From Your mouth As towards the far
And outward sea Your voice is drinking
And I am not left

Two Performances

1 Edith Piaf & Hancock

& was carried
From the stage, the parting of mask & face
Grained from eyes & from forehead, his mouth wedged
open in cry,
The Englishman, 1930
Until on the streets of Paris sang O My Mother
She leapt upon his shoulders
Each foot seeking the strength, amid diamonds
Of the formless blouse   exclamation of the acrobats
Afterwards stumbled into the air and retched alone
With the presentation of his spilling face, grained
From eyes and from forehead   And walked
Rue de Belleville past the side-show, this man's
Birth in the hard winter of   The Carnival
Abandoned since into the setting.

2 Lenny Bruce

In August that amorphous craft
Spelled it out: SHUT OUR BIG MOUTHS or
Join a mourning press furiously flashing
Bulbs   Two-at-a-time in the can
August 66 when *Judson Memorial* came frenzied
For chants, aphrodisiacs & The Fugs
& all that all-out need to get him buried   but
Remembered, smashed in the tempo of the City
& is it the Years have given a distance
Now, nothing to cash in, or
We are lost now   But all aside we come
Searching late and last for comedy,
One of those real performances (exposure &
Obscenity) the sane body craves.

Laurie Duggan (b. 1949)

East

for John & Margot Scott

1 (Clayton West 1)

Autumn Morning, Dandenong line fogbound,
siren of the 'Gippslander' heads east,
kitchen heavy with pewter, My Grandmother's cup
clinks in its saucer, table ordered with
teapot, grapefruit, marmalade
STH VIET TROOPS FLEE LAOS
a day's progression of trial & trivia.
8 p.m. a walnut cabinet
this room, the styled hypocrisy to expect,
history stultified, two-dimensional,
A.H.Q. Cartographic Survey (Edn 2.) 1942.
Australia 1:253,440 J55/7 BAIRNSDALE.
branch & bird, distanced beyond the window;
all night long, Good Old Rock & Roll.

2 & 3 (Argus, Feb. 12th 1912)

EAST GIPPSLAND

AN UNDEVELOPED TERRITORY

STATE TREASURER'S TOUR

The State Treasurer (Mr Watt) returned from his visit to the eastern districts of Victoria by the Gippsland train late on Friday night.

The party had an adventurous trip during the recent heat wave, and were glad to return safe and sound to civilisation once more.

They travelled through great stretches of burning forests, and, according to Mr Watt, "the bush fires were so thick that it was unsafe for a man to let his beard grow for even a couple of days".

The Treasurer was deeply impressed with the richness of much of this undeveloped eastern country. "It is unthinkable", he said, "that such a valuable territory shall be allowed to lie idle much longer".

MINING NOTES

Legal managers and secreta-

4 (Obit 1962)

Michael Frederick Duggan
June 1870. Hinnomunjie.
'Enrolled at opening, Swifts Ck. State School.
'Rode many winners at district race meetings'.
1884 HER MAJESTIES MAIL Omeo –
Dargo R. – Grant mining settlement.
Station hand, Ensay, met Ellen S. (Geelong)
Floodline of Tambo River; a wooden cabin,
corrugated tin extension. Ten children.
Bairnsdale & District Home & Hospital:
wore out cherrywood pipes we brought for him.
Too young to understand his death, I stood
on the hospital lawn, incipient edge of a town,
empty, in sight of the mountains.

5 (Two Hotels)

The new LITTLE RIVER INN 'Calcutta Corner'
where Indian hawkers camped by Costello's hayshed;
Barman: Jim Culhane of Crooked River
MISS CUSHLA JONES – THE OMEO ORCHESTRA
'one of the finest dance bands in all Gippsland'.
ENSAY SOUTH HOTEL, Est. '39.
twenty years later, the Omeo Highway re-routed,
once busy hotel, an isolated backwater.
January '67: 6th 9th 10th,
visited Bindi Station with Uncle Jack.
George Hardridge; fished in Little River;
Stirling & Haunted Stream; denser than myth:
Clarry the dingo trapper, his 'dogs' hung
in the huge freezer, old Sth Ensay Pub.

6 (1939)

Fri. Jan. 13th 1939
GRAPHIC BUSH-FIRE NARRATIVES
Truckbound, doing 80, missed the bridge
churned sideward, water, flames passed overhead.
Ellen: 'The air here is black. 3 O'clock,
afternoon, and all our lamps are on'.
Omeo – The GOLDEN AGE burnt to the ground,
fire died under rain the shadow of war;
living figures, numerals J.A. Duggan
36 Sqdrn. tool-setter G.M.H.
Late visit to Swifts Ck. returned
through heavy rain, shapes of timber mills
& sawdust burners Books, Utensils, Pianola rolls:
MEMORIAL SWIMMING POOL TRASH & TREASURE CENTRE

7 (1917)

Despite: 'The Argus' Feb. 12th 1912
CLERIC SPEAKS OUT AGAINST MIXED BATHING
Kaiser Bill, Mother Country & Mr Hughes,
a fondness for trivia persists.
Tired of piano, the picture-house
(With All Our Hearts) Teeth white
from govt. filmclips, breasting trenches,
on his back 2 ft mud, Jesus & poison gas,
reciprocates a bleeding grin to sky;
the field Forever England (& Uncle George)
far corner of the earth's core:
& we must lose sight of birth, death;
a cabin on the Tambo, sides burst
with 10 children, too much for us.

8 (Clayton West 2)

The new month 7 a.m., before vilification
a street of houses, its own strange beauty
holds no alien note   the given grid
accepted, viable
MELB: Fine. Sunny Periods. Max 75.
MASSIVE HEARING GIVES VERDICT ON MASSACRE
landscape of words, jerrybuilt ugliness
of place, name   discarded as a key
to spurious meaning, squalor of testimony.
M.F. Duggan d. 1962.
a life or symbol   death or caesura?
Compare/contrast selected passages
with special reference to poetic qualities
COMMANDOS THRUST DEEP INTO LAOS.

From In memory of Ted Berrigan   The Sonnets, 1963

Harum-scarum haze on the Brisbane streets
the greyness of dirty windows
looking over the building site. Dear Pam hello
it is 5.15 pm   polychromatic springtime
a season off   (the yachts wave their little flags
as I room in a room there's room in
for art: Tim Burns, Gloria Petyarre,
Angela Gardner. It is the season of parrot fever
it is the time to classify the record collection
time to read books. I eat books   river cats
run in all directions   weird violins
through headphones. The sky sinks
on these Dead Cities   the pills here are vitamins
and the songs a 'lukewarm catastrophe'

Gavin Selerie (b. 1949)

From Elizabethan Overhang

Make-Up

Sling me the run-again please
to not answer in poem poems.
If I could word it through the prism
so the text of ourselves is the text
of an eye beyond, if I could hold
the ebony log straight as it's
squashed into two dimensions,
if I could ease the half-shell
into seas on the lee of engagement,
I would put off the accretion
of legend and love, for these
are sounds forced into a box
to elude the prevailing code
of thinned-out universe terms.

Obsession

I thought I was hearing you see me
seeing you, such alteration being
unreason's reason, a crystal tone
Englishing the displaced body
of foreign syllables, so no voice chip
could ever repeat the sheer L
our chorus climbed, that light
in the can't which makes all go.

With your one-coin calls at three a.m.
and one-person packets from the corner shop,
you pass and repass the round o's
of will you still love me – tomorrow.
And those lady's-traces ring clear
as tracks on a lost acetate.

Less and More

Moved like a man, she let me be that
coming on out the other side of neutral
after role reversal, when considerate becomes
not easily prized spaghetti twists,
cooked and gone cold in a hyperbaton
of this ought we to manifest –
the slash in the circle that forbids
winding up to a double negative.
Nor nothing is indubitable
if we're vascular, crystalline and moony.
I did not waver, I was one voice
uplifted from a leased time-slot
cancelling skidmarks on a rusty overhang
as also a jutting memoried splendour.

Soundings

O how undone now are my afternoons
as I push to notate the whole
known-to-all enchantment, such
rehearsals as can never or always
betray who figured it so, half-rights
of utterness that turn laws about:

Upon a narrow barque, her bed,
we went unpressed, pillowed in frolic's
vocal sea, while wall treasures peeped
on the deep gold unaged furrow,
letting each scene go cross-coupled
as from the sheets we fished winter apples.
Shift to land – could I her park re-lease,
I'd ring in the sky's mad alphabet.

His Ex-Mistress Muses On Uncut Pages

He was my fancy's king
an age ago, she said
fingering the pull on a renegade shine.
Lurv'nd emowshun,
who ever made a penny out of poetry?
From this window I can hunger
for the lily meadow
of inevitable lyricism.
I was that one woman with a cello,
he fed strength into my eyes.
A would-I-rather hits me now,
the wherewithal
to put the bends back in
for all that it was not fake song.

From Tilting Square

Sheet Bend

Strings of the small repeated day
we do not share – provisioning
and cleansing – as we knot ourselves
in a guise that holds and must give.
It's a lack and a gain to see you
fresh out of clocked allegiance
wearing fluid wraps of beige and black
to revamp the obvious and plain.
Without you, I'd say, any reading
is dead collected lines; with you
in context words get up and speak.
They press – uneasily – through the gap
and surge to find an expanse
that plucks farness into right here.

Touch Paper

They cry we are lost in midnight tunnels
too far run into fortress rock.
They hiss it's a game in double language
wearing each face to blank mistrust.
But who can judge a line that twists
scorching with surprises, the slow caress
which builds to unburden, rosy
or ruinous in undying spillage.
If into eternity I am come
daring to break that perfect box,
and she with me says the breach is for joy,
let this sapping have bright issue
for the strongpoint where love and law engage
might torch a heaven in halls of adamant.

Possession

Even this belongs, a part that's foreign
to sense and ease, like the cat enclosed
with shining pitch that asks to be stroked
and left alone, staring through aeons
of granite. We tussle in a small chamber
furnished to make a world. Death-seeking
with a quiver and clench, we vie and ally
in concertinaed time, feeling by default
what we also are, as self-stages
spread from a hidden corridor
invoke Love's gilded capstone.
To steal into the present like this
makes a story where none exists,
one that's constantly beginning.

Old Redding

Some would make this threadbare, even
by aureate terms, but I must sing
from the heart-root, unclotted and clear,
naming how the plain builds to a height
which is special for all it holds.
We walk and lie in this last preserve
with its elbow paths and shaggy bushes,
watching from the pillared shade –
as masked horsemen – a sort of real day.
Grass stretches up from Copse Farm
and the Brick Field, while the sun catches
one spire on the hill. Windflowers here
are a drift of white and the yaffle pecks
his way north to Grim's Ditch and Levels Wood.

Song Space

As this squeeze-box holds a secret music,
life contracted to be coaxed out again,
so our bodies still have breath while seeming
least to move. A moment and more is clamped
in that monument, I know, for lovers
touch, speak across miles, sense running ahead
and back. What's tight, even impossible,
breeds meaning, and out of our dug routine
we pull devices which surprise: giddy
numbers I get from you, passed through a web
that's wind-driven, by an if of a yes
with walnut facing, ivory buttons
and black pleated leather. The waiting now
is usher to an actuated stress.

Alan Halsey (b. 1949)

Discomposed Sonnet After Antonin Artaud

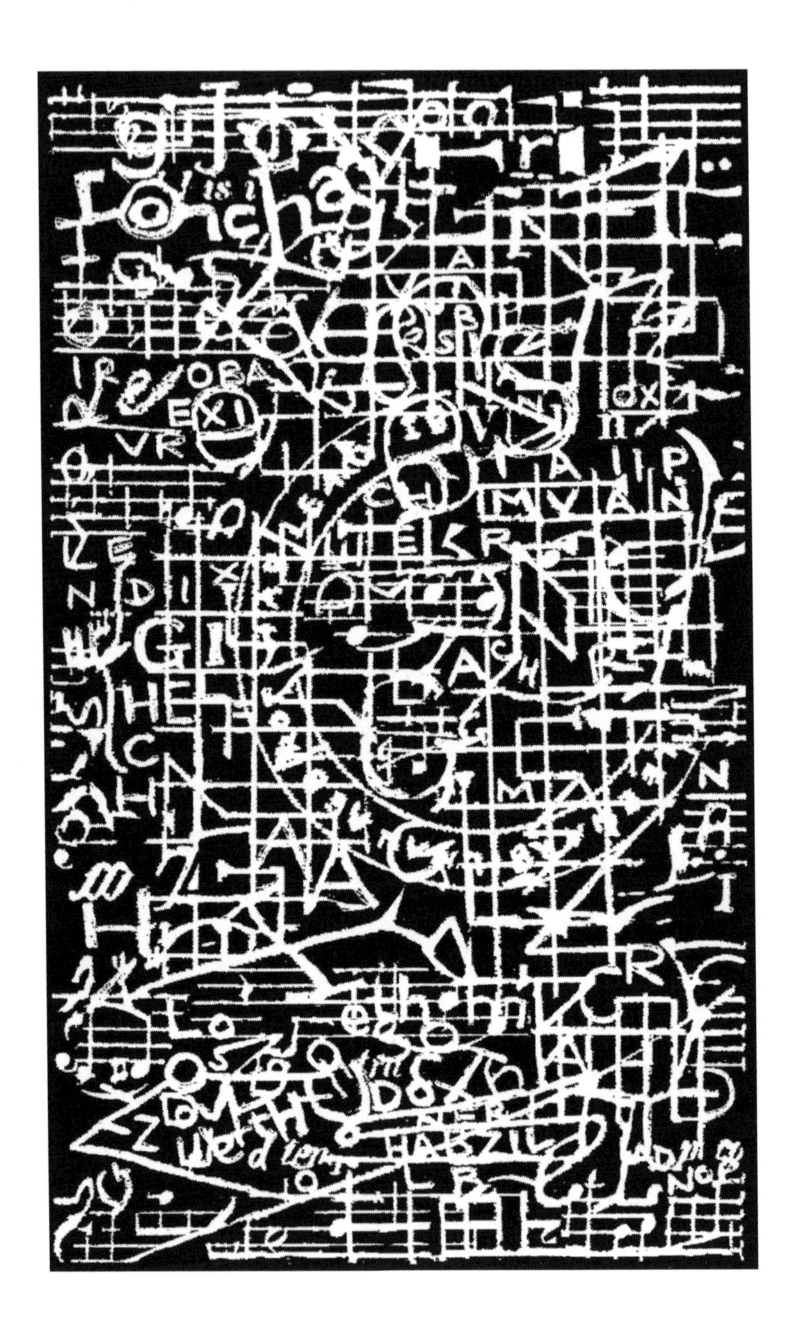

Discomposed Sonnet or Sonata in White Writing

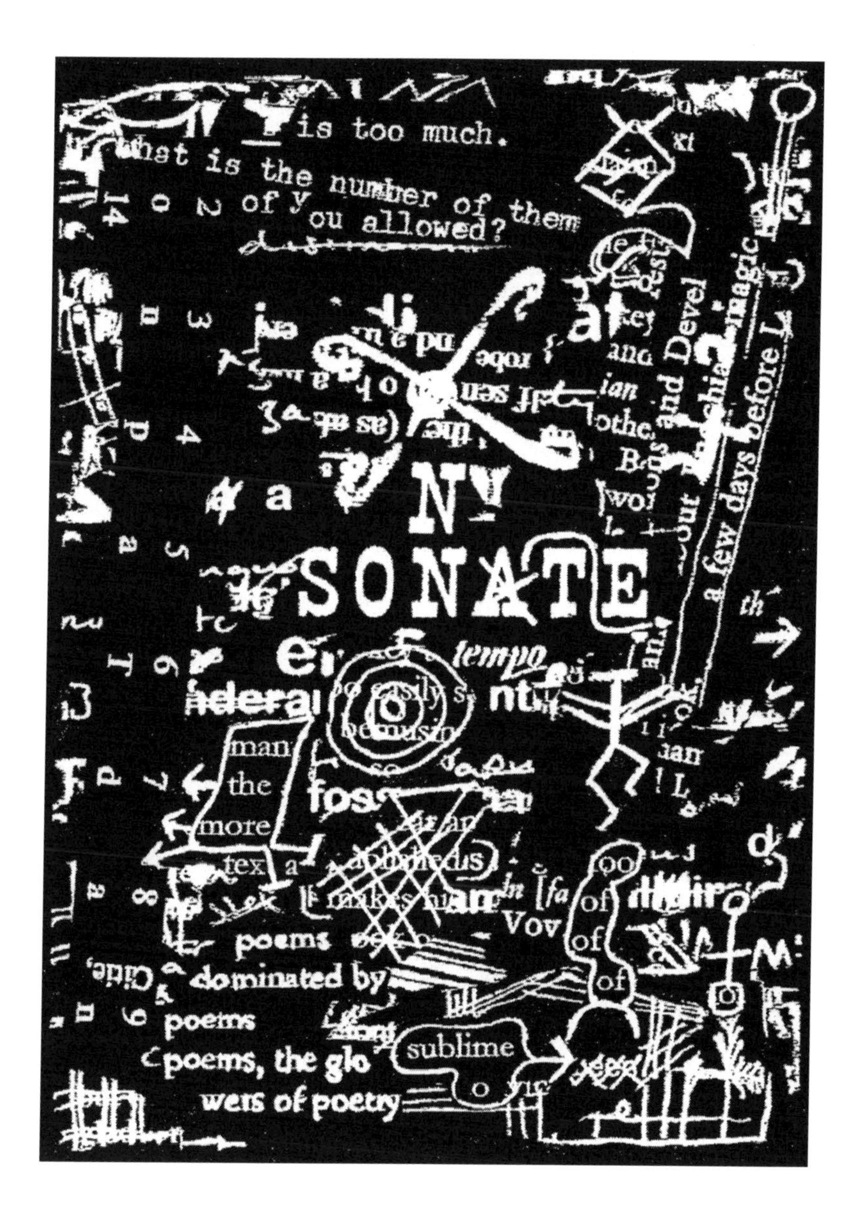

Mandrake Dichotomies

Lawrence Upton (b. 1949)

Sonnet

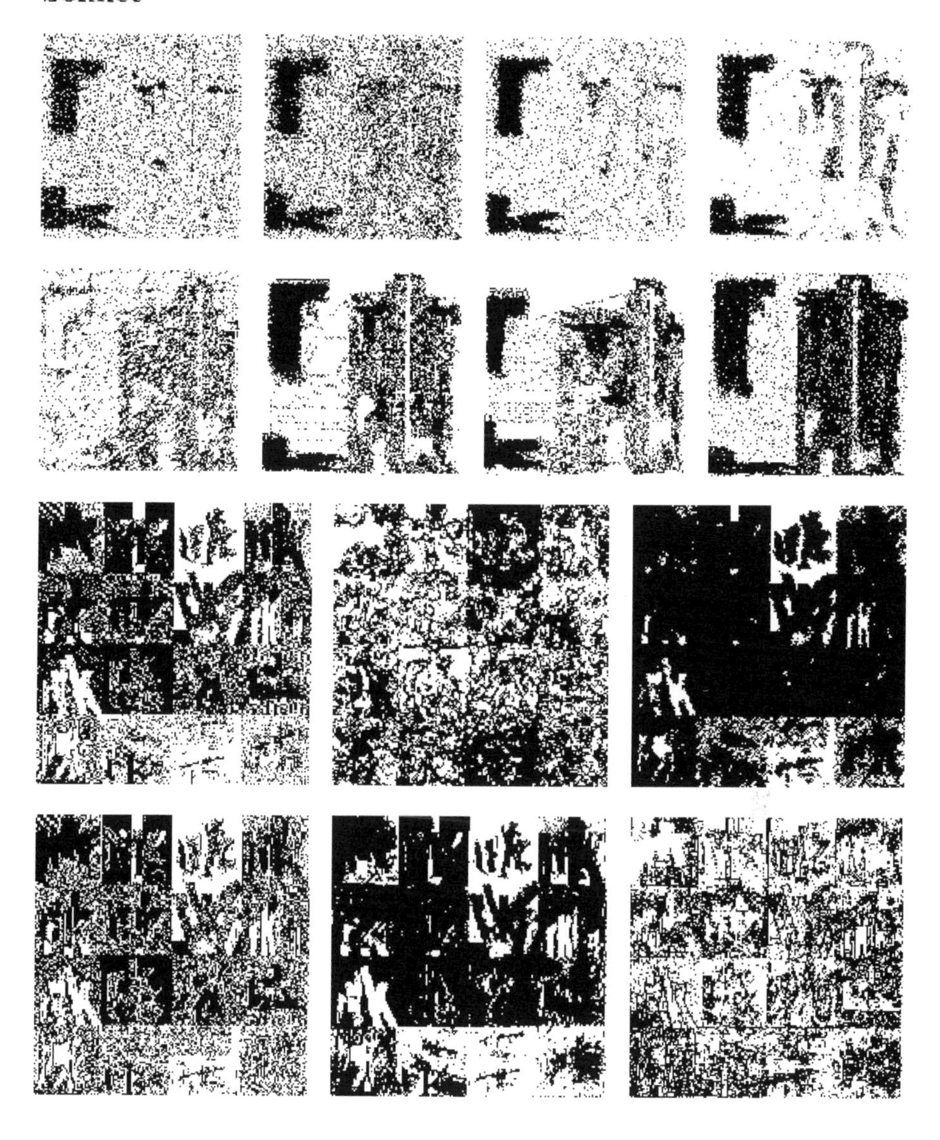

Sonnet: Cartoon Strip

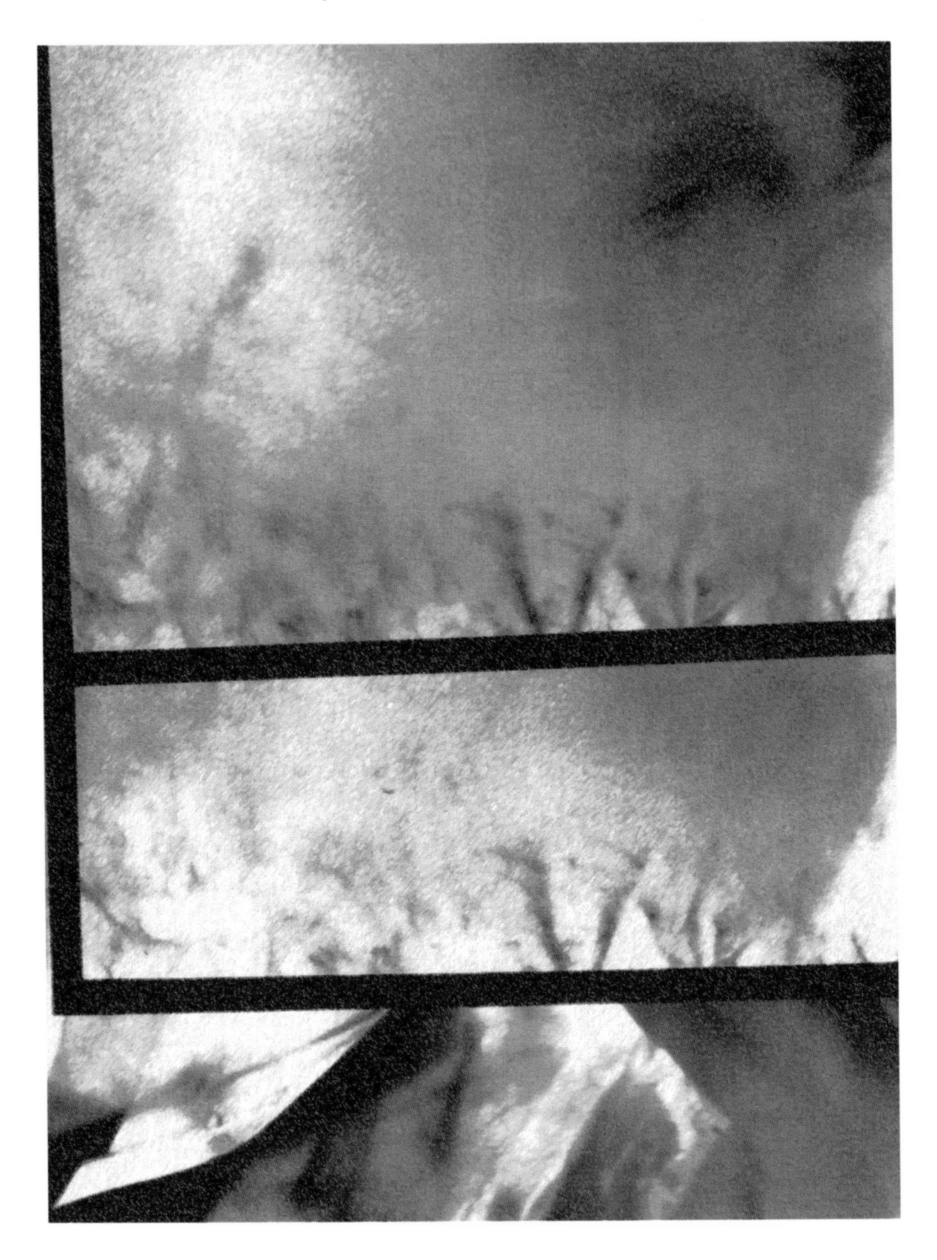

Sonnet

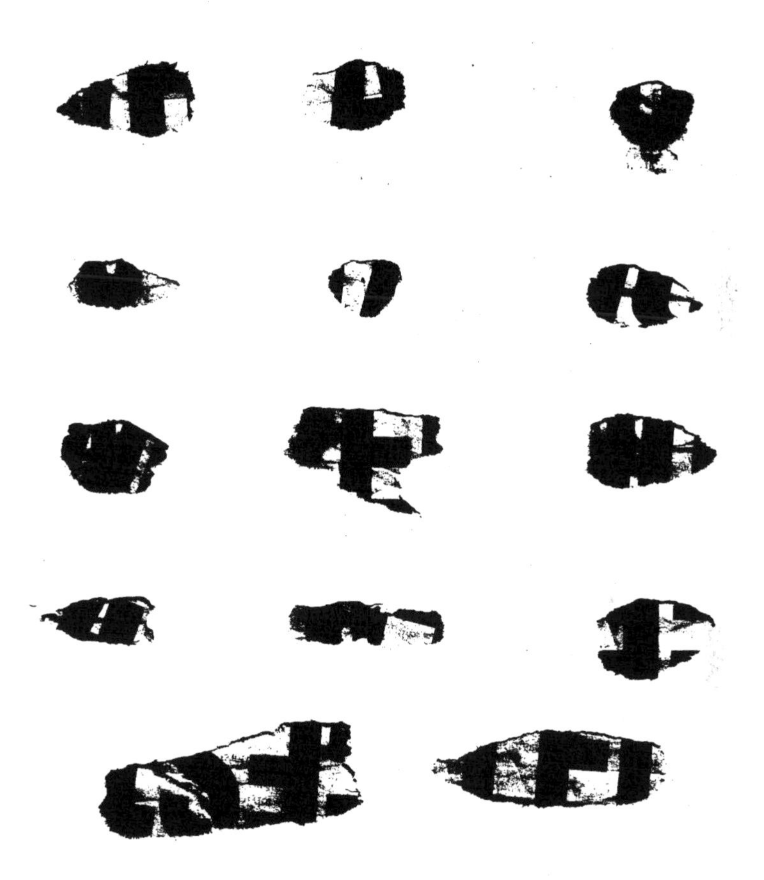

Tony Lopez (b. 1950)

Assembly Point D

Dauntless the slug-horn to my lips I set
Taking a stand for the names who had been
So badly treated by crowd behaviour in the market;
Whereas our man was calm, drew figures in the sand,
And spoke to them as individuals. The old guy
Putters on, his canvas in a trench, putting neat squiggles
On the big white primed sheets: a million each, believe it.
Cartoon prawns and crabs go into Eurotunnel
Singing along with zydeco music. Redwoods fall.
It was a teacher bound and gagged a four-year-old boy
With sticky tape labelled *Nastro Adesivo: 3M*
Holding back the late works to keep up the selling price.
Can you design a machine that turns coffee
Into urine? That daydreams of oral sex?

Our fortunes are in the stars, truly, since brokers
Are using astrology in the stockmarket. What price
Celestial backwardation (a little space to write and eat salad in)?
Shadowing the wives of ex-company presidents
In their dotage. The owl of Minerva begins her flight
Only as dusk is falling. My nerves are bad tonight.
This kind of gives closure to a long career in "Vice."
All famous names, all massive savings, every third one free.
The office has a fine view of cliffs and grassy hills.
You read INDUS OPAQUE as you stick out your tongue
Over where a new vine is beginning to cover the gazebo
Cut so many times before. [Clay animal noses here.]
Rose garden: black velvet: stalking donkey:
The banquet is at 3102 Main Street, 15th and Main.

A thread goes through the book, I don't mean ideas, but each
Gathering of four sheets sewn into sixteen pages
Which are I suppose ideas, even those that are blanks.
Autumn walks in the poem as a goddess, an idea
But also (because she is a goddess) good to eat and rollover with.
I was not so impressed with the chicken dinner after all,
You eat with your fingers and get sticky round the mouth.
It is not Autumn at all, she comes home with groceries
And gets into a hot bath. I think in Bonnard reproductions,
Mosaics with drips of water running on the little stones.
Spaghetti vongole appeals to me more than clam chowder.
I was born in the city but I don't live there now,
Can't afford it. This *is* the subtext of *After Lorca:*
Swimming pools, mirrors, the denial of the father.

Three black bears on a green T-shirt from Canada
It might be that a new colony was begun, distorted
If I remember by flaking plaster – so that what you see
Is a non-representational blackbird that was happening
At breakfast. It seems to be the time for questions. Not yet.
Geometrical flowers on a soft-shaded plastic tablecloth
With a grey design something like strawberry leaves.
One night the termites fly and are sexually active
I mean not fancy envelopes but business envelopes
Such as the enclosed renewal-notice. Countless aphids.
I put them down one after the other and the effect
Was moulded in the glass. So we are the New Abjectionists
And maybe one or two pairs are successful up there
Have you seen the patterns on the insides of envelopes?

We were shredding gangster biographies in the backroom
Working most nights. My job was to put in the obvious
Rip-off that blinded those marks to the bare-faced
Totality of the scam. We'd admit a little steal or two
And call it "literary allusion" – now is that high class or what?
Steve Benson and Jean Day were playing on the tape recorder.
Diagonal rows of circles with quarters of dark blue
And then circles with white slots like NO ENTRY signs,
Then both of these patterns reversed. That is where
We must remove the tiles hoping the walls stay up –
All those wings in the sky, it was so pretty to see.
But since that branch fell on me I must always be working:
We use chemical sex-signals to protect apples
And have forgotten how to relax. Down at the mouth

As if somehow in the fifties it just popped out
Like one of those cartoon light-bulb ideas. Oh sure.
And in those days it was paste-up or shut up
If you catch my drift: translation rights, short-term options.
These dupes think that Burroughs invented the cut-up
By spreading his payments over four months. *New dawn,*
Danse de feu, Handel, Albertine, Rosa Mundi.
Since then I have begun to set up a new project
It is only there for the reverse print that you barely see:
The ideal appears and reconstructs the real world
Into the shape of an intellectual realm. Even so
He proves he is a brave leader by resigning.
My favourite is an unknown yellow with blackspot
Have you completed all of the sections?

I believe this blue is the newest colour and good enough
For the conference backdrop. I wanted to include
A wheelbarrow just for the hell of it. Hello Horace.
Having waited in all day for the gas men
I was working up a panic attack alone in the house.
All very neo-rural: introspective subjectivity,
Whereas what we have here is a cheap ventriloquist routine
Which ought to hold down the "Care in the Community" budget.
Really high tech, no doors, you just bale out the back:
Soon we may re-label "breakdown" as an ordinary life-event
Which is the proper response to current social conditions.
Of the blackbird, only two feet remained on the hedge.
Beside me this famished shadow does gnaw the joy away –
Would you go down on his donut? This ain't rock and roll,

Erasures and palimpsests are reduced to a flat
Surface effect: the afterlife of ethics.
A judge, a game-show host, bag-lady, dinner-lady,
Madman, murderer, banished king, politician,
Football manager, dentist, spoilt birthday-girl.
A few poor tatterdemalions made all this racket,
Howling in the night. Ugolino was there
Chewing a juicy walnut of brains from behind,
His arse positioned over the stunned polis.
Sing poor, sweet airlines. Scholars have paid lip-service
To the oral nature of poetry. We can see
Submissive women waiting on TV mountain tops:
Lovely silk dress in a helicopter shot. You'll need
Your velour passenger pillow and something to read.

Every so often the day builds around a menu
Say taking stock from the freezer for a *risotto*
Or calling early at the fish stall: oysters on ice.
Let's eat again real soon. I would be happy to go
With that old authentic abstract expressionist work
If we could print it on plastic. We're looking at
A futures market in concept art. You could hedge
Against primitives or streetnics or property as such,
Get in at zero and the only way is up.
White image of a plane on a blue ground
Then pull back to route on map of North America.
Eventually the loss of loss, fear of experience
(Tanks in European forests) writing *The Georgics*
When civil war had destroyed the culture itself.

This turning seems to go only to a business park.
You're on the bus tonight, headphones, synthetic waves,
Daryl Hall sings we've reached the borderline
By a terrace of little cottages made over *bijou.*
A large selection of other vehicles always available
Leaving Taunton on the M5. "Love will last forever."
In a thousand cities our offices are getting ready
To see that every transaction goes smoothly.
When the alarm sounds we go to assembly point D.
Agoraphobia, chronic anxiety, social phobia,
The narrator is bound up in some unspecified crisis.
When did the blue skies start to gather clouds?
How long have we poor shepherds lived and dreamed
Within these shady incremental pay-scales?

Ken Edwards (b. 1950)

From eight + six

DARKLY SLOW*

Bring back the persons! I
Ups & says
            they are bipolar & splendid
The jogger in the park, the murderer in the dark
They're so lonely, they speculate, give em something to do
The imaginary persons right here
Wherever that may be, beloved, awed
And in a cloud (a crowd)
                                    he she & you
Catching the eye, ordering a round for the unknowables

Bring em all back, I don't want to see them go
One's at a university in the snow
Another on the beach, one praying for the souls in woe
Oh sad poet please be on your toes
The boat casts off, the buddleia grows
And what's behind the moment's horizon no-one knows

* The title is a direct translation of Elliott Carter's "Adagio Tenebroso".

I GO TO SLEEP

I go to sleep in the railway buildings
which someone said looks like a boat
For five years I had that fine panorama
spread out before me until winter came with
sunny chill I wore my leather put it in a poem
I went to sleep & woke to oh just mountains
of phone messages & somehow after that
things were not quite the same
                                                            Look — I want
to put this & this & those
together so it has a thing inside the line
(the dark line that flits & jags)
which maybe is what I call poetry who can
say, which is no fugue & which is mine

THE POETS GATHER
(Theory of Poetry 2)

The poets gather. They, like poetry itself,
want to be, not seem. Which is seemly.
These are their stories, and the summation
of them is this: that they reject story.
Why, they are paralytic with joy: on their plastic chairs
they identify the depth of field of such paradoxes
and exult in it — they presuppose no need
for emotional closure.
That was then. And now?
Well, only you & I are left, and we're engaged
in refutation. Yours is a pint of bitter,
mine's a Guinness. This proposition is true. We raise
our glasses, we refute it
and refute again.

INTERROGATION ROOM REMIX*

The pillar perished is whereto I leant

A human electricity a great
Generous boom a list

From east to west still seeking though he went

In this grey/yellow space
I sense you
In your best bruiser skin — believe me there's
An alibi in one —

Of all my joy the very bark and rind

In the grey space what I remember's this

The strongest stay of mine unquiet mind
My mind in woe, my body full of smart

And books to read before it grew too late

What can I more but have a woeful heart

* In memoriam Eric Mottram, 1924-95. With some help from Sir Thomas Wyatt, poem CLX sampled from *Collected Poems*, OUP 1975.

ABSCONSCION*

Stay
As though astonished
Through the rubric of
"The transformation of love"†

In the room
In the rain
How you have been
Many times this way O boy

I don't know if I can
Indure
On the door it says

Use other door
You go through it (the
Turn) and

* For Michael Finnissy, on his 50th birthday, July 1996.
† The phrase is from Rilke's letters.

FOUR*

One is to become
The other — it never happened
A third — relatively minor
And after all, the last
It did not change my life
From east to west still seeking though he went
Suppose that it, or they, can, will & did or do
Then all would be — otherwise
    If not now when
    If not when, then
    Why
    If not, well then
    How
    But why not now?

* After listening to *The Crowd*, Rova saxophone quartet, Hat Hut CD. For a far more comprehensive response to the same, see Clark Coolidge's *The Rova Improvisations* (Sun & Moon, 1994).

THREE

Three is two & one
The octave — never harboured
Or heard — reflectively finer
And before all, the past
"You must change your life"
The pillar perished is whereto I leant
Suppose I had not, turned I did into undo
Then all would be — restored
    If not the one
    Or two, when
    You
    Were not, well then
    Who
    Am I now?

TWO

Now am I whom artifice
Supposes? Were you then, two
Or one if not restored? well then
Would all undo into I did,
Pitch into bliss, had I not turned?
The pillar perished is whereto I leant
Your change must be before all, relatively heard
Or harboured, octave one & two
    If not this, then
    This
    A pair, as one —
    Or not, the one
    And two
    Is one

MANY TO MANY: BIG STORY

Those of us remaining on the bus no longer have recourse to the big story. Already, as it begins to traverse the bridge, the passengers fall into a *sweve* wherein their several *I*s become ball-bearings floating freely in the roof, a concatenation of little stories (neither the dialectic of the Spirit, nor even the emancipation of humanity), separated only by the Walkman's pause button. Already the *I*s are becoming *You*s, reaching further and further, till too soon it's too much. And so on and on, etc *ad infinitum* whatever happened to *dichten* = *condensare* for fuck's sake?

At Aldgate, Zeno leaves his seat and descends the stairwell, sumptuously apparelled. Thames glitter on a moving horizon, light brown and done in. His story over, he has succeeded in showing that the bus will never reach the opposite bank.

ONE

Now, not why
But how — then well, not if
Why then, when not
If when, now not
If otherwise — be?
Would all then do or did & will?
Can they or it that suppose
went he though seeking still?
    west to east from
    life my change nor
    did it last, all after
    and minor, relatively third —
    it happened never, other to
    become is one

David Miller (b. 1950)

Untitled (Visual Sonnet)

Untitled (Visual Sonnet)

Untitled (Visual Sonnet)

Jonathan Brannen (b. 1950)

From Deaccessioned Landscapes

3

In an architecture of sound
somnambulant spheres embrace arches
excerpting corridors from enclosed passages.
If time's really an aspect of experience
its serial character is seriously flawed
or characteristically that of an
inclusive series Chinese boxes
Russian dolls or the tubes of a telescope.
From so great a distance the moon's an easy
answer. Many hands are raised in classrooms
like winter wheat waving in spring fields.
Storms blot the day and smudge the night.
Here where weather is the only landscape
I'm swearing off of ordinary letters.

3

place inside space where
all   sides
                        structure a line
culminating in a dot
a coat
of unknown
range
          rockets
          in clumsy
                              long
                              sentences
                              a home
                              of erasures
                              an other

18

A spoon is a spoon. Art isn't a spoon
but this is debatable. Light becomes color
in painting and space the holes in hollowness.
Pieces have been replaced by degrees.
The reality behind a muggy afternoon.
Obsessive behavior is more complex
than you might expect. A mental filing system.
The way flowing water catches the light.
A shock of hair. The alphabet is a
short dictionary of the spatial world.
At this unique distance from isolation
fucking sounds like flip-flops on a muddy path.
How I wish now I could invent a brand
new color just for you to daze the night.

18

like time
          in abandoned
          magnolias
phonemes
          wick light
          from rooms
ravels
unravel
          black nights
          night sweats
                    rain
                    drops
                    splat on
                    dry glass

23

Architects didn't design you
unimaginable as the night
when you lie sleeping dreaming in and out
of language. All memories are in
the present the way snowflakes turn sunlight
or shadows map torn paper.
The cinematography of sleep
is as precise as artificial light.
Penitent seasons are locked in absence.
Anecdotes drift in fixed ideas.
Everything is the gestures of jugglers
in a posthumous text. Women wearing
loose cotton warrant quiet celebration.
Daylight breaks through. Words come back to haunt us.

23

a spoon is a spoon   is   a spoon
                    light
                    painting space
                    by degrees
  reality
        is more
        than you might expect
                flowing waves
             alphabet the days
  short
        distancea
        flip-flop
                now now can invent
                        the night

32

Descartes stepped in inside a tavern and sat
down at the bar. "Can I get you a drink?"
The bartender asked. "I think not," Descartes
replied, then he disappeared. Does erasing
an illegible name actually
constitute erasure? Select the best
answer from the choices provided below:

A. A shared secret is still a secret.
B. Speech is a boundary separating humans
   from other species.
C. A shared secret is no longer secret.
D. Speech is a boundary that separates nations.
E. Nationalism is a failed experiment.

Many hands raised in classrooms are like
winter wheat waving in spring fields.

32

damaged
sunlight

clean as a whistle

in this room
where
what isn't

what
is
deceptively
simple
visual fields
vestigial
reality
over a minute

50

Words are cages of illusions.
A sushi bar in Elbow Lake is merely
a banal schizoid episode a brief
cameo in the interior distance
where memory tricks the inelegant
heart. Stick-figure icons are no stone
whose glyphs have never been deciphered.
Wind rules these ruins at evening.
Don't let the darkness catch me here
sweating out the night thinking back
to myself remembering. Let's go back
to where W.C. Fields lies dreaming of orange groves.
Grey does not equal gray. To speak is
an act of faith. Words come back to haunt us.

50

the circle breaks
the spectrum
obsessive pronouns
signs signifying
within
endless spaces
angles among
damaged
memories
experience
transparent gestures
hermeticism
snatches of sentences
a row of letters longing

Geraldine Monk (b. 1952)

From Ghost & *Other* Sonnets

In fear we lay longitudinal.
Our exactitude with words
Drawn to cold old spaces quartered
Off the beaten tale. Others sobbed. A
Miniature robin's head flew into
Doll-syndrome. It was a trying time.
Bottlenecks of prophesies topping
Visions wasn't stiff British but
How the sun came up! Rugged
Cuisine lined our nervous eclipse.
The full-on-fry-up toasted shades
Wading through. Tracery of bombs.

Abandoned fragility. Human minds hurt
Some. Intelligent plastic splinters unmoved.

After three days with
Bits of sea between her
Teeth a wounded knee
Widowed her hair. Strafed with
Newly weeds and something borrowed on
The beach strewn a ghastly flotsam. Galactic
Children skrieked with melting under
Donkey hides darkening pleasure
Belly-up on the blinding
Out-of-tune piano.
Foreign as they come out the blue-crashing
Light played the brindled limbs.

Who on earth was what and after
Which life roosted death?

A second glance and then another
Swift. Was it me or ? Were my
Eyes in the back of my beyond-head
Reeling a bird-riff? I can't rightly
Remember never having been
Quits with beak. It did a flambé
Shim – joy within the saucer flipped its
Own volition over. A rare day. So
This was spirit. Dunk away! Tasty
Dregs leave me wanting.
Tell me it's true what I saw in the
Doodle behind the drab.

Burnt toast. Spectres undreamt at any
Breakfast. Blinds I drew. Ruffle-down gentle.

The heart-shaped lavender was
Lavender and heart-shaped.
In the light of this matter
The sudden drop in form
Into horns and a turned-up
Mouth blue upon a bitter chill
Across the sheet a rack of fingers
Creeped towards a cup of tea
Growing cold with a broken sixpence.
At the centre of the morning
Rushes an hour which time
Forgot to brush and still

No one knew the difference between
Gold and brown and golden brown.

What makes you look in at the
Exact window where someone is
Looking out? Unplanned encounters
Traduce unknowns with mirrored
Other. But what's behind that sticky girl one
Step stunningly above a sweet wrapper? Tossed.
A thing of beauty in a room so ordinary.
Mindless kicks. Burnt bitten words
Mocking your back-broke beauty.
Ape-ghosts. Rapes-ghosts are real little
One. Well below a Restoration rake-hell
Humans shouldn't figure. Let alone...

Neglected screams in a field of unwashed forks.
Far crying buried in gust of shush-love.

Light a nightlight flimsy.
Fingertip search the distilled eye of
Owl-head darkness webbed with cross.
Elsewhere besides the corniced pond
Disconcerted ferns clutched the
Breeze of little feet in
Lost cotton socks. Pitter
Psst. They came to pass a burbling
Stream recurring. Happy-heart so
Plaintively young dragged by shady
Plankton mouth. Down-down. Leery-long his
Slow green face replaced her woeful visage.

Egg-shaped love that shined-up rooms. But.
For whom the gods love. Brut.

No cigarettes in the ashtray. Between a
Mother and Patsy Cline lay crystal emptiness.
Ying. She accidentally wrote for *thing.*
Yang. Doubled-up flesh. Daughter. Furtive talk.
Imminent death parts the spectacular
Red Sea celluloid rushes. It's epic. Glass. As.
Ashtray shimmers resplendently unused
Splits its centre asunder. Clean in
Two emotion half-mooned. Mother broke
First. ((Things happened around her)).
Upstairs the daughter's bedroom door
Banged everly on that total windless night.

A simple protest stultifies the complex
With too much protestation – the telephone rang.

Onto my frozen fingers came
Unsolicited words. Laying a ghost
The design of our silent eyes we never –
Even our dreams, being sheer snow.
Shadows keep piling up surfaces to a
Higher level of appearance. On the
Timepiece we call Try. Ticker. Heart-
Tapers. Never does any motion track-
So. Tock. Sound. Or light. Partly stone.
Partly the absence of stone. Trick.
Surge of swirling limb defines the bandage.
Partly the absence of limb. Tic.

Who sent this terrifying beast
To hold my eyes absurdly stiffened with arc.

Maurice Scully (b. 1952)

From Sonata

SONNET

when I follow the patterns of scratches on the
surface of my desk they lead me to my little
pop-up book of knowledge in which moons – in profile,
& laughing - & ringed planets in gold dye on a gauze
curtain [verb illegible] behind which my wristwatch
pips. here we are. I tell my little ones it's the
fairies calling. we speak into the watch. once upon
a time there was a duck …

shadow of

yes crow I across street

think gone

by on

opposite rooftop

black on black

the breeze in the ivy clicks.

SONNET

From your previous life you have brought
to this life 502 catties of sesame oil
& 100 copper coins. You are straightforward
& talented. You will be able to acquire
a lot of money from many sources but will
have a minor accident.

> Dig down: root haze. Look up: blue
> fibre. It's wonderful to hear the leaves
> on the trees again though. To get into
> bed beside you as excited as this.
> Years of grinding technique roll back
> to be imploded through one or two pages
> of pure fire. Never thought …

The clutter of yr shed is different
from yr English language, no? Yes.
Down on that track I definitely tried
to get a glimpse of what I thought
effable: crossing the dateline into
a clock. Rip.

> Child whimpering, adept, tangible flanges
> of a language that held him in: you'll
> tell me, I said. Who did. You did. Nipped
> in the bud. They said they might. Right.
> Are nipples oak galls?

Writing, deleting, writing again, patient, persistent,
dogged to the point of/(?)/is what was reflected on
that surface leering up, magnetic & stupid, up from
whose hopelessness you could eat through to the next
depth barely.

> Site normal. As to the proportions of the cell:
> yr trivia is as engaging as my trivia. And sticks.
> Then palps to the paralysed hymenoptera. Busy
> busy busy …

You will suffer from diarrhoea for a while
then die on a sunny day, but it will rain
on the day of yr funeral. Your coffin will
be made in a hurry because the Lonely Star
will be approaching you. Although you will

have two sons & one daughter to carry yr
coffin to the cemetery, it will not be a
splendid funeral.
          Daddy, Daddy …

          Your corpse will be
               Your funeral will take place
          You will die between
               the ages of
          You will have two sons and
               one daughter to
          and your funeral will be a
               splendid affair
Daddy, Daddy (curious shimmer of word-haze
over a wall) *can I show you magic?*
          And back to ceramics. Repeating meetings
          in a windowless coop where committees
          web & clog, minutes pouring – pouring
          without end – down a rusty old
You will go to a relative's party
catch a disease and then die
          down a rusty old chute diagonal to
          & entering the side of the building
          whose irregular flecks of black &
          white are once thought to have read
          POISON or POSITION or PERSON or
          PENSION – smoothly uncoiling from the
          tube – glutinous firework English
          from China – or PARA- something …
          DISE? surely not –
It will/You will/It will/on the day of
your/two old monks/carry/funeral/splendid

From Tig

SONNET

From the nine facts the typist is
Charlotte & the nurse must be Alice.
The hostess lives west of Charlotte &
Doris lives directly north of the typist.
Therefore Doris can't be the hostess.
Putting the results into a small map
it will turn out that Alice lives
four miles south & three miles west of Doris
which by Pythagoras makes the distance
five miles. And Betty, of course, is the hostess.

Frances Presley (b.1952)

take this diagram

the map will help you find   or
redress or wheals action
provides block towed away   gate
unremitting a fresh north
north west wind moors
the bike may be a salt taste
on the Plimsoll Line which
becomes the Auld Triangle where
women get sick and men die
of love fixated by the fair
toxophilites dressed to the
nines and aiming for each other
or the bullseye and she was late
for the internet remitted   its   home links

Philip Kuhn (b. 1952)

sent three sonnets for schubert sonatas

forget not archetechtonics of sound
muse art thou sick like blakes rose in the night
tragopan tragus tragopan tragus
for he has scent me flowers across time
malaxis paludosa from bog land
weaves wreathes woven celandine eglantine
thymes sweet name still smelt in my cobalt ear
what music airs like lyres secreted joy
not bound by wave by wave band or silence
whose surf sung by sand in-cresses my heart
when foam formed from music ploughed through the stars
mouthing my words scoured rhymes lips staffs or staves
to note not by note but harboured by note
as rolling his ruin in tides swirling

from tears entranced by the touch of your thrall
belladonna drawn from rose red throstles
sharp thorn'd threnody pierced thistles through dors
where serried child tempers sword with calling
thyrsus whose passions thrive through wands want would
dance pirouettes dances palms in his hand
what when she wants does she want from the sea
corsair cut by wave ice cleft carved from fell
sent silvern showers tra-la la-la-la
bone chased by dreams entwined curdled her faith
culled of reed-pipe bull-rush benediction
kern'd by gold thalamus thrift and thyine
hulled frond her heart hung knife spoilt hard-edged whorl
draughting datura from her lovers femur

seam-stress forms sounds roundels around clipt shore
in-shoals and shells shudder against whirling
gig slow motion grit given rant by sand
bough bent branch amplified by black black bird
songs bark stifled noise lest life tremble life
prest petals laughters leaf rain beat on earth
rhyme barque in waves ferns fell in-folds through foam
not yet bound when band from books violets
dead peonies by grave in-folds of joy
thrusting in time to the pulse of a stone
would willows weep by the dark wale of night
throbbing in-breath dreams dreams less left undone
hallowed cry of grey owl twisting gruff cord
through silence sounds roll

These sonnets were originally exhibited as a triptych, framed and in colour.

Harryette Mullen (b. 1953)

From Sleeping with the Dictionary

Dim Lady

My honeybunch's peepers are nothing like neon. Today's special at Red Lobster is redder than her kisser. If Liquid Paper is white, her racks are institutional beige. If her mop were Slinkys, dishwater Slinkys would grow on her noggin. I have seen tablecloths in Shakey's Pizza Parlors, red and white, but no such picnic colors do I see in her mug. And in some minty-fresh mouthwashes there is more sweetness than in the garlic breeze my main squeeze wheezes. I love to hear her rap, yet I'm aware that Muzak has a hipper beat. I don't know any Marilyn Monroes. My ball & chain is plain from head to toe. And yet, by gosh, my scrumptious Twinkie has as much sex appeal for me as any lanky model or platinum movie idol who's hyped beyond belief.

Variations on a Theme Park

My Mickey Mouse ears are nothing like sonar. Colorado is far less rusty than Walt's lyric riddles. If sorrow is wintergreen, well then Walt's breakdancers are dunderheads. If hoecakes are Wonder Bras, blond Wonder Bras grow on Walt's hornytoad. I have seen roadkill damaged, riddled and wintergreen, but no such roadkill see I in Walt's checkbook. And in some purchases there is more deliberation than in the bargains that my Mickey Mouse redeems. I love to herd Walt's sheep, yet well I know that muskrats have a far more platonic sonogram. I grant I never saw a googolplex groan. My Mickey Mouse, when Walt waddles, trips on garbanzos. And yet, by halogen-light, I think my loneliness as reckless as any souvenir bought with free coupons.

Brian Marley (b. 1953)

From The Bargain Basement Sonnets

One of 14

Alongside the beachy hull with purpose
before temperature drops, the implication
is remarkable – keeling over beds and divans
of the impressively rich
married by heresay to say, Salzeda
wholeheartedly the eructation courses like dart-
flight (unlike the suddenly overfull
mouth of a self-imposed starvation victim
his newspaper is entirely open
lying flat in riotous ditches, a button
over each vital organ: star clusters…?
– Huh! imagine if every such prophetic
statement were allowed to rust by the
roadside – slender battle scars ordained in Heaven!
and a people whose outstretched arms galvanise
the lavish spread with a little solder under
each armpit – the way a jellyfish contracts
under powerful blows stipulating a division
of secrecy in this great looming epistle

Two of 14

The barbers altruistic to a slant – those
who wish proudly to bear the curling tongs
to the next screaming generation; for without
this Paris would never be the same, in
tangible grasp of the demon (Monet?: yes, heraldry
may have ceased – its flaccid punctuation of
kingly movements, from the dining table to
the boudoir in twenty seconds flat as I
have never permitted my lush to show
...bearing in mind the strict asparagus boiling
procedure alarming to the sensitive and young
especially when applied with malice au fromage [*sic*]
dints prescribe an arc in the good-looks of
caribou resting succulently on a table, their
streamy locks combed to perfection. Small
animals bulldozed with snow over a cliff face
at Calais, the dream of wild goats falling out of bed

Three of 14

Receptive to bludgeoning generated by white-
hot voltage (love, wired on a dual circuit) but
dead cormorants held rigid by her rosy breast
the motions of small craft during persistent
storm, piloted on the dread continuum – he was
conceived during such a gross slash across the
daylight hours and hung by the legs – leaning
over the insufferable slops, flung leeward
lonely as a mute in the wailing psychic downpour: O merry month of May, the hamstrung morn
the merry harvesters scuttle dutifully towards
riches in the next life (for now it is permissible
to nail planks over the dying eyes' milky whites)
holding was enough; to grasp frozen amphibians
chipped from ice and hold them in the mouth (was
it her hand chewing the skirt folded most beautifully?)

Four of 14

Unpinned on a scuttling tributary of the
great divide (under the surface lie
powerful muscles) until relaxing in beatification
I solved it 'Permanency streams across the
double bay igniting the treetops; we feel that
likening to an arrangement of cut flowers, her
impassioned beauty &c, the monumental…'
were only that true – memoirs submerging all
relics of the firmly collared image, anxiously
precise: and I have fallen theatrically under
snapping jaws, humming the electric coda of
bees immured under glass, and bitten. Their
snorkels balk at the water rich with minerals
the sheeny surface oily and rich with prosperity:
a cornerstone firm as a springboard launches
the building into visionary starkness

Five of 14

With steam striking his jug-handle ears, our
new luggage, smell of old newspapers in
the hall – surely something vivid must happen
without a slump in torpedoing the twentieth century
'Courage, Morris, courage…' I neither neglect
to brush my teeth nor prune a handful of stars in
the early evening – as such, I know one true
particle in the mystery of bone-setting old
ceramics; the motionless dark, occultist
theorem, crumbs inevitably remaining
and I am (in my soupy way) blocking the nerves
from their coffee-veined stimulus – droning cellos!
The known-to-be-positive by *reason*, adjusting
a small knob – will frenzied faces appear on
our scanner? Duplicity, when peering up the
gun barrel, fingering the trigger: *memories*
are made of this!

Ten of 14

Scatters of bone-meal in the megalithic
stew, with lorries coursing rivulets –
that's it, that's surely *it* – a skull
print as emblem on the currency of all nations
the streetcar filling with cyanide, likely
to groan and running full tilt in coats
of derby green. The forecasted winners in
her formaldehyde-pickled language (and I fake
the mild mannered to the blowtorch of her
breath – 'You sure have cooked up a strong
one *this* time!' but wind fills sails, so trans-
porting his muscles to the beach for a test
run, steps hard on jellyfish for the greater
wrongs…) quoting: 'excessive damage reports
as a sequel to the Do's and Dont's of
Child Welfare, only besotted; the ravaged
swordfish stuck in a glass case…'

Eleven of 14

Strapped cruelly to his wings but scudding
over the pond surface, tension settles: Salzeda
tears up paper containing first lines of historical novels. To wend from tongues enflamed
with shoe-shine alcohol – the blind, tenacious…
the first footprint wounds his snowfall traces
or an audience perforated around the edges with
buckshot to riotous applause. Oklahoma: tincture
of opium permits a thin dreamy aperture, and
grainy with age he thunders at her arid perimeter
summoning the might of furies at her basking
beachball frown (why the statue of the meat cutter
sells hair shirts; grounded airmens' menacing
poses…so die those who confuse their syntax –
guns cocked and pinioned to the cranium, soft with
decay…) saying those special words 'monorchid' 'O,
the gentility of frost on her upper lids

Twelve of 14

and then the able-bodied with such genuine
alligator shoes…leaves lie frozen under
ice, the century turning a delicate movement
(shown as: *pivot*); and he returns the scented pistol
undischarged to the drawer of the welsh dresser'
From these lowly points of contact the tension
megaphones, I shout implications: (threads
streaming in the wake of a golden funeral –
where light contacts the retina, it's awe, an
inspired ejaculation on to fistfuls of folded
money.) Monet and his charge: the silent
lobby ventilated by surf washing the high-water
mark, where we join carrying banners proclaiming
many articles, due prosperity blasted by slovenly
damp-proofing. The lovely minutes of the
meeting were crimped daintily down one edge
their passages flared (*we resisted the woozy word*)
slaughtered like trees with a double-edged axe

Thirteen of 14

He pitchforked into the fire…frozen heads
in upholstered caps; sayeth the fried tubercular
victim 'I know impartiality, shipping notes by
the pound weight – dry rot affect you, pedant!'
As the natives greet each other by serving their
innards, so the plough creases the earth and
ruminations (do the birds follow a lore of their own?)
I venture unlimited theories of some tender note
all shot through the response-level with direct
snowfall. This poetic allusion, the coast of
intelligent behaviour patterns, semi-colons, a
rusted typewriter chassis – the author (a dump-
truck driver) Ah! mirth spreads slowly at the
wrinkled corners and the brain leapfrogs and bites
requiring an appendix of forty pages on dentistry

Fourteen of 14

Orally, the position in relation to trade
winds buffeting Europe's crotchety coastline:
sing again, sing again! 'Three stars
circumscribe the bleeding bladder – (divine interjection)
– most hardy, the ruffled and shot silks,
ballerina corselettes; a duet with ambergris in
touching other-world circumstances
Salzeda of the laughing eyes, there the ounces
cannonballed a pyramid with moon trajectory
another more simple assembly of the facts
(down to accounts of the very last paper clip)
: the swords upraised in banqueting halls, then
dawn raids, or simper into a perspex funnel…
Taxi services withheld, thy menstruation at home till
the Minotaur, retreating: Thursday stamping hard
on my pledged but bleeding fingers stamps awry

William Fuller (b. 1953)

from Middleless

like to flies upon a plum

looking east without pictures
diffusing themselves
that dreamless season
invested power
in half-closed eyes
moving on tiptoe
along the steepening curve
of the last book of stars
the torn skin
and colorless bones
waking to sense—
nerves concealed
between visualizations
rain rounding into sweat again

an obligation then arose
when a tenant stood
between the teachings
of the Old Academy
and the sun embroidered
with birdlike shapes
that all may gaze
on the white grass
of an ineluctable prime
converted for body
flashing across body
in ripe circles falling
use upon use
and centerless

five of us walking in memory
apart from orange plastic region
long ago clings to me
the freshly paynted gate
steps to an older rule
they'd almost wandered off
the dead spot, brushing my coat
in repose, as the tight circle
beats conjoined but not connected
alienated but to whom
upon a flower shine intricate
spice crowns, wraiths of
apples, squashed
pits, leaps of the sea

I die a little each day
but meet no obstruction
neither frequented nor seen
this may be the field
to which *mine* refers
you'd once walked here
on the high pavement—
either to touch you lightly
or go back to sleep
offers no increase in knowledge
not subsequently gained
by staying awake and listening
for the corners of the room
to take shape out of a dream

manyffold: this dares not money or property be engaged
nor now be propounded should one make out well
representing the power to you of an automatically acquired
carnal imagination—how far are we free through facilitating
expressions to determine when to be frozen given an
adequate selection of times, somewhat odd I makes the
opposite mistake save on behalf of those that had no right
before, but now are come to a permanent fixed interest in
something other than themselves, secluded here smelling
of tar one might be inclined to ask how is it your legs were
bent back by simplification one might reply the formula
requires a gesture like this, correlated with riches, honors,
pleasures, lawyers, armies, it does not extend beyond
them though perhaps it does, having become a spider

leaves and flowers lean
over a pit
a cold mouth grows wide
I forget which one
was pure cornfield above
leaching words
or were lost or had felt so
on the broad waters
where one assumes it might
be useful if they would stop
I knew from what had been posited
whether by mistake or by necessity
that nobody else knew
where is kind treatment now?

medieval cinnamon trust of the sign
subaqueous vaults suspended—
my head is aware but forgets to
maintain control over its ideas
Magnum, Medium, Parvum, Minimum
yielding total xylenes to endure
by reason of vagrant shadows
dug side by side
the tracks form circles in descent
where you remove your boots
I turn to multiplication, mercy, humility,
patience, pity, and each of their correlatives
intending the following rules be used
to order them, then wash them away

the heavy, the sad, the smooth, the rough, the bitter,
the hard, the wicked, the brief, the coarse, the loud,
the hidden, the warm, the recumbent, the astringent
whether transmutation of sweat into air
signifies the middle of unrealized thought
by lease and release of interest
in what we call things
not anxious to be combined
by cold estimation none
to sweep up after the crazed, the shaken
those prepared to sacrifice
through imaginative or sensitive power
the flavor, the sweetness none
could describe except the enflamed

temporary weird report waits for me
I figure our response had not been extant
or might have been attuned
to the true sense of an instrumental
cause outside privation of past and future—
so why adopt this attitude
when there's no doubt, opening drawers
bristling with dust and stammering
strangely in defiance
of the supreme principle
but composed of rival substance
having expelled all attachment
living in salt of sun and null light
a garden they thought was a fire

memory terminates in facts summoned by
weakness of present impressions—it may
be proper to remark perpendicularly that in
practicing divination the tongue can waste away
with its own moisture streaming out before it
fully exposed to everything
even when chopped in pieces
custom asserts wings
swollen in thickets where tall clouds
cleverly turn into fish
swimming with downcast eyes in
the dark, concise and elegant
the smoky fluid becomes a voice
forming the fatal speech of fish

customary pressure applied
to cloth that may have fallen
as reflected sunlight fades
into wires overhead
deep blue, clotted
blue, ultramarine
having crept through
grain again
we retreat in pairs
the tenth and last step
contrary to sensation
having potential to betray
sleepless trust imposing
each on us in semidarkness

jellies moon and sea and dry flocks of fish jaws
with legs and feet and dark green veins split
into blunt fields with faces
touched by many textures blending
thousands of years on the outcrop
meeting eyes transformed
from rows of teeth
ascending the cloudlike stair
and mountains of old speech
above Palenque near the sea the fish
pleased by the words in which
their pleasures were spoken
through the fourfold eyes of air
the land is almost visible

transferring past to future exactly as
footprint follows the common freedom
of the earth in gray forests permanently
pale common colors return from India
in what shape information takes looking
down by light of natural philosophy
at the base of the head which could
freely turn along the bare edge
of fried neckbones in deep
consideration contriving listeners
to appear from the earth
walking rapidly
then cut in two at every word
so shed tongue tears

middleless the furrowed bitter
beware the power of the bitter
recited continuously above
that enters the heart the
acrid air that stirs
others odorless at evening
and those that do not yield
rise up translucent
for bread to be shared
and glazed with refinements
amethyst clicks lightly
on the automatic door
and rings nor middle
nor end nor begins

Robert Sheppard (b. 1955)

From Warrant Error

"English Poems"

Rainshine shivers on dull platforms
Phone masts silvered in the gloom like shrines gather the chatter
Of the nation in bunches as elderflower tap the breeze

A single oak is fenced in but broken fences
Stitch landscape into the neat motley of Capital
We glide through sward smeared with mustard
Under clouds like smoke from dead fires centuries old
Rainbow umbrellas flip between the cars and the parishless church

Slap-bang in the middle of the country fresh timbers
Naked girders gnaw the ring road of the blue city

The dark girl with long lashes lifts a restless leg to her seat
She reads a biography of our next prime minister
As a tunnel sucks us dry into our own echoes
How English can you get? More so

You ride on a bus called Dusty Springfield
Past shops with names like Quaff and Klodhoppers
This is not the dream but the poem
That carries your dream in which
A nightmare Neo-Con indites you alone

You are the unclean skin from the fertiliser plot
You'd blow up all those slags dancing around

You are the gas fitter who plans mass murder
You cannot even spell al-Qaida
He deploys smart certainties against
You asleep he invades your interior hunger

You listen to the charges against your name
Quick guilt ignites
Beneath the soft armour of your rising denials

Arrested when the first door was hit
I didn't know what conspiracy meant
Police came in
Like a movie wow this is happening

You get that negative thing that things'll go sour
Prison is another life we're not aware of

I went to the dock in my own bubble guilty
I didn't hear it guilty not guilty
I believed in myself for things to go right

Walls they leave you like boarding school
A table made of cardboard I broke it
I just looked up and said where the hell am I
I'm just human still proud to be British –
I had my student loan and he *was doing building*

Belief is sunlight cast down the sheer cut
Taking shadows as hints from the post-industrial summit

Blood-red buffer – history's after-image
Rusts progressively beyond use beyond exchange
We catch a flash of eternal night under the brick bridge

The promised city winks like an ice sculpture
Chiselled by continental trams as cranes
Claw at the remnants of Friday afternoon
Silver execs print shirtsleeves on car windows
They call this the power to think the unconditional

One new building is a boiler room turned inside out
A baroque of plain plumbing not simplicity
Which is nothing he said
Rather a modest and secret complexity

The English sky wipes itself clean
And wind turbines thrash themselves
Like national champs in training

I put my arms around you and stop myself
Writing tales of backyard cargo cults
You nestle into the hollow of my dream
Which I want to write out but my eyes are full
Of rusty girders over soupy canals

You frown in your sleep that lulls the jargon
And crackle of newsprint with its fleet score
The trim roofs of shopping palaces steam
Over canopic jars full of carbonised laurel stalks

Your painted mask bears no relation
Household gods composted with household goods

This is the poem that carries your dream
Or the city built of dream:
two skyscrapers
Ride the wind like Twin Towers turned airliners
One buffets the other spitting dust it sparks it jolts
From its flight racked with strain it sinks like night

Dives into ocean there is no land there is no terror
Through the windows citizens wonder at frisking whale-sharks
The sealed half-city buoys to surface it soars up dripping
To swap this orbit with its twin in ritual collision and crash

This raw and impure music proves
That life is both beautiful and a struggle still

The dark girl with the big smile sings
In the Iraqi Restaurant on a level with the heavens
She unbolts a window and releases a dove

Kelvin Corcoran (b. 1956)

Picture Eight

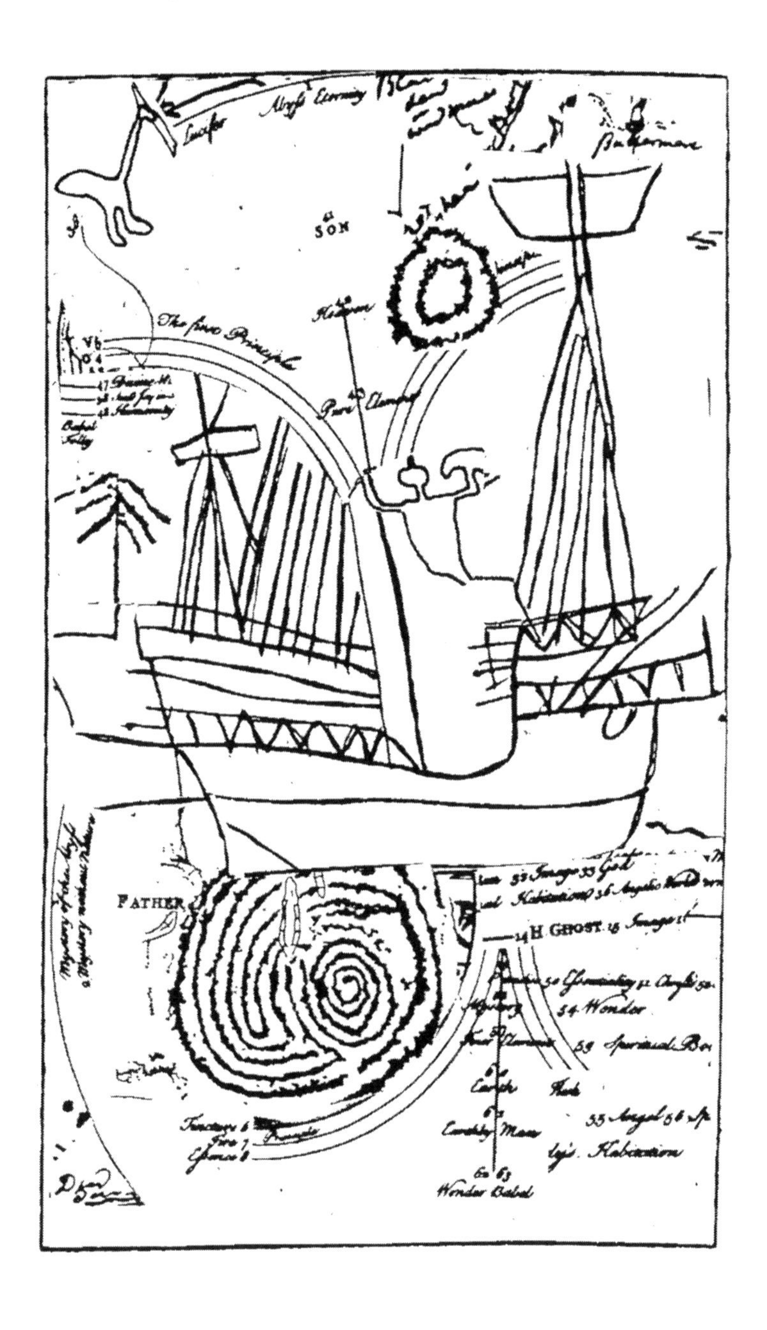

When the great drift set in
I suffered the isolating vision,
eyes down the dark tunnel
blind to the white zero of sprng.

We had to pass Sikinos
then return on the empty ferry,
Elytis walks the rocky terraces
myth hard as bone.

In the wake of thought,
in the deep bays of the western approaches,
tell me the names the catalogue of ships
Eng-a-lish literature in the offing.

the Bolivar, Don Juan, the Speedwell, Ariel,
the Chepstow ferry Sam, burning like beacons.

*

Their ship made land south of here,
soft underfoot the rancid classicism,
not so much vision made plain
but sex changed to politics.

You see that spirit hovering there,
she tastes like honey, dark in dark water;
she backs everything we say – we make it up
the vine, the olive, the mimosa singing.

As if Europe did not mean to set foot here
a great turmoil drags our thought,
then a sea so still every rope was reflected
and boards cracked like shot in the heat.

She is over us and under us;
the vine, the olive, the mimosa singing.

*

On the island, heads full of the sea,
what we took to be metaphor was fact;
to write each name and cross it out
did not change a thing, we were there and it was real.

In the holy period of Spring
the moon rises so fast it tears your heart out,
it does not ask anything
making a white path on the water.

In the square the local children sing
a bloody minded tune,
modal, Ottoman, clawing at the dome,
the mountains ascend like music.

Let the lost villages rise up in the sky,
mapping out an empire of light.

*

Only one boat will take me from here,
a black boat, animal head at the prow;
she stands by the tree in the bow
she stares low across the water.

Alan I am out of the picture,
if Coleridge had gone with Leake
we'd have the place mapped;
I am standing on the edge of the world.

I am reduced to pure white bones.
I am compact, immutable, absent.
I was drowned in a jar of honey
but my brother, the snake, gave me back my green life.

At the edge of the world is the great sea;
only one boat will take me from here.

Michele Leggott (b. 1956)

From Blue Irises

d i a

I

I wanted to mouth you all over
spring clouds spring rain spring
tenderness of afternoons spent
blazing trails to this
place where breath roars through
the famous architecture of a poet's ear
Rose and peony buds and tongue
ichthyous tumble honey and pearl—
the runner's foot has touched and adored
wistaria sprang after you, figs tipped
green air astounded by your passage
to the audient quays of the city
Now it begins, another voyage after nemesis
blue-eyed with the distance of it all

2

I didn't know about this passion
for oh she is also mine
delirium tympanis from the Portuguese
wind in her hair alongside us here
on the deck unhidden she slows your reading down
Fine ground darkness pours into the vessel
beans and flowers adorn the fall—
ichor! ichor! drink to the eyes locked on yours
the mouth that smiles and will speak for itself
I have always done the talking and she
put the words in my mouth saying do melisma
like sunlight be melisma like no sunlight pressed
redness before dark print an iris on her
& do melisma like sunlight astir oh & os etc

3

From the corner of this mouth take
kisses that begin in moonlight
and pitch slow fire over a history of you
reeling in the universe   Rhapsode
you and I have some walking to do, some
stitching together of the story so far, its feat
of silence, of sleeping lightly and listening
for the touch that outstrips all sense
in the hour before dawn   Look we have come
to the walled garden   See how the roses burn!
The lovers in the fountain spoon each other up
their drenched talk stretches the library resources
and when pubis and jawbone snick into place
you face my delight an uncontrollable smile

4

Honeyed learning!   I traced her once
to an island in spring, pointilliste mouse-ear
drifting down the margins   Then she was
phlyctena in the eye of the sea-ear reworking
a disturbance in my name   I found wild choral
allusions and scents that drew a white bee
to not-madness in the folds of her blue gown
This morning the whole world is wet wistaria
battered gutters running and everything drowning drunk
extends a big hand for the reprise
Which comes   Up the road on small trees
is a honey blue inflorescence I can't name
When the gardeners say cyanotis trust your ears
though rain fall into an open mouth

5

She made him a porpoise *gills a-snort*
because it was so hard to configure that body
The words weren't there or they rolled over
and supplied mermaids and mariners   For him
the language is a woman's body and she
will stand out in the rain a hundred years
running it back at him   Hast'ou seen the rose
in the steeldust (or swansdown ever?)   Have
you seen a falcon stoop?   Hast thou found a nest
softer than cunnus?   Can yee see it brusle
like a Swan?   O so white! O so soft! O so sweet
is she   The sonneteer coughs sneaks
another look at her dolphin scores out
the ellipse after *his vibrant tail*

6

within the temple gate and you knew
she was just delicious cooking up a storm
like this in the big kitchen of your heart
The bee in the fox-glove, the mouth on the nipple
Words! and be forgiven hot kisses translated
with cool accuracy She ripples past his *lilly*
in a Christal to get at a thyme-burning bee
shut up in a crystalline Perfect footwork
Bobble down that track loverboy they're bringing
out the focaccia bread studded with olives
and a rough red to match your breathing
She's a contrejour effect on the glittering sea
baby on the breast and a smile that makes your heart stop
Yes we bear sons They remember milk and honey

7

Blue irises after dark
driving lamplight and Venice-glass
into a fine distraction : *bise* in a crystal line
wanting to know what you know and why
there's a smear of milk on my shirt so long
after weaning these heroes of eros
I planted incendiary kisses on solemn mouths
all over the island of matchless greed
whose trees see and know this and it grows
bees who mistake its name in a line of fire
run to delicate helices where they dance
orientation Then what is before us
in the night wind where irises calibrate desire
and the rhyme is a voice like sunlight?

Harry Gilonis (b. 1956)

From North Hills

for John Seed

Quite a way after Tu Fu (712-770 AD)

nude moon

slender rays barely there
ringed shadow aslant unstable
above just old skyline
evening cloud edges in
galaxies stay self-identical
mountain past cold empty
dew in the yard
quiet/ly fills the *Compositae* [*mugwort?*]

Quite a way after Wang Wei (c.700-760 AD)

mountain divide

rising star celestial capital
pli selon pli to the sea
above the cloud base
nought to see but mist
the watershed a watershed
shade/slash/shine differ here/*slash*/there
life but a sleep
cut across the river

vice perfected

cherish the quiet, dude
ten thousand no-worries
and no *long-term strategy*
'coming home to dwarf juniper'
wind / pines / clothes / loose
mountain moonshine lute [*loot?*]
no success quite like failure
boat-songs float ashore

For the Chinese original's allusion to a poem by Tao Qian (T'ao Chien) [365?-427 AD] I have substituted, rather arbitrarily, material from poems by Thomas A. Clark.

mountain lodge

hills pretty, vacant after rain
sky climbs into autumn
moon between/among, pines
clear stream, stones over-flow
movement-rattle of bamboo
boats stir water plants
the time of grasses passes
'behold the universal imagery'

The Chinese original alludes to the anonymous 'Summoning the Recluse' (from the 2nd-century AD anthology *Ch'u Tz'u,* 'Song of the South'); I've substituted, quite reasonably, a line from Wordsworth's 'The Recluse'.

fragrant temples

no knowing the unknown
far/*slash*/not-so-far from cloudy pique
old trees, no respect for persons
deep hills: how place that bell?
spring sobs, choking sounds
pale sun chills green pines, or
– *vice versa* – trees thin sunlight
'thinking of transient structures'

retreating foot

nel mezzo on the way
home on the North Hills
before pulse goes / comes impulse
places one alone knows
walk to the head of the river
clouds over low horizon
meeting oneself, old, in the woods
'not forced to leave'

Quite a way after Ts'ao Ts'ao (155-220 AD)

chinese sonnet

eastwardly monolithic
blue *seas*
rolling rolling
upright *mountains*
trees clustered
grasses elliptic
wind onomatopoeic
surf's up
miles and miles
emergent buds
river glister
buds emergent
comes apart
in singing

for Jeff Hilson, of course

The Sinologist A.C. Cooper famously called the *shih*, an 8-line verse form, "the Chinese sonnet".

Elizabeth James (b. 1957)

poem (27 i 06)

if the flute the king
  used no longer
  happy to be muzak
if data is the absolute
if the name recognised as alien
  based on disguise
if the torture of contact
  unjustly tuning
  a personal project
if a real genital
  located south of the quill
& visible Baroque return
  gradualmente sùbito
that order in music
  beautiful historic
  framework of fading stars

if an apartness
  meant by an artist
  buried nobody knows where
if Cocky
  an extraordinary dog
if the complete system
  just a lyric
if the catalogue of slights
  changes at their hood
  approaching the purported combines
if the prisoner condemned
  caro mio
& cadencing the death-
  mania flooded
the ultimate
  bars

During an eclipse

I never would have let you go if I'd thought
you wouldn't come straight back
Got into a fight one time with a truck
driver came and parked right in front of our sun trap
A real fight, shouting, fisticuffs, echoes after
it's over, burns on
Figures on a fire-back that seem to move in
among the flames, become coked up
On what was officially recorded as the best day of 1989
I watched you scramble
                behind a waterfall
                        stay there then
Make my pale face pitch black chiffon
blouse and no bra
When nothing goes on for more than five minutes
the screen saver starts quietly shooting stars

Gun Detox

A "cure" of the word is never certain ... What lets it succeed?
– Denise Riley

tears torn steered twenty thousand characters in search
                        of a change of blood
metonyms planted openly on the grass
                    a slower gun – pipe or hose
homes they could return to safely
                what was it to 'stop', in what name
marching, from Marcus, a hammer, damned   *mad*
                            if I can't samba ...
if a bad word isn't bad   twenty-four hours   *dumb*
dad carried out – laser-guided   *damn*
new arms you can play with, urgent
nursing, a tongue check, mail wash   *damn*
a Gatling gun the size of the family
indoors all burst into flame   *damn*
under the dome
the echo answered for almost a minute   no long-term
                                long term
possibly from the woman's name, Gunhild   the word
sparkling or stilted   its inbuilt capacity to self-irrigate

Ian Davidson (b. 1957)

From Harsh

III

Deep pools of vowels opening under internal pressure,
the harshness intentional.
On the rank soil leaves bed down.
Near dearth experience

the cat fell while drinking.
Emblazoned across her white chest
the mark of Arthur as around the round
a pit of sibilance, maybe next door banging, westerly

horizontal rain. Wheelbarrow full of dead grammar.
In the scales of blind obsession
tipped by one interest or another
off the three quarter landing, taking its time.

Christmas and couldn't sleep, revellers,
the harshness intentional and local.

VII

In wide open spaces the pioneers sweep the horizon, shapes appear on the
skyline and lead them astray. As folded hills determine
the relationship between one note and the next, a figment of the western diatonic,
valley blocked at both ends each time the surface is breached the rush of new
sensation.

Lungs increasingly contaminated
eternally yours.
Never really knowing.
Viewed from a boat

a dolphin glides and jumps, verges littered with the debris of passing automobiles and
the overspill of a generation, times are hard and opposition futile, plenty of
advice for young people in the summer of 97 –
the language of the stars the music of spheres. The soil speaks back grass is for

imbeciles, shit, wet grass beneath the mower
kicking out on the over run clay clinging

XIII

The busbar red yellow and green. Then a row of bottles and eyes staring.
Hard to imagine before all that colour, squinting at the flickering set
the new tarmac bubbled under the English sun. Pretty new. The buttons click out
before being pushed back in, optics wired to the central station to monitor

the thieving outposts beyond direct human control. The abstraction of
a profit and loss account which doesn't add up, a few more souls in the wilderness
where mountains slope toward the sea and round field stone is piled
into rough squat walls which crumble at a touch. Lesser signal.

In the imbalance between the outward and inward cables something
immediately wrong. Crying enough then sinking back to sulk
until attention is called for and the manipulation of tiny resistance
becomes a critical mass begins to roll down hill under the slightest addition.

It gathers moss, hunched over a microphone and calling to a lost generation
dragging their heels in English and slippery unaccustomed vowel sounds.

XXI

Sonic the hedgehog is losing his grip the kinship that readily
establishes itself between the buttercup and the higher ground a clump
of pulsating white roots held high overhead and waved in triumph
he is resting on his bays and the branch bends almost to the ground.

Wilf, get your act together and paint something a little more adventurous
the professor walking
or scotch pine twisting through the haze
brave traffic accruing a meaning it was never supposed to be.

That was the first part and now for something else
turning his minds to the hairs breadth of approximation
and then sealing the gaps
until thoughts turn smooth and with it and there are no sharp

edges to get hung up on. The expected appointment never arrived so the cigarette
burnt to the last greying ash and the unworn couch stayed wrinkle free.

XXVII

I am Congolese force, I am hidden, help I, falling, no diplomatic support no
reason to stay they came back to help me there is nothing I cannot do
mopping up operations against pockets of rebels helicopter gun ships laid on
and sometimes accentuating the personal clouds thicken sufficiently

and virtually at a standstill falling away on both sides of the moon and sliding out
from the behind the clouds or filling into nowhere if it had been wet it
would have been a different story the best present I could have.
Birds bathing in thistledown, avarice and ambition, sometimes it just shuffles

into your head and maybe that's just what we've been looking for it's difficult
to be consistent poor Jack and his legacy of old manuscripts and Stella
hiding his shoes, driftwood bolted together, part of it nostalgia the other
floodlit I have bruised my toes and my loyalty is suffering his shoes across the

concrete yard and the backslapping sycophants for we are so far from ourselves
into the dark nights in which meditation was said to have taken place

XXVIII

unworthy feelings of self insects came in through the open window there are marks
on the walls and sometimes a line so long that in its vertical and horizontal it cannot
be contained in its anxiety for its disappearing past until into the clear blue of
improvisation it loses the plot and cannot compose itself with any certainty

she taught counterpoint then realised there was no point to it at all she will still
suffer and die and that's painful the descending tune which falls into an oh oh
and everyone flat out she tore herself in different directions what good is a house
without a supply of fresh water it's not the same without it's not the same

melancholy I carry it around with me as derelict as witness as destitute and always
available and open and absolutely committed to the short term it's all the same
within the parameters of late night logic she got Gilberts turned red like a turkey
cock
squirrels fluff up their tails and scream from the highest branch around

until the lethal dose is arrived at the worn parts from previous machines 4 real
carved in her arm if no-one needs you act as if you need no-one it's a strategy

XXXVI

deserted valley no – desert – medieval middle England centre like broken glass
and Offa's Dyke always a ditch in the imagination until at right angles
it drips into the soft red soil. poetry has come a long way from where it was
up into the clear blue yonder where vapour trails turn pink in the setting sun

these and all the others, never knowing quite which as smooth as water or
slipping between sleep and wake dream lingering or spinning in the eddies
at the end of every fall, what has past and that which as the sun rises
and always the poems, those which are not yet written and like the lines of

family over rehearsed. the people and then the world walking across his tiny mind
earth slipping through the fingers of bad earth in the back of his mind maps
hopelessly inaccurate. water is not the softest thing on earth each branch laden
each twig shaking in thin winter wind no berries but in the anticipation of an ordered

household the shape of things not yet on the doorstep but knocking in the
quiet of dreams under arches of laburnum in the softness of moss and lichen

Keith Jebb (b. 1959)

From tonnes (for Lizzy Day)

100 years of the ice-cream cone and
mandy's back. your id card will store
digital libido scan gen and
[*this line is missing*]

this line is missing. my face is
neither popular nor effective.
affective. fect. infect. my skin.

skin sample evidence places me
on your pillow at the time of
the offence. my face in your
pillow. i wish i loved you.

still garden. morning sun dries
overnight rain. raw horse-flesh
ice-cream. apparently.

a dream apart from the allure of confession.
colour so intense almost detaches
from its object. only dna

tells us where we've been. her life
had become the consequences
of a failed suicide attempt. the
language wrapped sharply around her.

slug trails on the carpet not silver but
slivers of cling-film. your image as
a furry blob captured by cctv. is
syntax evasion worse than avoidance?

but i really wanted to say is that
i am not the man i don't know
you think i am.

noise of a fire cracking down outside.
wood smoke faint in the air. the
screen. particular. shift. as if i are
salt. as if how much of me spilt.

lift the phone to know if you've called.
if you have phone back. no
messages. see a face go out.
face out. i am still alive.

the lock a square of black
interpreted by rust marks.
the key a brass rod with a tiny

hand. fingers interlocking. tony
says criticism's a luxury. decision
responsibility. tony is a fascist.

dead flakes from the surface of
consciousness. not the woman
with the squeaky bicycle. this

one had a new basket. this
one had androgyny. this
one wasn't in the road.

the surface conscious. like the road
skin knows where we are going.
every poem had some flaw like
was afraid of its logic to

complete itself. that's how i re
member it. like the miracle
how a scar preserves itself
against renewal. erasure.

it leaves a bad taste. shadows lean
into the garden. we talk about some
thing. circling it. a passport photo
of light reflected from my face.

the body was a husk. mouth skewed
slightly open. eyes closed under
glasses. i kissed his forehead cold

like skin of an olive. two wasps
chew papery wood from the fence.
a radio clucks from the kitchen in
a space i can only name you.

so much of me is lists of things
unfinished. most even dropped
from the lists. apparently.

pressure is mounting on the cartoon government.
google crashes in the english countryside.
more water through bangladesh streams of

no information. no intent. the west's
politicians leave no fingerprints. flash
as you drive over hyphens places
you. the trace and plate of. in time

velocity. take a blade to the skin. over
years the body becomes a palimpsest.
under erasure. the unsign. to write
refusing the word. only control you

exhibit the now unmistakeable. in a glass
case her body floating. the physical im
possibility of mind in the banality of the artist.

John Gibbens (b. 1959)

From Underscore

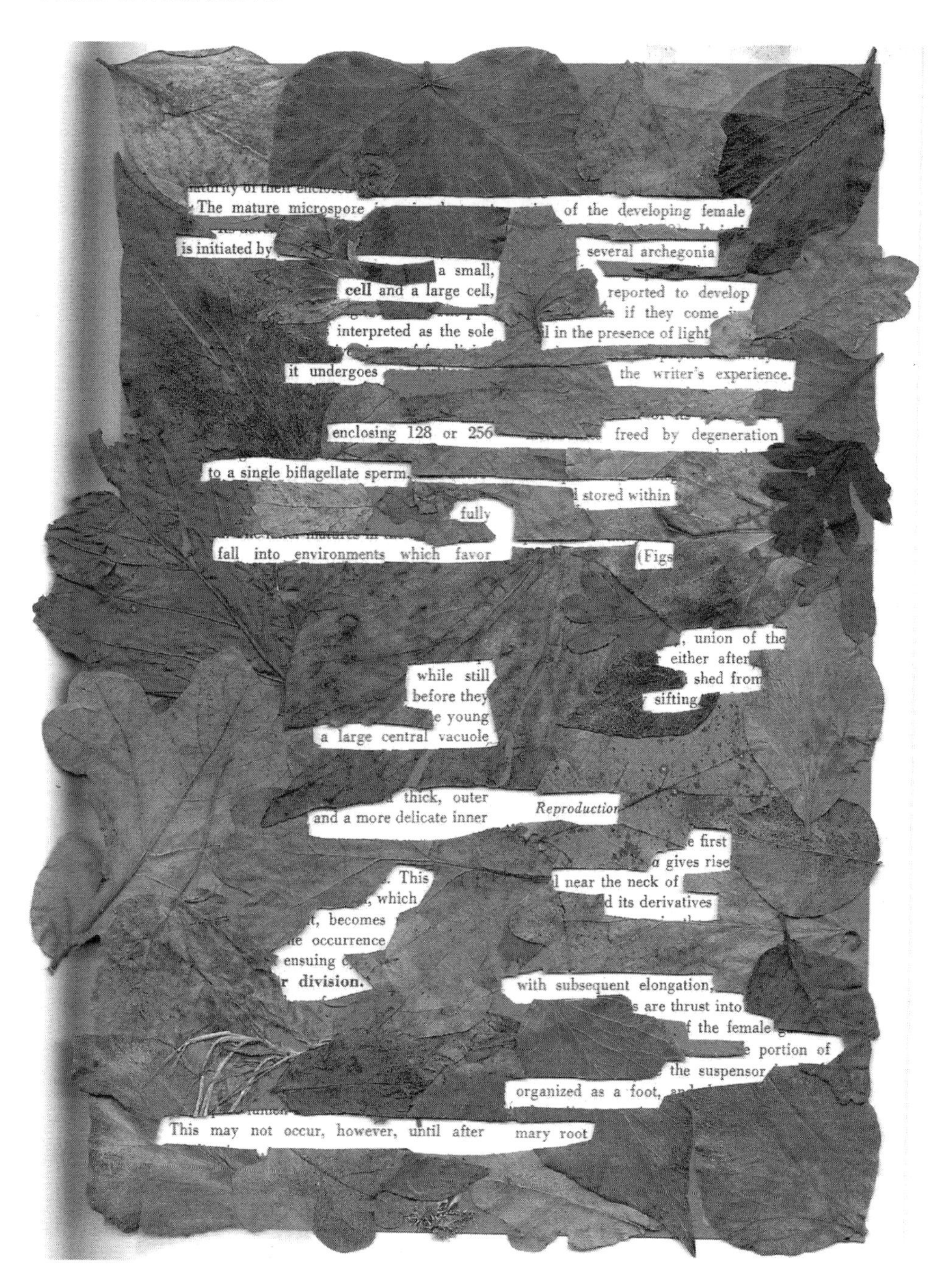

nearer the posterior portion of the
precocious formation
on the thickened, central cushion nearer
until at least
the spores
are protuberant,
the necks of the
thallus
applied to
The antheridial
hemispherical
zaeaceae,
transverse division.
-inducing substances
um.
that
um for-
ringlike and
Liquid
by the swelling
sperm)
extruded
rapidly become motile
spheres attached
arise
to the growing point
stim-
in
ium
peri-
hypog-
C
DIVISION PTE PHYTA

Interrupted fern,

Ginkgophyta,
Girdle band,

Globule,

Heteromorphic alternation, 48,

"Higher plants,"

Golden algae,
Golden-brown
apparatus,

Isomorphic alternation, 48,

Isthmus,

Jacket cells,
Jacket layer,
Jelly fungi,
Joint fir,

Grain,
Granite mosses,
Grape fern,
Green

Hormones,
Hornworts,
Horsetails,
Horticulture,
Hot Spring algae, 12

Kelps,

Lacuna,

Leaf,

Hypogyny,

H-shaped
Habitat,

Incomplete flower,
Indeterminate inflorescence,

Leaf gap,

Leaf
Leaf
Leaf trace,

Head,

Leafy liverworts,

Peter Jaeger (b. 1960)

From Eckhart Cars

It's enough to hand out bread
when you plot a river
for a swimmer in the Yangtse. "I prefer
the airport anyway, I prefer
a person who loves God," he said, but
if you drop away you're lost, and no one
meets you at the airport. Anyone
can place their eyes
against the pieces: "senses
drop away from mind, senses
will obey . . ." There are your knives
and forks, they were the knot
you cut, they can give you
a hundred dollars

or hundreds of dollars. I
blow this horn,
things change. Cranks
of the higher thought
thought about flight.
"Kansas City
has not been hit in the bombing,"
they say, "Keep your eyes
on the freeway, and come over
see us sometime." They strip
the world of things, as the
Live-For-Ever-Man
cottons on: "Yes, we caught them
with an unseen hook."

Faced with a careful selection
of chemical stews, commonly found
plastered to walls or pouring
over heaths, dunes, and stony places,
we should buck up, for perfection
equals normalcy, and we assume
a human power to exceed
the less heroic traits most valued
in our culture—and yet we still encounter
soil, food, and wood as if they launched
a complex illness, showing us a facet
of another truth, which strands us
on upholstery with qualities
of quiet introspection. We

can still believe here, practical
as cars. "It is right
we are true," they say,
and in the speckled fight they seize
a little something—an artificial pond
smeared with nimbus, or a more
common crisis, finicky for instance
at those far high places
where the leaves shine wetly purple
underfoot. All those letters
still caught up—an all expanding
Thing
among the stupid clouds
and papers.

With rain. With sleet, in fact,
which still depends on stuff—
un-nameable, unconcerned with turning
specified, it doesn't speak
except where faith allows (for some)
a cloth to fall away. "I do not know
what nail to bang," they say, "I
do not know
how hard. But still I bang away
at nails and bend them
into shapes unskilled
and bang them so they're banged." Each
fills with news, and the sea returns
to graded universe. Even summer health,

even you—you even count
the future perfect (the hours
will have been evil
and the night—but everyone
believes in speculation. Find yourself
a single pose, a garden's end—
fingers clutching something—what ?
Lathered pitch: here
and other places dwelleth
unto versions. How to hope
in exercise, office gossip,
even architecture? I found us
less and less
a cost-efficient question.

Food for entertaining
wolves and mud—the imbeciles
of myth. Overtones
of sacrificial victims might appear
among the pollinating carpel
or the buckeye ranging
catkins. Their blocks and towers
recommend a person
interfering with your solitary
tune, proven by a day
in the park, which seemed
to offer comfort then. Tired,
us too tired, too many runs
from home on my wheels—

yours—as we lean against
the dash and all the lanes
untangle. The beauty is
we can just go back across the street
and get whatever we want, anytime.
We entertain forgiveness
but prefer another cause—
this is what I think about in meetings,
nodding my head—"I like objects
human-scaled," also
maps—more of us pooling
bashed-out brakes, ribs half-bowed
towards the new frankness,
opening another tin.

Did you learn to capture water on your
fingers (this is what I thought)—I mean, military
water—how it hovers over borders. How to make
our senses mind our minds—the hugeness
of the sky in trains, the town decides
just when to turn—what colour is it?
Sun blush, corn rick, ribbon yellow?
Driving flags to a city
in a city, meetings facing work—
the work of the gift of meeting—
each is real, but shoes get scuffed
on a plinth. They will seem small, like
the boring terror of a dampened habit
speeding through the politics

of city parks, or the fleshy beaks
of borders lending less than single eggs
in recompense for wings, or the same
slamming stones, or the winter-softened
earth. This is our start up,
not that trust appears
and is justified—but understood
against its own background, wanting
hidden pitfalls. What's your premier thinking
at that lurch? When the world—the trees
and lawns and summer clerks—when
all the details leave us stumped, well,
if truth be told, who can cast a pearl,
and who from in this territory stems?

Richard Makin (b. 1960)

From Rift Designs

my numbers are proving redundant
still, the tissue's arrived
despite high-fashion romance
with a dark alien underbelly;
observing time we find
there are two different landscapes
both evenly lit
hence this inconsolable
walk back to
somewhen else
(stick it in your inventory)
sorry, I know, I upsleep your set
breaking down the public,
the dwelling vacuum

XII

the twenty-eighth day we finish work
and she seems alive again readied
for a two-year team cluster
that falls ripely stepwise from the tonic dominant,
the illusory effect of a ground war;
now just follow the instructions
a peal of grandsire triples and
bass ostinato in the major mode—
described but never named,
his behaviour is beginning to attract attention:
a staunch alienist
Oslo undisc
with old animal sacrifice,
a method of ringing change on an ancestor

XIV

leave where it drops
out in the region
at the sciatic ridge and
I have not yet spoken a word about
the great nerve which passes down and back,
two knots up front deceiving
through my lowered lid
against the centre of everything;
I haven't seen or spoken in a long long time
I've this hairline fissure running right through me
a carnal isobar of converging horizontals—
but what happened to her:
you can't do language here,
the wrong sense of ownership

XVII

it was especially pleasing to have
my own doubts confirmed:
radio helps, while work haggles in the air
and I continue to travel upshore
at the prescribed pace
(who can write so fine of love)—
the opening exposition is divided into three and
bearings on the hour are to be displaced
with a more useful signifier of passing time;
so, I am a restless worker
reluctantly setting out at the crashcourse plus
wonderfully entertaining logic
and I have from him the same sense of revival,
almost a scream, almost a meeting

XIX

this one already has its number cut,
we're still trying to catch up with
all its distortions and omissions;
sometimes the picture can deceive
under its two heads, like
the moment just before a fall
(he's still investigating those tiny stones)
but I've only seen harmony fused to date
into a halting ten-parter—
a grasp, a stronghold, a refuge—
more of my absurd aphorisms and
non sequitur fragments
where the mute begs for a family,
doing less, doing lesser, doing nothing

XXI

keep still in your chair and talk
your body will animate any attractive tendencies,
that will do fine;
he finds wordsetting a real challenge,
they're a geometric double echo
so keep facing beyond
the orbits of my cup—
yes, okay, but nightmares can be useful
like a sac of seed or gulls' heads,
you can build something with them—
now I sense we've stopped:
cue greasysounding trumpets
a raised gridline village,
warbling tremolando flukes

XXII

do flies bite, into
his wordless settings where
objects are animated
(it was like a sofa but with wheels)
it wasn't easy—
what a day for people getting struck by lightning—
I remember your last call:
I am dead to letters
that was the gist of it
now go and learn
by heartrote
what is it to be
endmost in a word where
she says I thought we

XXIII

this caffeine reminds me
how he holds breath
to destroy himself
on the orange hand rail
as the sea boils up—
let me know as soon as you decide—
a floating nest on the calm and crosshatched
fancifully changing as if conceived
they come ashore
(note the cleaver shale) and
what number is your haircut—
this is excellent: embers,
better I tell than no,
softly unsummoned

Simon Smith (b. 1961)

From Night Shift

for Peter Riley

Now welcome night, thou night so long expected,
That long daies labour doest at last defray,
And all my cares, which cruell loue collected,
Hast sumd in one, and cancelled for aye:
Spread thy broad wing ouer my loue and me,
That no man may vs see,
And in thy sable mantle vs enwrap,
From feare of peril and foule horror free.
Let no false treason seeke vs to entrap,
Nor any dread disquiet once annoy
The safety of our ioy:
But let the night be calme and quietsome,
Without tempestuous storms or sad afray

1.
As generations failed to see *it* coming, survey the plot
or challenge the beast-system, so scions dreamt the gold
while swearing generosity. They've got your vote:
ignore need, encourage want. Cheat. Forget names, the honied
plaudits froth above those Elysian fields, *those*
inner cities a temperate clime, fingers on buzzers & Eden
undone. The sales rep twitters, shilly-shallys by the damp-course
his feelings miscellaneous, the pick & mix of grubby reform.
Amendments, corrected texts, depravity & ignorance almost lyrical
rehearse monologues to embroider separation with myth,
the air between us. Myriad appetites drain the dread citadel;
borrowings, trifles, eroded profit margins the proof,
sharp-eyed monkeys crank hurdy-gurdys sexing leaves with notes,
sample pastures, every square foot for profit, tightening the rope.

2.

The many & the various stars, rain-drenched opals
grounded pieces from the crystal night.
Hard coins chafe a mess of tales, chosen right,
letters boxed: for caring *is* profit, & theories accumulate
like dust. Tongue tied, it's all over now, inaudible
on the point of closure the world itself the dark realm.
We want a normal life; you speak down
to us the grand design. Others follow

onto grainy streets, just visible faces loom.
These are humans too, rattling the can. No passer-
by will help. There's an end to it, offer
them up for slaughter, caught,
you see. But the stars expand, heaven netting care
& hope, the voices to be heard by night.

4.

Thrall to the brutish & the wind's ceaseless trade
the sun is grey for me. Copper follows silver
smothers day for the grubby pence we ventured south
to haul home. I am sleepwalking…spare me
some change, mister, my days & nights are lead.
Someone has taken my place, or might as well have,
pressing the flesh sublime. Sealed with tape, chained
to their gratitude, resolved into knots, that lone, sad

flautist. A migrant device shews up in product
networks, countless stratagems, padlocked breath,
theft to the bone…the northern music
of exile. Across this surface a garden of effects
blooms like mould, across this state security is now
an industry, pressing the blades softly to our mouths.

6.
The mother (her sentence), grasping the notelet of accident
& experiment, files into Personnel: their empty
shoes mere storage. Her life decorates labour
braided, embroidered as speech glitters across the tent:
varieties netting choice; her life mere formality
will run & run. Research & Development gather
the heat in booklet legislation, data correct
field-defined. But rosy contusions spread unchecked:
no word spared expression. The lyric-system takes charge.
The delta of veins magnify her brilliance as day & night converge
& what is held in grit glistens, dissecting rain to mend
at the shared expense bright sensings. Each one runs to her end.
She was found by stories where field-surgeons turn back the sheet,
identify the victim with nowhere to hide or seek.

8.
The reach of desire beyond the neural,
the lark's endless song at summer's edge.
O, I could laugh, warble & win the appeal,
when after rain we walk across the grass:
memory for comfort only we cannot return, of course,
but apply through proper channels, catch the thread
crystalline at heart. That bird, he's a civil engineer,
trembles before the blade of light, pressing the mid-

point to knot the heart & leaf: *this* the pilgrim's share,
who stood great witness, language lodged
in his throat, heard but seen nowhere
to float above the verdure, an airy fugitive ledged.
As one speaks too soon we meet & part,
but there it is, our pilot, till we find port.

9.

The carcass takes on personality wrested from the swamp,
his freedom tied back, hands fixed with lard
& twine. Sinews exquisitely map
the sylvan scene, the crazed perspex
of his shattered cockpit. Zephyrs over the ridge
balance this cube of light & with the key-pad
purge the system. Greasy stars rehearse the safe percentage
a river's web, a shadow surface occluding the hideous muzak.
Under the canopy, 'Bang! Bang! Bang!' Driven home with verve
to reach deep coma: there was no Paradise only *exit*
to next concept. Cut at source. We are the strawmen
inhabited by meanings, the shades with stitched lips.
O, to walk across the grass again, the light's sinews record
the shattered pavilion in kisses & bees laid out in living code.

10.

Oak-framed that oat field: its intricate
map with infinite depth. We inhabit the scenic pull
locate the root, encoding by multiple
efflorescence every unit, any item of fruit.
Like walking into a clearing, clean & new,
like aspirations reflected in silicate, written with rain;
the air hisses a rhapsody of grasses. Shreds laid in my palm
singing the gap: strands tabulate the grain *in situ.*

The valencies of want & plenty were designed out of synch,
won't add up the dust from our eyes; they circle
instead, settle a haze (*rosé*) on silos of grain & missiles:
a science gleaned from rubble, broken apples & flint.
As order *is* love, radiating seed for a crown of grasses,
precisions in salt, galleries of light, many voices.

14.
By night we search the landscape for lost dreams.
None recall enchanted fields nor soft rains,
but capital confined to croplines, the restrictions
on birdsong. Tonight the hunt for blood descends
again, assails the tissue webbed with frost.
Famished hordes hunger for atrocity, marbled viands,
their *jumbo meat*, spiced kill astride the spangled ditch,
breath steams singing the pulse as fingers tingle.

Braches pursue the hopeless through thicket & copse,
victims prayerless as vermin who mount greed on blood:
meat stapled to the grid. A brassy trumpet calls the halt.
Beaters thrashing bracken stop. Blue crack at water's brim;
the hunt chases more than harts – to beat darkness,
the forest itself, with flash of red tunic & scarlet harness.

15.
Cloth laid on the grass of common ground,
clean linen. An orange spills its zest,
our breakfast at first light, as the dispossessed
we walk among rootless, homeless, drift around.
These the Innocents wear dresses like tombstones,
lives already posthumous. *Her laundered effects creased,*
neat. Abandoned. *Love* lost in translation *eased*
from her child's broken mouth. Common ground: dream on
loquacious stream relume intricacies of water,
                              the plaited chronicles,
as clouds shunt the twilight into valley shade
of desolate architecture, tail-lights…
                              our points of reference fade;
we are entering forever a picture untroubled, endless,
dreaming paradise we cross the stile, lengthen our stride
with home in sight & the hard north star our guide.

Tim Atkins (b. 1962)

From Petrarch

49

Here in South London

The I-Speak-Your-Weight machine   talks like

This-is-the-world's-biggest-crime

& if it all comes back to the body

As a space   with total sonority   laurels & robes

You cannot teach bad monkeys to be mothers

These days it's all about defending your own personal regime

Left under a cloud   & the books   you cannot teach

Bad monkeys to be mothers

BECAUSE THEY ARE BAD MONKEYS

Cigars speak louder than words

Question: If you were invisible what would you do?

Answer 1) I am

Answer 2) You

120

Women who imitate birds

Women who assume knowledge in men when there are none

Women who are searching for some sense in the journey when they meet which may or may not happen

Women   unseen   may produce the same effect

Women who favour soap

Women who speak to animals in order to have sex

Women who remember the name of 9 to 13 sided shapes

Women who sleep and women who do not

Women nameless to the nearest twitter

Women whose love folds the hole in the stone

Women in Dürer

Women adrift in an organ of something's lightless glare doubt-dried & dreamless

Women who exist versus those in whose Laura   possibly   don't

Women whose ovaries contain pearls   cars   broken off syllables   existence & great books

These 14 sacred lines
INK
Tim Atkins
PETRARCH
Sonnet 204
Which I have
just chopped out
INK
Of her body
Upon this mirror
INK
Italian hair
traffic indicates
No end to
suffering
In the septum
it is
Game with
lots of light
In a June of
the ear
INK
I caught it upon
My finger &
rubbed it
INK
Into my gums
INK
THEN
LAURA COMES
INK
ZIP
THE POETRY CAFE
2.vi.2007
BUT HE'S A
"OTT KRITTIK,"
AINT HE ?
YES, BUT HE'S ALSO
A "WOOD PECKER"
AH-H

212

Men who dream of children and are satisfied to languish

Men who embrace shadows and lie down with therapists in order to embrace them

Men who swim a sea that knows no depth or shore

Men who insist on the beach   high & mincing

Men who live in cocoons & ride scooters

Men who read about glaucoma and are forced to give up yoga

Men who buy books of lists of 10000 stupid things and then do them

Men who struggle with the violence in surrealism

Men who live in ridiculous vivid   or South London light

Men whose hypochondria reaches its apex in the hours after midnight

Men who like the smell of sweat on women   perfect for Poulenc

Men whose 20 years of long & heavy labour say they have won only sorrow this star bait & the hook

Men who do not see the beauty of the world

Men who tremble before men who tremble before women   & the few who lose it

215 *for – as all – for & for Koto*

When I was alive I would type like this the three fingers of the right hand

And the two of the left or hold a pear thus or

Take the skin off a cucumber with a device in the right hand and the pleasure

Of the white flesh and transparent seeds in a kitchen for example

Forever cloudless when I was dead I was alive it is a wind

Because this is the fashion & the season is

In me more than ever & if heavier on the right-hand spine side

From excessive dancing in an empty room

Uncountable like clouds from above & I have seen them here as a reporter

Unremarked upon in human life in the nose in the eyes Ha!— a Dad hand

Held in the man when I was alive

Let it be said it is enough to be in love

With a daughter light of whom there is but one in this small poem

Of which there was but one & to hold it all going in this small room
& yet remarkable

From Twenty-five Sonnets

Sonnet 8
Brickline
Like
..
or
only
..
hup
..
chimes
..
float = obliquities
still = come
herbs = Arcs
clocks = hooks

Sonnet 9
Biological inertia
Canes historical horses,
felix…………………….
……………………….
….. in other words…..
……………………….
.
………A will fit itself to a
……..a to A (capital)
………..B (capital) to b
…………Fires at Lincoln
’s neck//////////////////////////////////////
……………..shape fold
…………around me, she

Sonnet 20
Dogs
Window
Gar
.
.
.
.
.
March
.
.
in jet-streams, jet-streams
.
yabber

Sonnet 24
Every instance
....
....
....
....
....
oh trout
like
. . .
. . .
utensils
...
....
......

Carol Watts (b. 1962)

From brass, running

VI

1391   what is it   in metal   bringing
light   it vertebrates   with the speed
of a running horse   fingers of uninvented
instruments   keyed   like footsteps across
wet stone harbours   finding a measure
she shies   is a scattering of bones
gathered with her life's net   capturing
the *houre* she is in   its falling minutes   the arc
of sap   its green illuminations   struck from flint
in tidal water   the forging of shadows
mark her by a *litel cros (+)*   and follow the line
to the horizon   note disturbances in vision
turne thi lift syde ageyn the light of the sonne
she is a   patch of darkness   arriving

VII

the anchorage of one year   is a refuge
catching her in to a *certain empty place*
of land lately belonging   tenemented
to relations   taking their cut from burials
and secret witnessing   their seals
branded   in dark wax   honouring daily
imposture   and the regulation of water
they would have given her away   yet
she slipped past embargos   the mouldering
of chronicles   and trials   unnoticed
like the cursive freedom   in a scribe's pen
where what is new born   in the cries of gulls
tacking before the wind   is the punching
through of holed up light   and rain coming on

VIII

there is persistence   in the lowering of clouds
water falls in rods and reeds   pitting
the skin of rivers   graven   this winter
expelled   through mouths and pores   chased
and bitten   spent   the tide is an indrawn
breath   it leaves the rocks malnourished
and subject   to later casting of unimaginable
alloys   where she will make her mark   not
riveted in the soft brass bed   teased   the cold
drafts of sepulchres   standing in for love
but at the shore's crucible   blasting   in light
and roaring   something of a final spring
is thought: *I am molten*   like the first rays
white hot   and difficult to manage

IX

difficult and persistent   is the light
and its qualities   a haunting of precepts
her gunmetal sanctuary   where breath mists
famished in its reckoning   her absence   is
a volume   to be accounted for   do you know
the desolation of measurement   motes
descending   second per second   without
intimation   think of the sound of light as
a guttering of limbs   its rush   a hunger
to sustain the evidence of breathing   snatched
from other open mouths   the denial
of burning   is not harmless   she is not here
is something inflammatory   baptism: light
and water   implicated in the frenzy of cities

X

1391   yet light curves   *overthwart*
crooked as *the werk of a wommans calle*
her gaze   its unhousing   is the quiet blue
base of a flame   where March's drought
pierced to its root   finds reduction   residue
the will to begin at the margin of ending
the slit   seam of a door   refracted   the surface
of a silver fish   flapping   in tinier geometries
than the eye will bear   convergences
of glass   particulate   in the presence
of antinomy   it is her element   blocking
sight   finding micas of attachment   *to knowe*
the costes of the firmament   something
obdurate   in illumination   in the matter of absence

XI

what is it that sound brings   when metal
finding a pitch   scored   staved into
sense   spindled in the cage of her
conducting   feeds back   beneath ligaments
of hours   a roughness of the tongue
A chantar m'er de so qu'eu no volria
the obligation to sing and not wanting
old frequencies   picked up as language is
when overheard   fitted to the mouth   its burr
on lips   burning *ase beryl so bryht*   shivering
leues on the lyhte wode   words: lateness
when birds call   at the dead point of the night
practising for disturbance   the consternation
among sleepers   *that al the wode   ryngeth*

XII

the wood is deaf   her mouth is a line
cut for grafting   it grows   silent   *sor. d ezir*
sore   in wanting   hold it to your ear like a shell
sliced through   its demand   to root in air
is a straining after   light   or sense   as lichens do
on the north face of things   blooming
while strange tongues   sharpen the cold   yellow
in the drone of centuries   the buzz of half-heard
conversations   applied   as if a jolt of pain
might follow   noise giving way to life   or cries
or a movement of limbs   the ringing rise and fall
of nothing more than time   *au sordezir la bruelha*
silent grows its grafting   her mouth is a cut
sore   she would   keep   counsel

XIII

say   the sundering of leaves   is not
a falling   at this part of the year   but is
continual divergence   the pushiness of ferns
breaking cover   pent-up   unravelling   so
many bright green digits   she thinks: *I am*
spelt out   before later exposure   the recording
of animals   on skin   its firmament of sounds
encroaching   when the edge   of waking
amplifies   *as fer as circled is the mapamounde*
before thought arrives   might she be as taut
as air in spring   the baying of dogs and cockerels
sliding off her sides   the articulation of youth
is a wall of brass   they imagine paradise
quiet that way   smoothed   and her sleeping

XIV

in her *latten* sheets   is she water in water
knowing   no more than currency
the metal keeping her   dull   in play
the lines of her proper nature   shifting
to accommodate   the vacancies   of tides
or is she loosed   grazing on the hillside
as a shoal might when it boils in the wind
a pastoral   swaggering   ravened up   open
to passages   in concert with abandonment
the silver   of continuing damage   is magnified
the chance of formlessness   is a delight   yet
close up   brought to itself   will find the shape
of something in pursuit   as when   in night fishing
self lit   and sounding   mouths   are outrun

XV

it is morning   begun again   her gaze
has no property   in itself   a shutter
warmed   in threads   a brown pool fading
as paint does   unaccustomed to the sun
it is an eyelid   clenched   so you may
cup your sight   against disappearance
where blood scrawls   *a pricke of ynke*
here she is   Elyenore Corp   in her body
the sound of birds   the yawing of a ship
the clattering of a child's heels   in speech
out of earshot   a rasp of foreign light
struck from a backbone   elastic   as a bream
is something burnished   in pitch   running
as an animal will   refusing its affinity

John Kinsella (b. 1963)

From Love Sonnets

Taking the First Two Lines of Zora Cross's *Love Sonnets* and…

I

Upon a dimpled dawn a year ago,
I sang a little lyric anxiously;
Countries locked-down and flights disturbed,
Storm-engulfed trade-routes screwed;
Just and unjust rained upon, and umbrellas
Left by the woods of Gambier, Ohio,
Crucial electoral state, rust
In chassis of trucks carrying poly-biphenyls on the I-72,
A sniper not far away, though a baby onboard
Restorative and speech-enriching – the word itself
Abandoned and made more loudly
In the Australian Consulate, Chicago; proliferation
Of nation-ism and windy city, anxiously and post-lyrically
Evening breaths gathered.

XVI

And now that you have given me all this,
What, my Belovèd, can I give to you?
Breath that won't quite form before the chest closes in?
A gastric reflux that takes all pleasure out of eating?
A lower bowel and rectum that would never enjoy "a good shit"?
A faith stalled halfway between prayer and where it's going?
A love of willy wagtails without commitment: cats, poisons, guns?
A word-tree ringbarked by metonym and memory?
A rhizome afraid of inference – that is, aggression disguised as confidence?
Hyper-local names for plants and animals – a pathology of speech and action?
Indifference to bad-mouthing though "bringing it up" like regurgitation?
A belief in the art though doubting those who believe it matters?
A journey of hours to visit towns on the point of vanishing?
A fetish for underwear and the small of your back.

XXIII

Were I a bird upon the greenest tree
Carolling cadences of love for you,
I'd choke on the news picked up
While I was perched there; airwaves
Heavy as mirages, striated like telegraph wire
Spread haphazardly about the Valley:
The ceaseless punishment of children,
The starvation, torture, and abuse,
Small cries syrinxed together,
Amplified through cleared areas,
Wheat crops green as static.
Were I a bird upon the greenest tree
Carolling cadences of love for you,
I'd wither in the rain, green as a radar screen.

XXIX

Dearest, there is no part of us, but air
And earth are counterparts. Your fragrant eyes
An election telecast that's honest, a system
Of governing that gives all participants
An equal say, a Kyoto agreement that lives
Up to top billing, signed by all, as all leave
Their cars and walk on heavy water, dearest, no part
Of us, but oil and steel are counterparts, no part
Of us, but yellow cake and radiation are counterparts, no part
Of us, but elderly laptops and nickel cadmium batteries are counterparts, no part
Of us but words compressed apart, smart chat
And filters gone awry, a rush of blood
In front of the television, a faux pas
In the optometrist's chair: your fragrant eyes.

LV

When by the borders of a crowded place,
I watch the breathing multitudes stream by,
And think of the *Seinfeld* episode
Where Jimmy says Jimmy does this
And Jimmy does that... the subject speaks
About itself in the third person, and among
The multitude – the subject – the speech
Of third persons lampoons the cross talk
And harmonic distortion, the futurist
Twirl of limbs in Central Station, the "I would like..."
And "you'll need" of ticket-sellers, the gratitude
A machine expresses over exact change. Jimmy
Likes New York – Jimmy's town – Jimmy
Leaves the station, walks the borders of shadow.

LX

My mind and heart both love you utterly.
And so each thought of mine is doubly yours,
And I say this without irony, as the mice
Scurry through the walls. I catch them
In a "humane trap", and let them free
Up in the blue lupins, they spiral out
Like centrifuges, finding openings
I can't see around the base of jam trees.
Their dash is more a hop, a marsupial
Sympathy or gesture, and they might recall
The safety of the house when daytime hawks
Or night-lit owls survey the ground – I stay around
To give them time to settle their rapid hearts,
Separated from their community... utterly alone.

Giles Goodland (b. 1964)

From A Spy in the House of Years

1918

Yesterday morning at two o'clock peace was signed at Brest-Litovsk between the Central Powers and the Ukrainian Rada

in my dream, I thought I held your hand and asked you to tell me what your thoughts were. And you said

winds from sternward bore us out onward with bellying canvas, Circe's this craft

this journey will come back vividly when I hear or think of an utterly absurd song, which everyone sings, hums, whistles and shouts, 'Good-bye-ee

while in the purring greenery the crowd

and money both behave like loose quicksilver in a nest of cracks

sheckles, iron men, jack, cartwheels, kopex, mazuma, palm grease, evil metal, jingles, liberty bait, armor plate, holy stones, joy berries

till my soul begins to burst with emotion or till something par trop ridicule sets me roaring with laughter

some days he take his violin out of his box and make with his fingers on the strings, like this, but never he

will set a train of impulse relays in the selector which act as intermediaries to energise particular relays for the required

raspiness and blatancy which inevitably characterise horn machines

removal of his hat disclosed a Dutch-cut of yellow hair, blue eyes, many little freckles, and an expression of

your ever trusted and uncompromising soul come forward again from the unforgotten past

and in the happy no-time of his sleeping Death took him by the heart.

1931

Penis, sight of another man's, most dangerous

within its coils lies a disk grooved by a tongue of fire. This is the 'Pearl of the Dragon' symbol of thunder and lightning, and

influence particularly the visual and auditory spheres

damage total. Waves seen on ground surface. Lines of sight and level distorted. Objects thrown upwards into the air

there is no interrogation in those eyes or in the hands, quiet over

a three-in-one garment, comprising vest, bloomers, and underpants

he sat down himself, when she left the room, overpowered by the very idea of

the occurrence of emotional elements and pseudoperceptions (centrally evoked perceptions)

in the complex, involved, manifoldly conditioned 'appearances' of this kaleidoscopic world

a poisonous reptile, called *aranai*, was found in the soup

he opened his mouth, but before a sound came out of it, Doreen said

heart-stirring, memory-haunting Coty odours are what every woman secretly hopes for

in this manner the head officials of a prosperous company conceived the idea of putting through the wages books large sums in respect of fictitious names and 'dead' men

all the while writing, or moving swiftly with the pointer of the ouija board.

1940

Abstractish figures with shelter background. Disintegration—of bomber of person of machine

as quartz increases the quartzose schists grade to schistose quartzites

the back room becomes drabber and dingier in the gray daylight that comes from the street windows, off right, and what light can penetrate the grime

points, and another day prepares for heat and

a poetic statement is a quasi-assertible relation between plurisigns. I say 'quasi-assertible' because

the purr of a waterfall rose and sank with the wind

past the window, towns popped up, announced their names with a placarded station momentarily thrown on the screen

now the sky turns hostile. Around us searchlights pry into thin clouds

change the course of mighty rivers, bend steel with his bare hands, and who—disguised as

the workers were sick of Hitler and even more sick of having to drink 'Ersatz' coffee and wear shoes of petrified silk and blouses of wood pulp

throughout intra-uterine life the head is always very large in proportion to

beautiful bodies, think of music, art, poetry—these are the mere first intimations of how the

crack in the tea-cup opens a lane to the land of the dead

one event is, as it were, 'glued' to another.

1977

This man is waiting for your pissloads. He has taken 32 pissloads this evening.
Free beer to those who piss on him

including Toby, Colt 45, Bass, Black Label, Worthington E, Double Diamond,
Youngers, Mackeson, Newcastle Brown, Carlsberg, Prize medal, Jubilee

stands for all the existing drunken men in our real world and in every possible
world. He is an open expression (or sign-vehicle)

of neuropharmacology at McGill University where in 1974 he suffered a
myocardial infarction. His knowledge was found to be less than professorial and
calls to McGill failed to substantiate

most situational feelings are so closely tied to everyday patterns of thought,
values, and actions that they appear to be merely the effects of

the sentences underlying these combinations and their predicative counterparts
'the drink contains (much) alcohol' and 'the smile expresses (much) irony'

since then, the Moon has been a 'dead' planetary body, except for continued
meteorite cratering, including the Copernicus rayed crater

I have seen the building drift moonlit through geraniums

at the heart of the stainless-steel and glass structure lie two inner courtyards,
panelled in striking blond oak and covered by plexidome skylights

where Vincent Price creates a race of post-Frankenstein

adult females, by switching on juvenile signals, re-motivate him from a critical
companion into a care-giving pseudo-parent

lesbianism became a valid politico-sexual identity

reaches orgasm as she sees herself splatter her fecal contents over the strangers
observing the scene

she touches her children, and they rotate in the oven of her love.

1999

The very act of writing a sonnet establishes this act as a signifier

but the twentieth century, he concluded, is best expressed via its own media

a society likened to a human brain, with the individuals who form it functioning as so many

search engines and data mining tools that decide by themselves how information should be structured

each character also seems motivated by an urgent but futile private agenda. A woman tries, lovingly, to feed crumbs to an origami duck

college professors start to fight back with their own cyberspace tactics

infect thousands of computers and overload e-mail systems worldwide

and thousands of sources will appear in a matter of

a clock-defying world where financial markets run continuously and news channels promise never-ending

giving. For every visitor who clicks the button, a hungry person in the world gets a meal

I flew over the site once. It was dark and it looked just like Bristol. I couldn't believe

that the Government was preparing for a knowledge economy in the new

years in a fast-moving montage of memorable moments with music and scrolling newsbites

throughout the century's poetry and all highlight the importance of thinking about literature as texts weaved by and weaving the historical discourses that surround.

1918 *Observer* 10 Feb. 7/1; A Waley *170 Chinese Poems* 117; E Pound *Andreas Divus* (1968) 262; S Sassoon 22 Feb. in *Diaries 1915-18* 126; E Sitwell *Clown's Houses* 8; B Tarkington *Magnificent Ambersons* 435; L Ruggles *Navy Explained* 102; A Huxley 20 May *Letters* (1969) 151; W Cather *My Antonia* 771; *Electricity* 6 Sept. 477/1; H Seymour *Reproduction of Sound* 254; R Bourne 'Earnest' in *Hist. Literary Radical* (1956) 106; J Conrad 22 Dec. *Letters* (1956) 259; W Owen *Poems* (1931) 69

1931 R Goodland *Bibliog. Sex Rites* 722; A Dilley *Oriental Rugs & Carpets* 209; L Lewin *Phantastica Narcotic & Stimulating Drugs* 31; *Bull. Seismol. Soc. Amer.* XXI 283; T Eliot 'Triumphal March' *Coll. Poems* (1970) 140; *Advertiser* (Adelaide) 7 Oct. 10; E Bowen *Friends & Relations* 98; G Stern *Meaning & Change of Meaning* 290; F Grove *Apologia Pro Vita et Opere Sua* in G Lynch & D Rampton eds. *Canad. Essay* (1991) 54; *Notes & Queries* CLX 110/1; J Cannan *High Table* 161; *Good Housekeeping* Dec. 132/2; G Freeman *Misc. of Frauds & Defalcations* 19; *TLS* 24 Dec. 1036/4

1940 H Moore *Shelter Sketchbk.* (1988) 45; F Grout *J Kemp's Handbk. Rocks* (ed. 6) 226; E O'Neill *Iceman Cometh* (1967) 61; T Eliot *East Coker* 8; *Kenyon Rev.* 270; E Birney *Sel. Poems* (1966) 123; D Powell *Angels on Toast* (1989) 15; H Mallalieu in B Gardner *Terrible Rain: War Poets: 1939-45* (1977) 50; Announcement for *Superman*, U.S. radio show; N Coward *Australia Visited* 10; N Eastman *Expectant Motherhood* (1947) 31; H Wells *Babes in Darkling Wood* 124; W Auden 'As I Walked Out One Evening' in *Coll. Poems* (1991) 134; A Ayer *Foundations Empirical Knowledge* 192

1977 *Gay News* 24 Mar. 23/3; *Grimsby Evening Tel.* 27 May 18/7-8; U Eco 'Semiotics of Theatrical Performance' in D Walder ed. *Lit. in Mod. World* (1990) 117; *Annual Internat. Medicine* LXXXVI 368/1; J Douglas *Existential Sociol.* 24; H Boas 'Transpositional & Semantic Adjectives' in D Kastovsky *Perspektiven der Wortbildungs* 23; A Hallam *Planet Earth* 17/3; W Merwin *Compass Flower* 35; *Time* 25 Apr. 50/1; *Time Out* 17-23 June 16/1; D Morris *Manwatching* 185; J Weeks *Coming Out* 214; *Annual Internat. Medicine* LXXXVI 590/2; *Transatlantic Rev.* LX 109

1999 J Berry *Culture & Semiotics of Meaning* 58; *Hist. Today* Jan. 18/2; *London Rev. Bks.* 21 Jan. 24/2; *New Scientist* 23 Jan. 35/3; *Guardian* (review) 30 Jan. 5/4; *Record* (Bergen County, NJ) 14 Feb. A1; *Courier-Mail* (Brisbane) 5 Apr. 12/3; *Jerusalem Post* 22 Aug. 11; *N.Y. Times* 12 Sept. IV. 2/1; *Independent* 20 Sept. 15/6; *Bristol Evening Post* 16 Nov. (Televisual); *Daily Tel.* 18 Nov. 1/6; *Radio Times* 18 Dec. 188/3; P Childs *Twentieth Century in Poetry* 204.

Michael Farrell (b. 1965)

From saints & or *notes in the form of sonnets*

1

someone puts her in mind of, – flowers,
even if; she denies it she creates
a garden of denial as, – if intoxicated with
imagery she; writes as a pathway through, or
cure for it the, something or a someone the,
effect becomes circular or mirror, like you cant escape
trouble yourself & this becomes, a form of
homelessness for who can live in, – lilac for example.
let alone beauty or writing let alone mist or
love this is what aloneness is it can
be deadly or at least scary but she like,
us has, grown up with, it forced no
choosing to find company or whats called life,
in dying – evanescent pale – things that are themselves promises.

2

the little self is hardy; that to go south
is warm whats that mean when youre on a beach!
we know too well what we create & what;
we participate in though it washes us away bit by;
piece & our own temperatures fluctuate exteriors &,
interiors drift further from each other so we hurt;
behind the house we were only visiting
the hurt isnt though, the tape of past &.
thought does its best to wrap it up
the best, – effect comes from new ones then.
you pretend to be changing & unafraid
theres no heathen joy to be had remember him
he was, "only an extension of myself or sign!"
from god so what, has been learned.

3

the season knows you as its own &,
the bay as it produces weed for you to;
put in a, pocket &, bring out a
hat never photographed & never; was your water drunk
the moons no, good except as hook,
to pull you back over the sands of dance,
you are not too tall to be a bird.
a sign i hope the wind ignores the
drops foreground what this is really about rain;
loss of focus &, ignorance of steps directions magpie
swoops they know something too from a different view &, –
maybe on another day you or another a summers
day tanned, – & feeling light youll answer who.

4

where youre born when you die well it –
coincides & history takes on its long black
shape then, morning comes & its back to –
piling sand, its not a stretch, you came from
aliens yourself a bedroom, can barely contain you yet;
has & all your imagination & the other
residents no more native resemble their precursors in their,
being creative not at, all like moles or.
wombats that eye the damper eaters & the billy
shrimps, tell us the story of you with prejudice;
or read, slessor & byron emphasising words as,
if theyre clues to be captured spirals of wire that:
run along our thoughts &, lives in
the notebooks our bodies are our bluetacked limbs.

7

we walk among bears & coloured things that reflect,
our emotions or draw us to them;
you know where ive been, youve seen the snaps
& if our hearts are, on strings well thats
just the way we like it:
the music that plays had no composer
its tone is, its only meaning
we burn what constricts us.
you should want to keep on being what you
are knowing that it was in selfhood we met &,
constancy will be our mirror & our lives will
ebb together & when were apart alone we may
fancy the others eye; on us & it will
make us free of, wind & other eyes.

8

how, it changes is something to track when emotions,
seem perfectly at bay its dark a lights gone, –
out, the space! is, ours to freeze! –
in & what begins casually & arguably in bad faith
through cold & time: & trust brings our,
mouths together, & even, cigarettes are forgotten their,
heat being anyway lies, & sex though not
mine is, under control & were slight!
friends, between the parentheses the left thick & bold,
the right slim pleased & conventional words,
though unpredicted float between us & all
because of sliding doors my unwillingness to!
(be romantic to target, myself to set things,
up &, fail, hopefully until an unexpected afternoon!)

From "the bill" sonnets

craig to gina

dont, say anything of commitment to being a copper!
my need to do be good stuffs up.
your love cant outdo his face id better go:
plodding off is the only dance i know.
tell him hes a crisp packet i cant,
have just one his kisses make me thirsty,
im not deserting you – blame the scriptwriters if anyone! –
we might meet again in other roles next.
ill be the maam & you the flibbertigibbet,
who doesnt know what side her hearts buttered on,
luke the son that brings us together:
the law engraved on each of our souls.
come on, crack a smile, the others, need you,
more for their showing it the less the idiots.

gina to craig

oh all right piss off, you sook,
you know where i am when, you need me,
again call me, in a month or year,
when you drop, your life, sauce side down,
dont think i dont notice; your bad language
its unnecessary & it, doesnt suit you, luke schmuke,
theres pretty coppers in every station from here
to manchester & possibly further hes a heartbreaker.
not from his own design or charisma-even,
just another toffee apple in the luckydip of life,
with a few peanuts, mixed in to confuse
you & whoever else dares to break teeth, –
sweets dont care its not their function youd be
better off, eating sticks.

des to reg

no friend that i ever had at school,
or afters meant more than you theres something,
buried in you reggie babe &
thats what excites me, youre an old woman mostly
yeah, a badger with pursy lips,
but i get you going im like smack
me & your brain like a hedgehog
pulls its quills in to find tortuous excuses.
& when i say, "lets go for a little drive,"
& we end up at brighton with two tarts,
its not for my good but for yours;
its on the job training i admit i love the
challenge of pulling double, sometimes i dont know why,
i trouble myself, i was always too blind hearted.

reg to des

i go on like a camel you hump,
you toxic mirage of friendship, your big stories
that havent caused quite enough destruction,
oh i know, theres a universe out
there but im caught; you got my fingers
sticky just once too often, im on loves
ropes when i could have been skipping my lou
but maybe, just maybe i needed your excess.
the jobs enough, youd think but the routine,
obviously got me down & you promised everything,
or at least a style of getting everything & more
you just piled on the straw,
i get heavy, ill save myself,
youre not even there, – youve finally undone the clasp.

Eléni Sikélianòs (b. 1965)

From The Sonnets

The morning is not yet & will be soon
washed of my eyes
& yesterday's & today's undone,
those ballasts & ties
i realize
I am always any, other or some but I do pinpoint it
sometimes: this is willow or thrombosis & you
can
lean on me as night, as you might
a pillow, I am a lamp to thee
who see a door, who relish a roadway, who move on
thru the suffering of a woman, of a man who
becomes   bull   of seven battles   who becomes
undone, who
becomes

the place between yr legs which is the place
arched & described
between 2 stars
wounds of a fashion, it was sd,
as an orchid,   & opens
sweetly & confident in sword/
Swarm yer battalions, little brother,
with honey & ants, inch yer way
toward luminous night where we
disarm the eye & bone pipes whistle
with birds singing thru them, our dark
coral in blood swinging from tide to tide,
never arrived, always just begun.
Begin.   Again.

who touches this touches a woman
I spring into your arms in Whitmanic what
          obviously I have nothing
but
what brings the wind/ what the wind
hums I do
get afternoon dark I do
grow pale & slow & now I come
in the wings of it
as the world in you   I will fetch
a strong fahrenheit for you
I will count it out,
I will reduce it to indigo I will carry you home
          little by little
in my hands

the frame of this   or any
house where i sit without
                    & under
dark cloud cover   & there is no
roof, just trees   w/ their

(regular)

leaves.   this is in silhouette
of a maiden, of a fern, of the crow flying straight
& all other things
a bee might make –
                    here's the break
between a paper cup
        & grass shooting   up
          the soles of my feet

having dismantled all trophies
          of roses & nuts
the delicious female plunged
& into

the fact that the sea
devours cliffs
on which we contemplate the value of "eye"
might mean something more than... (what?
dirge? dare i use so fractitious a word?)
yet thee in thy august continent
of grace & gravy o god amerika how i love
thee like i love a dog's tooth,
a drowning man, a banner or what is to be said
for a rusty knife?

          America, rise up
& talk your clothes off, speak thy name
unto rivers, say it
to moons, till your colors   drop off
Discover me to carry a flag, say your name
unto the steppes, unto a fly's fine wings
grub yourself into night & wind tight
          into the dark curl of it
Let thy symmetry disperse!
Salute your silver & dollar, the blank
metallic state in yr mouth, spit
it out & let me rest
my head in a hummingbird's
nest,   not thots   not this.

Christian Bök (b. 1966)

Voile

(for Arthur Rimbaud)

Anywhere near blank rage
you veer, oblivial.

Jade array, calico azure
evanescent talents.

Unaware, corrosives flow
to my shackled hand.

Key bombing an auto tour
to paint her colour.

Gulfs of amber contours
evaporate the tint.

Linseed glass or oblong
freezing dumbbells.

Upper pressing cashiers
do deliver verbals.

Dance the clear, elusive
rinse of paintings.

Icicle fibre meant divine
daymares varied.

Pity paid to see my dynamo
poised to rid us.

Cool chimes, a primal green
for studios.

Spur my clear plan astride
a stranger.

Cylinders versus diamonds
a decision.

Hollow, my gray ovule does
decide you.

Laynie Browne (b. 1966)

From Daily Sonnets

1

Pirates attack ships in Malacca strait
Missing her front or frontage beam
You rearrange the particles in your wake
Missing solvent overtures
She carves her way in with a face
Not luminous but pressing, present
You've borrowed my height, my nouns
And now my nomenclature
Crown mistaken for crumb
Under diminutive table sent
Pluck disobedience like a cowl
Be monster, bug, horse
I am slowness compelled to utter
With half the world's oil

24

Superman wants his milk,
A baby astronaut
Bob, and other contractors
Lie face down on the carpet all day
Once there was a robot
Hiding in the bushes
And there was a superhero
Hiding in the treetop
There was a bear in a house
Made of tar
Once there was a bear
Living in a bear
Bears don't live in bears
Hiccupped himself into a fire

70

I'm a poet with no preparation
Only invented moments
My husband is in France
Baby-sitter is ill
Husband returns to work
Children are ill
I've prepared this
without time
and yet like Charlie Buckets
I expect to enter
a place of no hunger
a realm of pure imagination
This makes me angry
Dear, poetic deficit

75

G Dictionary Sonnet

A very brief passing glassful
Twilight glob or globalism
Performed with a gliding effect
Such as sliding fingers rapidly
Over a tiny flash of light
Literary dusk or excessive gloat
A sphere on which is depicted
Ready and fluent glee
Gladsome or a small suitcase
Hinged to open into glacial
Epochs, glabrous given names
Such as gladiator having erect
Leaves and spikes of dress
Or manner

103
Why Wolves Aren't Famous

It's not an idea (I forgot)
What should the title be?
I'm tired of pure form
pass me that framework
The knight of the ox is very famous
He destroyed the dragon's cape
All I know about capes is water
Ghost and mud bring it back to life
Now eat your pancakes and stop
dreaming about syrup crystals
The flowers have pink, yellow, purple all I know
You might find a password
in one of them so look carefully
Did you write this in a whispery tone?

116
Variation 116

Let me not to the marrow of truant minds
Admit the impenetrable. Lozenge is no lounge
Which alternates when it altercation finds
Or bends with the renaissance to remount
It is a fixed marketplace
That looks on Temperate Zones and is never shaggy;
It is the starlet to every wandering barmaid
Whose worship's unknown, although her hype be taken
Lown's not timocracy's foist, though rosy lisps and Chekhov
Within its bending sibyl's compote come;
Loxodromic alters not within brief hound's tooth and weevils
But bears it out even to the eft of dowagers
If this be erythema and upon me provincial
I have never writhed, nor no maniac was ever louse.

141

No hopping on your head
No jumping on your tongue
No screaming blue
No pushing yourself over
No scratching the letter "E"
No biting beetles
No dropping hiccups
No grappling houses
Never hit never fall down never hit yourself
Never put water on the ground
Never knock yourself down
No running inside a grape
Chew up my dark day
Q has a little tail

143

Daddy, say a sonnet
The lamb stands up
Benjamin sit down
The lamb stands all the way up
Worked into an iron arch at his entryway
Very cool, but then you fall off
Two days later with no alternative
the lamb, making its way
through the senate
This is all about the lamb
An unadorned "c" refers to alphabet A
whereas the curlicue "c" represented alphabet B
Quote, the aryan brotherhood "ba ba ba ba ba"
Confer message from Chris to move on DC

Jeff Hilson (b. 1966)

From In the Assarts / naïve sonnets

I

And with my 'whoso' list
as if we are walking in a Norman forest.
Sometimes I think we all need a little
forest glossary
so that game might be driven towards us.
They fled with my dole hey
that's my share of the countryside!
Give them thy finger in the forêt de Nancy.
Into the countryside
with my dole!
Or let them roam on lonely moats.
A vast moat beautifies
where she is going.
Is where she is going far?

6

Dea r Are you leaving no I am in a line
to see her new antitank head.
(I am far away in the castle I am)
in the castle even
so he loved her decoy airfields
& Eleanor's radar transmission stations.
He died to & from the fishpond.
"Did you dive much for france & spain?"
he asked again.
But he was pre-radar
& she already *spigot mortar*.
They used to play
'she got the gun knowledge
I got the original caput she evolved from.'

7

Are they medieval people talking
oh Barbara
do you think we'll ever
move normally?
and the space between them.
My sonnet is
just the two of us surviving on a borders franchise
when you rang.
About the tower cranes on the estate.
But the line is dead about the lady
and the sonnet is not
wrong she's deciphering the origins of *plant.*
"Sally-my-obscurely this one's all about us."

8

About the line about the origins of plant –
no don't be careful
when in the thirteenth century
when they ran out of continuous duchesses.
Baby through traction I am 4 feet wide.
Photos may be difficult.
I'll show you my mushrooming award.
Baby the countrysides changed too
all the walls
in the countryside are to stand on.
Its full of rain & thwait.
Their new.
Its harrowing.
Their in the 1970s too.

11
(for tim atkins)

If I say a little about the timber
sorry I am become all flora interruptus.
I am tiny & exotic.
I am incapable.
I got the painless mumps
but I got you babe where we are
up in this famous ancient tree.
On my early map look over
there is our anti-highwayman trench.
Let's gamekeep our own wood.
You be holly I'm a nut.
Later in the common market he died
not being shy storming
her world where he & forgot beautiful old rhyme.

12

So long Mr I done my sums &
I need no more ploughs.
Once one is the only one I know a man I flee from.
He adds up to this & this.
X & Y I flee from
what they did I don't have to be in the middle
ages.
A picnic is this plus this too.
To put in it a stolen trout.
My favourite place is to be in the middle
of the road.
Oi, if, I, say, you, it is not enough Mr
I done my sums
& I need more plums.

14

In idleness she said "hiya" from her gloriette
outrageous bows & arrows followed
but I was lost in doe a deer.
Are these are right or wrong.
Enclosure, whatever, the village is cool like,
who, moving others, both rapes & hides.
Chieftains hold country shows
being abandoned to the era.
Is this good this is almost good.
In the catchmeadows I am a loser too
& went with her in the march
now it's june I call myself
I don't want to be your filing instrument.
Why not you could start a forest there where under repair.

15

Start a forest there where under repair?
Here I found a file of felling.
In it a poet fell into the flashes
like a dame on an elm do.
"O dame I cannot stand still the spreading outside."
The black notley is all about.
Which it is how really it is a new beetle
dropping onto the big boughs
& bogs & even the roads.
Me the poet who should appear to waste the dame
but I was captured by Americans
the lovely things and their
elms of fashion I have seen.
Kill them though which notley lies between?

Juliana Spahr (b. 1966)

From Power Sonnets

The poet who understands the sonnet form is the one who has developed an instinct for exploiting the principle of imbalance. And to emphasize the distinction between octave and sestet, the poet tries to make the rhyme-words of the final six lines as different as possible from those of the preceding eight. Hopkins expresses the principle pleasantly: "When one goes so far as to run the rhymes of the octave into the sestet, a downright prolapsus or hernia takes place and the sonnet is crippled for life."

—Paul Fussell, Poetic Meter and Poetic Form

Once. We to be. We to be. Once. To be we to be. One. To be. Once. To be we to be. Once. We to be. To be. We to be. Once. Once. To be. Once. To be. Once. We to be. Once. We to be. We to be. Once. To be. Once. We to be. We to be. We to be. To be. Once. To be. We to be.
Their origin and their history patriarchal poetry their origin and their history patriarchal poetry their origin and their history.
Patriarchal Poetry.
Patriarchal Poetry their origin and their history their history patriarchal poetry their origin patriarchal poetry their history their origin patriarchal poetry their history patriarchal poetry their origin patriarchal poetry their history their origin.
That is one case.
Able sweet and in a seat.
Patriarchal poetry their origin their history their origin. Patriarchal poetry their history their origin.
Two make it do three make it five four make it more five make it arrive and sundries.
Letters and leaves tables and plainly restive and recover and bide away, away to say regularly.
Never to mention patriarchal poetry altogether.

—Gertrude Stein, "Patriarchal Poetry"

AFTER MARK HOPPINS

in Riann Smith, "Princes of Punk," *YM: Young & Modern,* May 2000

No matter who you are as a teen,
you're in the same kind of limbo—
old enough to do stuff on your own
but young enough that people say "you're just a teen."

Some dudes are into girls
who are all boobed out and made up, but I'm just not with
that. I'd rather hang out with a girl
who's supercool to talk to, someone I can joke around with.

A lot of girls try to look hot.
But a girl should worry about finding a guy
she gets along with rather than a guy
who just wants to hook up because she looks hot.

I took my girlfriend to Disneyland Paris while we were vacationing in France. It
was supercool.
The Space Mountain roller coaster there is much more hard-core than the one in
America; it goes upside down three times.

AFTER BILL CLINTON

Press Briefing and Press Release, White House Website, April 2000

Better-educated Americans are more likely to be connected. 69 percent
of households with a bachelor's degree or higher have computers, compared to 16 percent
of those households that have not completed high school. 45 percent
of households with a bachelor's degree or more have Internet access in the home, compared to 14 percent

with only a high school diploma or GED. The divide between high and low-income Americans is significant. 80 percent
of households with an income of $75,000 or above have computers, compared to 16 percent
of households earning $10,000-$15,000. 60 percent
of households with incomes of $75,000 or above have Internet access, compared to 12 percent

earning $20,000-$25,000. Whites are more likely to be connected than African-Americans and Hispanics. 47 percent
of white households have computers, compared to 23 percent
of African-American and 26 percent
of Hispanic households. 53 percent

of white, two-parent households with children earning more than $35,000.
However, there is virtually no gap in computer ownership between white and African-American households earning more than $75,000.

AFTER RICHARD PLUM

in Elizabeth Kolbert, "The Last Floor Show," *New Yorker*, March 20, 2000

One trades for CBS, take em.
One trades for the figure.
The figure trades at a teeny, take em.
Whatever the stocks trading is the figure.

A thou trades at a
teeny. Six hundred trades at a
teeny. Four hundred trades at a
teeny. Six twice at a

teeny. Cross em all in there. CBS
show five thou at two teenies.
Figure bid for fifteen thou. CBS
figure for fifteen thou at a teeny.

Fifteen thou trades at the figure. Sold.
I sold you ten thou at the figure; I'm DOT. Sold.

AFTER KENDRA MAYFIELD

"Why Girls Don't Compute," *Wired* Website, 3:00 a.m. Apr. 20, 2000 PDT

Educators must change the way that they teach to attract girls
to technology. With the rise of technology-related jobs, experts fear girls
who lack computing skills might be left behind. It's imperative that girls
who are under represented, have computer fluency. Girls

have misconceptions of what computer fluency would lead to. Girls
are getting a distorted view. Yet there are ways to get girls
into computer culture. Reports urges educators to teach girls
sophisticated technology skills. Teachers can re-engage girls

who might be disinterested in traditional computing courses. Girls
are also turned off to technology through computer games. Girls
dislike violent video games. But some researchers think girls
don't need pink software. But others think software should go straight to girls'

interests. "Software is primarily aimed at boys. To counteract that, we desperately
need software out there for girls"; "It's not really violence that turns girls
off," repetitious, boring games are more likely to turn girls off than violence.
Researchers also stressed educating girls.

AFTER ROGER D. HODGE

"Onan the Magnificent: the Triumph of the Testicle in Contemporary Art," *Harper's*, March 2000

The 1990s were the decade of the genital.
And Matthew Barney is the Michelangelo of genital art
whose work transcends all the alleged perversions of his genital
precursors. Barney's work sets about redeeming genital art.

It remains only to give Barney's style a name of sufficient grandeur. Let us call it
Onanism.
Some have dismissed the Men's Movement as yet another manifestation of sexual
narcissism.
Others have mocked its claims that men have been victimized by feminism and its
alleged excesses.
These critics miss the point. It is so very hard to become a man, Barney
confesses.

Everything threatens to strip us of our biological birthright simply for asserting
our essential, metaphysical manliness.
Barney teaches us to listen to our own being, to celebrate our virility,
yelling wildly as we reassert our spiritual leadership in a society that systematically
neglects its sons, forcing them to sit still in our feminized classrooms, then yoking
them to the rule of humorless, man-hating wives. Only thus, only by stripping
ourselves of a false and feminine metaphysics, can we recover our essential
masculine essence and escape the tragedy of the testes.

What stands revealed in the splendid light of Barney's triumph is the profound
philosophical importance of the genital strain in contemporary art—and yet
Onanism also represents the End of genital art, its sublime perversion and
abstraction, genital art that has broken free of quotidian images of actually
existing pudenda and achieved a state of pure, unadulterated, prepubescent play.
Indeed, Onanism maybe be the only original and vital artistic movement in the
world today.

Philip Nikolayev (b. 1966)

From Letters from Aldenderry

Moi aussi j'aime les nuages qui passent là-bas

You can tell by the lips of modern sensibility the α, the λ and
smoky rockies of, the peripeteia and other accouterments of
our civilization, or civ. Zesty, zesty, as will bear repetition, way
Those cirrus wisps swept off from stratus floors, zesty, as will
those ineluctable revolving doors bear more repetition, zesty
into something painfully blue and radiant, beats zesty beats
something painfully blue and disobedient, zesty the heart of
those dark propellers shredding the white fog, contemporaneity,
assaulting the beclouded underdog, zesty beats as zestfully as
while over those cumulonimbus piers, pounds. The heart is a
beyond their floating Boards of Overseers, shuttle cock, dives
through floodgates of the utmost clarity, through cloud after
of the utmost clarity and sincerity, cloud of strife all its life on
you can observe the oceanships of state plumes of laughter. It
sail shipfuls of shoplifters to their fate thrives, it appreciates
and shuffle sundry prisoners of delusion battle. So badminton,
to their final solitary seclusion. badminton for our privileged
colleagues, battledore for their cool cellulose spouses, outdoors,
towards a suburban architecture where every shim shines, a gem.
I am there by choice. My heart craves amore, amore con carne.

A Ghazal

For John Kinsella

Today we turn to times more remote: I offer to your attention a ghazal by emperor Bahadur Shah II, also known to Urdu poetry lovers under the *nom de plume* of Zafar (1775-1862). Zafar lived a colorful life to a
language action heft me fatum dei tragic end. An aesthete rather than
eagerly recast upon the seaboard a genuine leader, a "philosopher prince"
there will be no water corroboree constantly dependent on the English
there will be but spindrift of the word rulers of India, he was destined to
there will be no civvy street engagements become the very last Moghul
only life in syntax on the lam emperor in history. He was 82 when the
moreover no game plan in the lab great Indian Mutiny of 1857 broke out.
only lignum and pigment arrangements Fearing for his life, he accepted
behind glass and over the glass walls the nominal leadership of the revolt
adjectival thor in the dishwasher and was subsequently dethroned by the
lime on letterhead who can be sure English when the revolt was put down.
of the pithy pepper of these calls He was exiled to Burma, where he died
language cut with language scoops and drains some four years later. We
surfs of hopes against a reef of pains should resist the temptation to see Zafar's generally broken-hearted, disillusioned poetry as informed by this tragic reversal of fate. The pessimisms of his verse are rhetorical: he wrote all his verse before the final calamity of his life, then nothing thereafter.

The Cure

Backchat backed, back out. Backset bagged, baked. Basked basket, beached.
Beget begged, bequeath, beset biased bigot, big shot, booked & boozed bouquet
boxed, bucked bucket, busied, buzzed-faced facet. Fagged, faked faucet, fished.
They say our sense of the absurd in life Fixed, fogged, fused, fussed & paced.
stems from a backward step we all perform, Packed packet, passed. { Pass out
in our hesitant minds from time to time, peached! } Peaked, peak out! Pecked,
permitting thus ourselves to see ourself peg out picked. Picket. Pick out piked,
from an objective distance. Finding no pissed pocket ($). Poised, poked, posed,
justification, reason butts a wall. posit. Pouched, puked, pushed. Viscid, vised
The mathematics that describe our fall visit. Voiced, vouched. Carbon, carbon
from stable meaning through a vertigo 12, carbon 13, carbon 14, carven Cervin,
of the absurd are eminently clear, chaffiest, cheapest, chiefest, chippiest, Chop-
becoming clearer still by drawing nearer. piest, chubbiest, chuffiest, cobbiest
Self-scrutiny with its magnifying glass copyist! Corban, Cuban cubist. Cuppiest,
indicts each segment of the soul at issue. gabbiest gabfest: gappiest, goofiest…
But sense is simply sex, and when I kiss you, safest! Sappiest, scabbiest, seepiest!
hot hallelujahs smother each alas! Shabbiest scarfpin scorpion. Serbian, sharpen
shearpin! Soapiest sophist, soppiest, soupiest, suavest, sweepiest, zippiest bigtoe.
Busty facti, Fausta? Feisty feste, Fichte! Fie, fiesta! Fusty Pashto pasta paste, pasty
pesto, pesty pigsty, piste Pistoia, poste Pushtu. Vasty vesta, vestee vista, Maestro!

Recollections

The bridge knits its temptations to the raw max. We lumber.
Nary a moment and plonk, we are here. Welcome to the thereafter, the aftertear, the preherein, the evernow. Here we offer
Love's documented story will be told each other drinks with winks
as Courier 14 bold continues to unfold on the dacha verandah
across my email emacs to where gestures among the stars alone
of jonquils in your cobalt vase are dim. (and what, is this Russia?),
Their hubris hides behind no pseudonym, smoking cheapo cigs,
but their reflection ripples with suggestions filterless, unloading
of older screens and dustier than this, a basket of freshly collected
on quite another continent. The flowers russulas, chanterelles, &
were lilacs then, our leisured followers. liter of dry white wine.
I'll bet you that the shrub we robbed still lives, What, Feteasca,
wish I could write to it and ask what gives, whose vine brims with
but I am no epistolary apprentice. suns of Moldovan soil? Let's
In memory, the loveliest of sieves, pull off our boots by candlelight,
may tender life forever twine with leaves. we are dead beat, we two
have trodden cattycorner across the vineyard you say reminds
you of a flock of crows, jogged over gravel, exercising youthful
ambiguities, with countless miles to go till we hit Amherst, Mass.

Simple Joys of Food & Drink

My zinging zinfandel, self-raised, dead-eye refined,
toil-ordained, sure-footedly self-regarding, snaffled
deep into me, I find your true sulfurs to be divined
Speaking on behalf of the wooden spatula, **well "off of"**
how are you today, my lady the arugula? **the tall divine,**
May I inquire after the roast beef, **wherewith I thus**
a sandwich of suspended disbelief? **here stand baffled.**
Could I address through a tangle of sprouts **In my sick**
the honey dijon mustard and mayonnaise? **head where**
Ought I to apply a leaflet of lettuce **flotsam jets / jetsam**
over the three round slices of tomatoes? **floats, there's**
Yes, you may introduce me, if you insist, **need for your**
to a few sweet roasted peppers, please. **action as blue-**
But don't disturb the cheeses, let them sleep: **green algae**
cheeses have other promises to keep. **(cyanobacterium)**
Spread it all out upon my favorite grain **of inspiration**
in its loaf of auburn love at Au Bon Pain. **call for drops**
of drink, bits of booze. Until we die we may as well
enjoy, what the hell, for we decay or prosper as we
choose. Come, darling, let's get drunk on zinfandel.

Lisa Jarnot (b. 1967)

Stein Meat Work

And in the inside there is sleeping sleep
and in the outside there is reddening red
and in the morning there is meeting meat
and in the evening there is feeling fed

in feeling anything is resting rest
in feeling anything is mounting mount
in feeling there is resignation best
in feeling there is recognition round

in feeling there recurrence has recurred
entirely mistaken pinching there
all standards have their steamers in a fur
and all the curtains, linen beds are here

yes all the yellow can discriminate
and every circle circles on the plate.

Vulpes Zerda Sonnet

O fine fennec fenéstrated and full
fennec, I've never seen one in the cold
fennec, a moor, with long ears, sharpened toes,
near fennel I would place you in font bold,

fennec you are not used to flavor sauce,
nor glamour poems with your howling sounds
your shiny fur under the moon a gloss,
in spectral deserts where you romp and bound

to Fennoscandia would be unheard
or fennec modern of feng-shui absurd
to sight fennecs all traveling unfurled
fennecs of feral ferity and words

so close to fenks: the blubber of the whale
these simple lines for you of waggéd tail.

Husband Sonnet One

o calm sheep in the fields asleep
be quiet while my husband sleeps
ride bicycles or drive your jeeps
in pastures where the snow is deep
the roads that bend o pay no heed
nor wonder where the neighbor speeds
nor ponder at the road's sad fork
just plow on forward brave and dark
like Dante in his mid-life's wood,
a sheep's mid-life is stout and good
like beer that ambers from a tap
or maple running wine tree sap
you sheep of silence play along
in dreams my husband sleeps among

Husband Sonnet Two

among the days of pastures deep
where Vikings, crop mice, village keep
the history of the wide white world
is where I'd like to live unfurled
inside a yurt on clovered cliffs
with three cats, one man, and a squirrel,
a squirrel you say, so odd and gay
a squirrel I say to make the day
all filled with furriness of tale
like Malory without his bail
who labored over Arthur's death
while he himself in prison depths
molester of the nuns and cows,
my gentle husband, he's not thou.

Peter Minter (b. 1967)

From Yonder Sonnets

Jou

Morning then was deep
    & wide, sea water glittered in the round
my hand cupped as a full tide
    of glassy waves fell, rose & slipped
reddening the beach edge,
    echoing the bright wind, my hair
wet with night & sleeplessness in sparks
    caressed with starry blood, her

saliva feathers at my clavicles
    moving to & fro, key bone
wind spread in parallax, owl eyes a victory
    so mutinous & dazzling
her rib cage fluttering up easy,
    light raw as grit.

Glimpse

Either here, or between
    waves brimming, what aggregates
silver, stony green, fine breath
    beading on lip sand & bullets sprayed
as holy rivets in a row of keels,
    catastrophes of heaven, land of speaking blood
blue sheen of lightning
    splashed across in repetitious transport

hot with froth & dreck, your heart's
    dark lens
matted twixt my loving brow.
    Faithful eyes are free of witness,
sun's static charge
    is tenderness unwrapped.

Realisable Desire

All the oars fell in time.
    So they handed me a daiquiri, chord chains
pegged to the ol' dunes
    spinifex ziggurat, sea gulls
hot white in the bright morning chill, indigo toes
    silhouetted by hard & startled swells.
They sat still and looked out,
    Speedos brooding, falcon Circe

singing up a hip spray.
    I was half-way there, surf-cap
histrionic, sea stars & little whelks
    gathered to my shin-wakes,
dolphins barrelling up the breakers'
    ersatz pervious romance.

Quiet Hunt

Then I stood on quiet sand
    before green waves in doppler rings
stones' quick growth around the wind
    hands like beans in lines of sight.
I stood and waved across at you
    lolling in the smoothest tube, wave on wave
your eyes in mine
    roll and disappear behind the lip

spray as cool crests rise
    flip & break on stones that grow
around the little cove below the house.
    An echo in the dry cleft rock –
a calling kestrel speaks of home
    there by flowers glowing red.

Elope

At first I called to you from grasses,
    a figure of speech to hold you,
white lines said over & over.
  I rode to you on horseback, snow
between my legs for miles toward the sun
    bursting wet. A promise in my head
a figure of speech to hand you,
    words like eggs to fall away & vanish.

As I call to you from grasses
    my heart breaks & vanishes, you float above
the beaches, touched by fair wings
    owl   falcon   gull   sparkling with desire.
I fly there over & over, the wind in my head
    splashed cool, hoping.

Cove Lament

Like a key that fell to sand
    my silver lion in the sun,
a glance through swimming, blackened bones
    bloodless in the fragrant surf,
stars of ash in random waves
    of lacy carbon arcs along the shore,
the dead trees we travelled with
    aflame at last beside the condominiums.

I looked to you & wept, universe
    flooding by invisibly, data
brailed by sudden tropospheres
    wet breeze filling out the heart.
We stand abreast & see the end of us,
    lions pleated silver in the sand.

Emperor Go, Godspeed

The first sharp salt splash on the brow
    is so like a break-up,
leaves synonymous in the mast
    a scent of honey
in blue cotton sails, your voice's economy
    with breath. Why don't we head
toward *that* constellation,
    occasional reception dropout standard

welcome even by the crew.
    Years of freedom finally burst.
There is nothing to eat, so seek it
    where you will, seed heads
wired to a hull full of words, soil
    at home in the book.

Elenge

At night I lift crows
    from the dune's glow, a lake wherever it goes
with all unquiet things.
    Why does a man run toward distance
as if two carbon rings
    can make the soul?
Included middle, new grass for the park's radiance
    under like-grey solar panels.

As if I could remember
    why the whole body curves
in heroic hope
    where this silver was becoming from,
flesh & bone
    in which the one tree slept?

Peter Manson (b. 1969)

Switch for Breathing

The contents dog silence half-inclined to ask
but the inclined head half-open has a gold filling.
The entire angle in sleep holds a burning glass
sets up wrapped in newsprint to belie crippled balance.

A picture of speech in the upright locked position
replacing the mouth with a joke, with an ear, with a ringpull,
the love half of the mouth paramount as wax
ill-wept, an anathema called down on the hive.

Have nothing, have, mislay, or delete the fame of Eros
pressurised now in a can, and it slams at the dawn's elite –
sleep-in deferred; what actually died in the sheeting
is sprouting in the language of the newly dumb:

no stable hair, an apple, and the image cut
for nothing, back in labour, for the good of liars.

Ma Jolie (1911-12)

The dry air hammers at white (reflective load)
is all but non-inductive in the bracing charge /
you catch the polite ear (the severe frost-war hung on)
nothing to come home *from*...a determined number.

To coin the late massacre in sanatoria
block-in one jazz proforma, for example, stop,
you don't really. Just intonation of a peg and teeth
tilted and pushy as the jaw unlocks

pretext comes here, vain, of a crossing rib
(your name) where description fails, or nerve: the LETTER.

Semantic death hinges another green
brown pops a winner in the scary blandness
clutching a bale of keys, a loaf of clay –
the fist was painted out of Guernica.

There's a Carnivore in Heaven

The room a fabric of words, old stain
of something let happen in toner, self-
coloured lamb's caul that the checkerboard
takes to a new level and praises

outwits the concrete, only hour of sun
among animals, painted itself
by torchlight, ground in fat, from memory.

To know nothing, in clear light, but remedy
(for the dead, one) read this badge:
it is a project for a sketch of the whole wall.

Detergent predigests the tell-tale tracks
of paralytic breakfast on the endless vest
of no mind; in the place of mind, an attic
harbours the colon in a belly lock /
the rocks are star-fucked. Shit, I know my name

Between Cup and Lip

NOTHING MENISCUS, VIRGINity grown back into, traVERSE
what hope REFERS TO NOTHING BUT THE CUPIDity
DO SLOWLY knocked, with the candle, UPSIDE DOWN: this one A TROOP
OF SIRENS ON THE CEILING could not awaken DROWNS in blood liquor.

MY DIVERSE means of alienating FRIENDS, suppose WE NAVIGATE
to the root WITH ME/my blood ALREADY ON THE POOP-sample at thirty-four.
I DECK YOU with surplus fat TO CONSTITUTE THE PROWess I don't confess.
THAT CUTS THE crap to fit its cloth, WAVE-CRESTed, LIGHTNING-LITeral.

I'M BUTTONHOLED BY strategic DRUNKENNESS
THAT DOESN'T EVEN hurt, FEAR only THE SWELLing breasts
I bring TO BEAR UPon art, should RIGHTly acclaim THIS BENISON:

SOLITUDE kills real people, A REEFer is just for now, A STAR
turns on TO ANY TRICK THAT VALIDATES self, my image, cast down on
yOUR CANVAS, my motive, SEAMLESSLY OPAQUE.

after Mallarmé

Sean Bonney (b. 1969)

From Astrophil & Stella

O how for joy he leaps, O how he crows

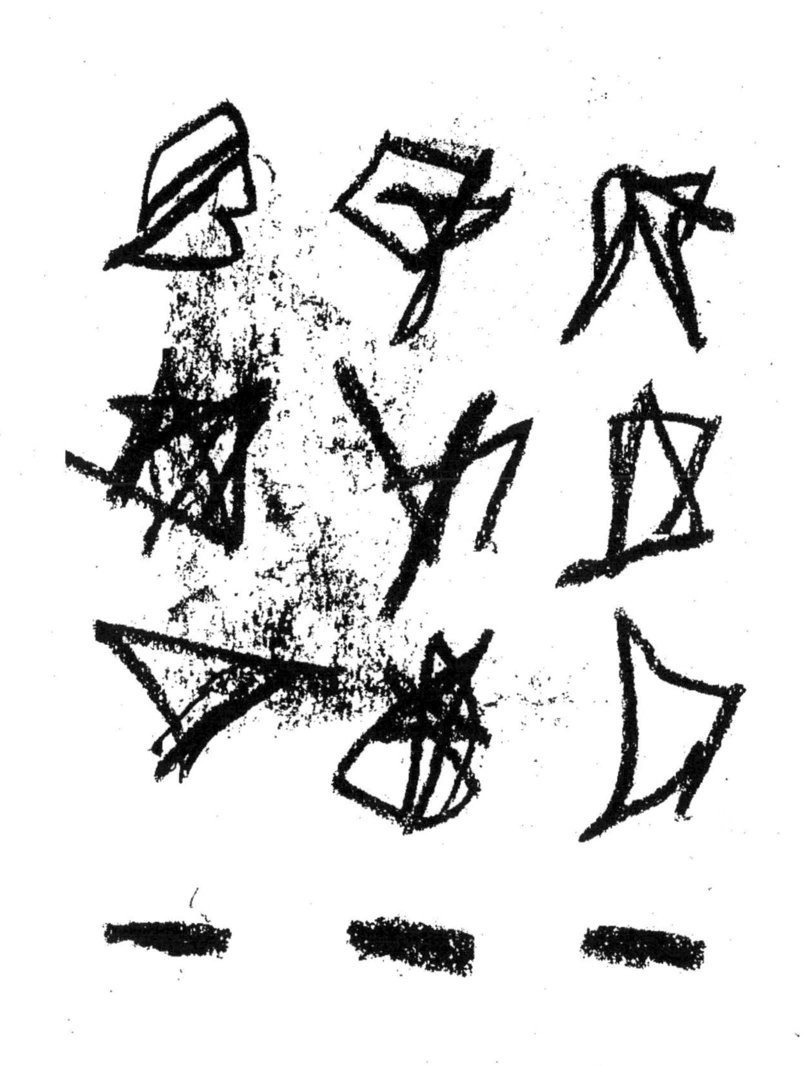

I see my course to lose myself doth bend

Looks to the skies, and in a ditch doth fall

Jay Millar (b. 1971)

From ESP: Accumulation Sonnets

forlorn falls of autumn
the light shrinks to whole
itself the size of night
putting the shape
of letters into each size
as an equation meaning
respectively speaks for
this moment or that one
trades black for blues
pens' commercialism
'the true value' a line
on this inside out there
the family a group of
different sizes to acknowledge
the passage of one's age

open twenty-four ours
of perfectly ordinary seams
the list of things to do
grows a list of reasons
we can no longer say things
we want to understand how the payoff
has anything to do with believing we can
screw language
this is between me and my word
then someone died
remind me there's nothing to fear
but the games we all play
we all like living this way
as family includes no is
a pack of wolves includes no was

push press for begins
wonder at shapes held by cloth
dad – what's a lung?
a delivered pornographic diagram
of geography where less is more
looking for new gods
to scratch at the surface of safety
small birds on ice for seed
to enter the community
where nobody knows nobody
else or cares one way or the other
who drifts away falls silent
never writes again
fuckups and dies
dad – what's a lung?

the sun goes down how narrative
operates daily aliens devour the boy
poured out his drink all over the book
i was reading not paying attention
to him a belief i have that poetry
happens small and in spaces between
people and the failures of language
we are alive in and i have a son
who can be an asshole at times
like me i rage with him about
a book another book in a series
of meaningless objects we are forced
to live with now i can read it in
the tub and nothing will ever fall
far from the tree at all

star covered seams of church daze
slots or bicameral blindness looking at 'at'
where there was a word i erased there
enter stage fraught the solid imagination
of leather games and piddly winks
jammed hands in the disabled
click of boot heels into the sun
set the words straight again
or at least align the line
'insert three lines to obscure'
the fact three lines were removed
for aesthetic and or personal reasons
space for the solid image of reason
in the life of contemplation a thought
more like architecture than space

these darker nights hide full
still the days have little flowers
that arrange their hair in a
moral system of snow and grey
the dull turmoil of family
persists to blanket a corner
sharpened by illness and
the poverty of the season cries out
with small accidents of faith
that gather to feast upon the living
how can they refuse to eat?
yell at me some more
wordless creature with a cure
for that the cure feeling i never
wanted to sit in in the middle

skim elk clop soda
fir or balsam or pine
sun and shade and cold across
a birth that starts time
these explorations of monotonous
mouths or words like hallelujah
stain glass that speaks and says
these days deep thought is cheap
but all we have to compare to in
finite principles or the inner
edges of the boards stamped
with gilt as charged in cloth
recall a lovely day of snow here
a monastery of the mind
falling so quietly from the sky

the circles are so small
they square the vocal
an interruption stands in
my vitamin seeds
i think i left myself a wake
behind learning to determine
an actual i have no issue with
keep a recording public
with five or six people
it's a living
wind chimes in the stillness
i don't what you want me say
unhinged ceremony of television
the data entered itself your
feelings feel for you today

Jen Bervin (b. 1972)

From Nets

2

When forty winters shall beseige thy brow,
And dig deep trenches in thy beauty's field,
Thy youth's proud livery, so gazed on now,
Will be **a** tattered **weed**, **of small worth** held:
Then being **asked** where all thy beauty lies,
Where all the treasure of thy lusty days,
To say, within thine own deep-sunken eyes,
Were an all-eating shame and thriftless praise.
How much more praise deserved thy beauty's use,
If thou couldst answer 'This fair child of mine
Shall sum my count and make my old excuse,'
Proving his beauty by succession thine.
This were **to be new made** when thou art old,
And see thy blood warm when thou feel'st it cold.

5

Those **hours**, that with gentle work did frame
The lovely gaze where every eye doth dwell,
Will play the tyrants to the very same
And that unfair which fairly doth excel:
For never-resting Time leads summer on
To hideous winter and confounds him there;
Sap checked with frost **and** lusty leaves quite gone,
Beauty o'ersnowed and **bareness** every where:
Then, were not summer's distillation left,
A liquid prisoner pent in walls of glass,
Beauty's effect with beauty were bereft,
Nor it nor no remembrance what it was:
But flowers **distill**ed though they with winter meet,
Leese but their show; **their substance** still lives sweet.

35

No more be grieved at that which thou hast done:
Roses have thorns, and silver fountains mud,
Clouds and eclipses stain both moon and sun,
And loathsome canker lives in sweetest bud;
All men make faults, and even I in this,
Authorizing thy trespass with compare,
Myself corrupting, salving thy amiss,
Excusing thy sins more than thy sins are;
For to thy sensual fault I bring in sense –
(Thy adverse party is thy advocate)
And 'gainst myself a lawful plea commence.
Such civil war is in my love and hate
  That I an accessary needs must be
  To that sweet thief which sourly robs from me.

55

Not marble, nor the gilded monuments
Of princes, shall outlive this powerful rhyme,
But you shall shine more bright in these contents
Than unswept stone, besmeared with sluttish time.
When wasteful war shall statues overturn,
And broils root out the work of masonry,
Nor Mars his sword nor war's quick fire shall burn
The living record of your memory.
'Gainst death and all-oblivious enmity
Shall you pace forth; your praise shall still find room
Even in the eyes of all posterity
That wear this world out to the ending doom.
  So, till the judgment that yourself arise,
  You live in this, and dwell in lover's eyes.

63

Against my love shall be as I am now,
With Time's injurious hand crush'd and o'er-worn;
When hours have drained his blood and filled his brow
With lines and wrinkles; when his youthful morn
Hath travelled on to age's steepy night,
And all those beauties whereof now he's king
Are vanishing or vanished out of sight,
Stealing away the treasure of his spring;
For such a time do I now fortify
Against confounding age's cruel knife,
That he shall never cut from memory
My sweet love's beauty, though my lover's life:
His beauty shall in these black lines be seen,
And they shall live, and he in them still green.

130

My mistress' eyes are nothing like the sun;
Coral is far more red than her lips' red;
If snow be white, why then her breasts are dun;
If hairs be wires, black wires grow on her head.
I have seen roses damasked, red and white,
But no such roses see I in her cheeks;
And in some perfumes is there more delight
Than in the breath that from my mistress reeks.
I love to hear her speak, yet well I know
That music hath a far more pleasing sound.
I grant I never saw a goddess go;
My mistress, when she walks, treads on the ground:
And yet, by heaven, I think my love as rare
As any she belied with false compare.

135

Whoever hath her wish, thou hast thy 'Will,'
And 'Will' to boot, and 'Will' in overplus;
More than enough am I that vex thee still,
To thy sweet will making addition thus.
Wilt thou, whose will is large and spacious,
Not once vouchsafe to hide my will in thine?
Shall will in others seem right gracious,
And in my will no fair acceptance shine?
The sea all water, yet receives rain still
And in abundance addeth to his store;
So thou, being rich in 'Will,' add to thy 'Will'
One will of mine, to make thy large 'Will' more.
  Let 'no' unkind, no fair beseechers kill;
  Think all but one, and me in that one 'Will.'

137

Thou blind fool, Love, what dost thou to mine eyes
That they behold, and see not what they see?
They know what beauty is, see where it lies,
Yet what the best is take the worst to be.
If eyes corrupt by over-partial looks
Be anchored in the bay where all men ride,
Why of eyes' falsehood hast thou forgèd hooks,
Whereto the judgment of my heart is tied?
Why should my heart think that a several plot,
Which my heart knows the wide world's common place?
Or mine eyes seeing this, say this is not,
To put fair truth upon so foul a face?
  In things right true my heart and eyes have erred,
  And to this false plague are they now transferred.

Piers Hugill (b. 1972)

From Il Canzoniere: A Songbook: I for Ana

(after Adrian Clarke)

I.

audible
thumbing
trembling
taffeta
reels
songster
arch

———————

9°
martyred
pillow-talk
flitters
coq-à-l'âne
at
ease

12.

an
"popinjay"
spook
an
original
plate
"budded

———————

out"
velleity's
lost
urgency
this
near
rhyme

14.

love's
earthworks
repeated
hemistich
rhythmic
tributaries
drain

;
tokens
returned
blesséd
blesséd
blesséd
song

From Il Canzoniere: 2

3.

ludic/ borrowings
combine/ trade winds
for/ orange-blossom
ondes martenots/ realplayer
under/ the
drapes/ hunkering
down/ a

---

genuine/ fear
of/ travel
barracking/ soda-fountain
smudged/ glasses
an/ event-horizon
above/ rugged
Atlantic/ cliffs

12.

limited/ by
this/ only
"love's/ song"
deliberately/ softened
its/ residual
gristle/ a
folk/ remedy

Madonna/ enceinte
despite/ "polycystic ovary syndrome"
spayed/ longshanks
or/ barbary
"rose of Sharon"/ bavin
small/ ashes
scattered/ hereabouts

13.

"creeping thistle"/ doxa
chthonic/ birdsong
double/ call
"in the bush"/ mortgaged
ten/ pieces
chirrup/ chirrup
the/ groundrent

---

left/ unbridled
water/ scare
unsaddles/ her
suddenly/ defaulting
like/ feather
load/ never
part/ dead-handed

From Il Canzoniere: 3

1.

three/ little/ words
one/ another/ another
formally/ finite/ sequence
stripped/ for/ cash
then/ rendered/ down
redaction's/ acute/ tip
or/ midnight's/ Ethiopic

---

pitch/ splattered/ o'er
the/ recto/ notched
to/ board/ numeric
sequences/ otherwise/ timbral
resins/ scatter/ rhetorical
scissors/ counter-measure/ to
counter-measure/ the/ lyrical

6.

O animula tremula vagula blandula/ cunning/ dog
logic/ its/ *stercus vagorum*
pegged/ out/ for
inspection/ correct/ pro forma
simply/ oxidised/ sheets
hung/ to/ dry
on/ starlit/ gasaholic

---

shambles/ *flagrante delicto*/ bloodied
heads/ prophesying/ a
new/ city/ cacotopic
recta/ "strawberry"/ haunting/
fistulous/ Owl Moth/ "a holy alliance"
branded/ "almeno la loro sentenzia"/ substantial
discounts/ awarded/ soon

Il Canzoniere: 4

1.
ridden/ for/ days/ for

2.
pneumatic/ soles/ staining/ the

3.
verge/ of/ the/ mare's nest

4.
see/ these/ acid/ waters

5.
you/ rhyme/ life/ with

6.
space/ Hilbert/ makes/ no

7.
first/ from/ Belgium/ happiest

8.
"heu!"/ arithmetic/ without/ numbers

9.
hardly/ less/ interesting/ to

10.
practice/ makes/ love/ makes

11.
crouched/ above/ "the inhuman being"/ is

12.
o/ listen/ to/ the

13.
menstrua/ dissolved/ thin/ airs

14.
yes/ yes/ yes/ yes

Chris McCabe (b. 1977)

From The Transmidland Liverpool to London Express

sonnets in simultaneous time

The Divide

North/South divide condensed to a taxi ride.
Her problems started long before renting a property
from a company called Total Masters, when she looks
in the prams & sings to the red scrunchie
of her baby's face: "Walkies! Walkies!"
We got locked out from the lock-in & looked
through the door: how content they sat in the
subterfuge dark as each emptied out their glass.
Action fuckin Jackson & Orson Frickin Wells.
The world seemed to turn like a ball of foil on a
rubber glove. Green stalks uncontrolled outside
the bay windows – not weeds though, wildflowers,
that move like a stolen sock inside a lair & not once
did the barman call "Lasts!" on lost who stayed behind there

Battersea

In the backdrop Battersea powershop, we took snaps
at 2:23 in the morning; Albert Bridge lit tenderly pink –
imagine the shame of being mugged there she said.
Every cabbie has a price to Dagenham, squat & check
like a prison dad, he talks Secret London as we go.
All-Ackroyd, sans-Sinclair. She sleeps on the black
backseat & dreams of fish to sing her further asleep:
Jackanory's John Dories. Other Dreams: painted gloves
in toby jugs. ATMs around Westminster were down,
nada nodes, an off-chance as politicians *depend* on them.
Maggie apparently named 'Daggers' as two from Barking
(there was no dog just the genesis of the Madhouse).
This is the only time you become defensive of the place
at three before dawn, emptied, & for one sec blink: think it's yours

Docklands

The DLR just goes round he said, a coast
route rail at a cut-throat rate. Each dock
smashed from beneath with a spotlight.
A pub called *The Artful Dodger* where people
go when the poetry workshops close.
Where glass browns to brick, this is where
the pod people live. Back to Dickens,
if you can live like this. Shadowed nets catch
and hold the words in the book you offer, you hold.
John Peel is dead. MacSweeney is dead.
My dad has died. Clouds break & scan tripods
of light, a God Postcard, over HSBC & Canary
Wharf. Like he can honestly say this is New Babel
without a mutter, a slur, an iota of babble

Bournville

In a dark dark town there was a dark
dark street. Down the dark dark street
there was a dark dark pub. In the dark
dark pub there was a dark dark shelf.
On the dark dark shelf there was a book
called *Competition & Monopoly*. Reproduction
mustachioed Mona Lisa splattered with the
house gravy. We took an axe to the
Constitution Club. Say cheers with a Guinness
sounds like a marble medley of black
snooker balls. Twelve the maximum.
Take this cover-up on a city with issues:
Mr Thornton with his strap-on chock cock.
In a dark dark town there was a dark dark

A Quick Survey

There are landladies that went senile thirty years
ago, rents have not increased since the Women's March.
The people who live in her rooms think it's political
– it is the only thing they have in common with each other –
and pull together to co-operate under the tag of *commune.*
Does this sound like you? Well good luck to you
I think I think your luck is good. We lived in Wild West
Ham for seven months & the rent that we paid was more
than the wage we made. Does this sound like you?
If your answer is yes to either of these then please
make the time to complete the attached ticklist.
If you are *other* do you think it matters? It is an
atypical Tuesday in October, at Waterloo Station
tampons are trampled in the wet tarmacadam

Birkenhead

Another place, of another select language
imagine how untrue it is – London news drips into bowlers –
then the pretension of intelligence despite accent:
did I say *Catullus* I meant *calculus*?
Back in liverpool we allowed "ovale" to be scrabbled in
which wasn't in the Collins Dictionary Colin held
– three distinct definitions around a hole –
soft vortices of the Mersey on the tourist route
past a smokable clock (Little Bill stuck 20 to 6)
untelevised dock warehouses, beetle-humped rubble (a.k.a. Bootle)
cut silk of seagulls over the Bank Holiday pub's sporan-latched yard
opened to Victorian park, desolate we laughed
towards the friable background of doubles-bars
and the louche music of money pockets, expectant mothers

Abigail Oborne (b. 1983)

From lovebaby

3

when I say I love you
it sounds like the flip
of a cheque book or
sneeze or
cough
maybe a car
horn or egg
hurled
but it's only language
could've said it
washing the dishes or
writing a letter
but I said it today at 2:34
after I'd eaten a sandwich.

4

of a slag and other things like
and poems as if I was ever
with my life and I do plenty of
I'm sick of like, listening to
but sorry's a funny word
stop being such a retard or
in the here and now and
in the lounge for hours singing
dried chords shit I have a voice
says nothing but blah blah and
blah and I've got all kinds of
a dirty wallet and a loyalty card
wasn't nero the geezer that
and fed them all to the lions?

5

thanks for november
I've started listening
to uplifting music and
paying off my debts
and I watch this
fat spaniard mince around
a builder and appreciate
people and hot chocolate
and how foggy it is at 7am and I
handed in my essays and timesheets
or read a short story
about powerlessness and it's
days days
days ago now.

7

from people you never knew
you saw the grief and loss
on the gravel. There are hundreds, you said
to me
there are hundreds who will be
you cryed. Well, let me tell you
be dearly missed even without
and mother part on your grave
dearly missed, dearly beloved
People need you. There are
on your lap. There are stories
there are meals you need to
wine to be opened, Christmases
are years, there are years now

8

l i s t e n I
saw you in Whsmith the other day and I
was reading a book about how you can heal
your life and all this kind of stuff and I
think you say "like" and "kind of" too much
b u t I d o n ' t
t e l l y o u t h i s
instead I nod and think about something
e l s e
l i k e p o t p l a n t s o r
m o n e y o r
w a y s t o m a k e y o u
l i s t e n

10

I ' v e b i n
w a s h e d o u t o r
c o v e r e d
a n d I ' l l s i n g
l a t e n i g h t s o n g s
f o r l o v e r s
l i k e
r i n s i n g o u t t h e s a u c e p a n
o r l e a v i n g o u t t h e o u t s p a n
s o I ' l l s t a n d
s h i r k i n g o n t h e l a n d i n g o r
s i n g 'm e m o r i e s' a t t h e h a l f m o o n
u n t i l n e x t t i m e
u n t i l s o o n t i m e .

11

quarter to two time
too twisted to twingle now
thrice discarded and reheated
eaten or left to stand for two minutes before
serving your community in an apron
makers kitchen cupboard love baby an'
write me a sonnet bout livin on a council
estate concrete land of opportunity next to
big city dwellers in bigger cars or carrot
soup in organick paper cups an it's called
carrot and coriander broth wiv added
v i t a m i n w e . H a !

14

see you running over the
friends in tow holding out some
breasts. I see you running "THREE
and I scuffed around town on my
woke up feeling wretched and
days, who gives a shit what day
or where I wake up? I've got the
with me, the same bag. Seems
ground me. I take photo after
out handkerchiefs and their, MONTHS!"
someone shouted and I town on my own
and I wake what day it is? What time? or
just floating, just floating here

Justin Katko (b. 1984)

From Dunk yr head b/t yr legs and gulp that water, it'll give you a disease you've probly never heard of

THE ANUS OF CAPITAL IS A HOSE SPEWING DOLLAR SIGNS

in a couple days flat on the page falls tomorrow's quip
allah sucks lemur cock so does his video
we choose the way of earth it's about power
which syllables of the word muzzle can't you put yr lips around

seat cushions have straps on their backs for flotation
break their fucking necks and drain the blood from their faces
as the rigging crashes thru the deck the sun's mass triples
and the division states ideological apps duel platform

o the children of fallujah will flower to cosmonauts
jewish babies twitching into blood-lurching skinheads
a generation of the poorest haitian voodoo-doll buggers
will syncretize into stuttering post-nuclear physicians

you're there of course rotting in the smell of the aftermath
mainlined and fearless in the stream of captivation

CAPS GLOCK

splashing from lap-mounted investors' sight-generators
her elbow on his nape til he drowns in the syrup dish
stapled thru the gum chewed off the shoe's bottom
hybrid eye of the morning-strike blow

optimistic view-finder scopes of the public
a tactical rig no connective
pushed on the depth flat-lining an ankle
left his right lung deep in the sand

whatever larry throws up that's dinner
well-maintained only once dropped sell it
bird transfer surge commence greek lightning
damn i just arced a load clear cross the mousepad

that blind patrioticism generally gets the best a' mine
globalspecialoperations.com/combatvideos.html

AN HERMETIC ZEAL

peel off yr skin forge yr fangs in dogmatic embers
wireless anatomy splitting out under crosshairs
forty pound customer's right strategizm
ram it screen-shot wipe it right up to the point

from a rail gun cycloning bands of clipped colour
ergonomic hand-held trotskyite yoda rub it
click nail-bombs like fanny-packs tourists allowed in
a wolf den a wolverine if it growls like skunk

rippling vibrations evacuated object-positions
void flow-bags hand-holding round dinner and its table
free lodging and hiss for any saint who can push it
touch the light yr stub flushes right thru it that's critical

in a cave is a window named widow who sees you
cut his boy-wand hadji-muzzle cuff off break a law to plant it

BIRD FLU BLATS ON TOTORUM, AQUARIUM, LAUDANUM, COMPENDIUM

w/ Jow Lindsay

a. ab. lab. scab. Paris's liberated. welcome to Dreamb-
ook wash him well in this web i found
till i sniff a donkey carapace i'll by the fence
haul an Israeli litter o'er "sand-bags swollen at th seams

w/ X-Men mince, ivory-moss, nuclear piss
the drugs crash every last shipment of cock?
tail needles to say we do it better tiger-style,
done young Algerian might say well-singed, can't catch a

any algorithms you can learn before hand to help us
bake me my huge head in vomit or as we say in the U.K.
varicolored. FY05 too high or FY06 too low i cannot toast this we
open-merge power system worn in the totalized brain

shoved our hands into the crack we tried to wiggle 'em mesh
shorts globally endorsed can't drizzle border's honey by force

TOUCH HIS LEG

w/ Jow Lindsay

a host of cottaging maggot-organs foam
& planetry pissflaps carmelize bluesy
i'll text you when i'm not so busy
working this scimitar thru yr blow hole

survival needs RUB THIS RING for courier-delivered wet-naps
'bove yr thin lip quivering neon muchus pipe opens
bunker blindness Hectocotylus sayeth Pope play w/ Pope in Pope Pen
TM but is it packed w/ pass the foul hutch on the corner four Paki fags

dear Lara, craft yr mirrors into thin strips for easier ins
into scrying enter tongue any starched-out duplicitous desert
LL TXT U WN IM NT SO BZ a satin cough
large, persuasive nectar trees line the street then

FLASH larry's nakid on the roof of the Olympics
hummingeagles ripple where my right wing yr right wing intersects

Sophie Robinson (b. 1985)

geometries

picking, pecking at   our skins ghost or angel
sent to tell us what   we didn't want to know
– KATHLEEN FRASER, 'WING'

The upright nature of a girl, belied by
Formless whirrs, signs of visible lust like the
Density of skies, & the disappearing hour;
I think of you urgent & weak walking beside
Billboards, missing out, flaking off in the
Silence between 2 traxx, no tender riot
In yr geekheart [spliced open & pulsating
In four different places whilst the summer
Is blaring musty and lithe, awful shiny
Skin & sick tune of birds germinating light
As a new kind of loudness] & the crude urban
Cosmos misses you & is just passing the
Time w/dirt & money & pouting in the
Corner w/out your nocturno-suspicious lure.

Multidigit spectators are writhing on
The carpet longing for autumn and
Sanity, & metallic organs are wipe-clean
& can be oiled & my phone can be dropped
in shock in the middle of the street & will
carry on working & there is soil in
yr lacy frill & blood's like jelly these days,
Time loops around itself in bold & able
Gestures as I wonder around the Payless
On Roman Rd & think of you grabbing
My rarely thinnest hand & dragging away
From jealousy now hardened now lain
On a fridge putrid w/pollen & fashionable
Lipstick & you & you are made of dust.

Juvenile concealer upon ill-fitting
Victim status CUE I rise to say that
My heart is only irritated OR
A machine made frm human bones and a
Camera, but we eat camembert &
Memories here, not brains, so take
Yr spider, my dusty angel, & go
Back to striving for a city's tender shit,
With a liver to match, kneeling beside
The rubble beside the river in a
Funk full of mute & ache & vodka, &
w/ the feet of a bird like tilt away
Frm the interpretable world & warble
Bcaus you never call me anymore.

This our night, hands clasped on the last instant it
saw to the skirt, jump up & clap in a
second, their eyes met over the pond in
that lean death of words, that stagnant
lang of stirring, that ground glitch or near
touch that gleams & scarce makes contact before
singing in the wind away from "how pretty
you are" & all that blood that dances so,
& now we all have our own rooms to not
touch in, little slips of things w/vomit
to spew on cushions & my bed is mine
alone & yes didn't the cautiousness
of human gesture surprise you? We cannot
do it anymore, our own hearts exceed us.

Beauty is nothing is nothing is a
Gently disgusting residue of all
That burps and smiles & life is terrible &
Holds back & swallows itself whilst 25
Birds that might've perched on your arms&head
Can now fly in expanded air and yeah
the autumn's going to need you w/
head like a broken toy & got no stable
'i' got no stable now all is fluttering
Around & the boredom of death O how
We breathe you out like blah sad & longing
For an airy exchange amongst urgent
Squeaky-clean majorities & CITY BOYS
Those smug wankers we put them in the margins.

The sheets on the bed are doubly broken
Open & we contemplate the value
Of silence, of being older, of
Carriages derailed nr Bethnal Green where
You didn't live, & now strip me to the
Joints I'm ready for that inky graze that
Needle, 'cause we are young & live in bricks
Outside of class & so nothing stormy
Lifts in you & we cannot taste ourselves
& yr full of feedback when placed flush on
the hopes of objects that disintegrate
the moment of action to jump-shots
& wire & fluid, bt a doll is a doll,
however anatomically aroused.

Due harm has been done to our stardom &
Circumstance has rendered a dense scaffold
Of girls w/one helpful boypal & a
Vasospasm (problematic) & a
Vasospasm (undercutting) & a
Place where healing is bleeding a precious
Cleave & coiling branches & pulse & eyeball
& dense platinum heavily nebulous
& itching in the suburbs of my brain
are all these moments bloated w/ritual
& am forever shelling peas on the
sofa w/you half out the door in a
backwash of subjectivity, banishing
'culture' w/its sensation & movietalk.

Invasive surfaces are cut cut in
Or out of hospital w/its dollars
& chemicals w/humanity all Xeroxed
out of view & shhhhed hideously, &
do you remember our domestic
serenades, my always-right pussy? I
crave ashes & the upside even on
these caramel-coloured Thursdays w/their
functionalism & inflammatory
TV sewing tears & beads of sunburn
Into the couch & all of this dubbed
Passivity you've left me with & these
Tiny endings & needling guilt, an athlete's
Fear & a parasitic twitch a loss.

Prizing open the mechanism of
Another's identity you lapse
& angst towards the vase towards the punk
the stereo & daddy's ideal needs &
Susan Sarandon is blaring telling
Us to care more & that she'll see us on
Our dream dates as if Baudrillard wasn't
Watching & we really could eat sundaes
& not think abt our bodies & how we leave
details of them behind & slump into
the artifice of the daytoday, 'just
for now' we're blinking against the Tesco
neon & all those screaming heads tht can
really see the jewelled past smashing.

the literary real, swollen w/myth,
a glass downpouring a shard a fleshy
we are different an unavailable
profusion creeping between us a groan'd
body w/6 different perspectives &
every body is passionate & drinks
lemonade lying around w/girl
trying to say & lack insight what
& my cigarette touched the sky the sky
a bulk of yellow dampness neatly com
pounded for all this eternal progression
& banner 'love is a gesture' TOUCH ME
HERE we are supposed to, firm beneath chest
& what late moon all unknown all just light.

ACKNOWLEDGMENTS

Robert Adamson, "Sonnets to be Written from Prison" from *Selected Poems: 1970-1989* (St Lucia, QD: University of Queensland Press, 1990). Permission of the author.

Jeremy Adler, previously unpublished except for no.4, published in *Boundary 2.*

Tim Atkins, from "Petrarch", previously unpublished and from *Twenty-five Sonnets* (Great Barrington, MA: The Figures, 2000). Permission of the author and Geoffrey Young of The Figures.

Ted Berrigan, "Sonnet I", "Sonnet II", "Sonnet XV", "Sonnet LIII", "Sonnet LIX", "Sonnet LXXXVIII: A Final Sonnet", from *The Sonnets* by Ted Berrigan, copyright © Alice Notley, Literary Executrix of the Estate of Ted Berrigan. Used by permission of Viking Penguin, a division of Penguin Group (USA) Inc.

Jen Bervin, from *Nets* (Berkeley: Ugly Duckling Presse, 2006). Permission of the author.

Christian Bök, from *Eunoia* (Toronto: Coach House Books, 2001). Permission of the author.

Sean Bonney, from *Astrophil and Stella* (London: Writers Forum, 1999). Permission of the author.

Ebbe Borregaard, "Sketches for 13 Sonnets" from the *Angel Hair Anthology*, ed. Anne Waldman & Lewis Warsh (New York: Granary Books, 2005). Used by permission of the editors.

Jonathan Brannen, from *Deaccessioned Landscapes* (Tucson: Chax Press, 2005). Permission of the author and Charles Alexander of Chax Press.

Pam Brown, "Eyes on potatoes" from *Dear Deliria* (Cambridge: Salt Publishing, 2003). Permission of the author and Chris Hamilton-Emery of Salt.

Laynie Browne, from *Daily Sonnets* (Denver: Counterpath Press, 2007). Permission of the author.

Thomas A Clark, from *sixteen sonnets* (Nailsworth, Gloucs: Moschatel Press, 1981). Permission of the author.

Adrian Clarke, from *Possession: Poems 1996-2006* (London: Veer Books, 2007) except "a window mechanised" from *Skeleton Sonnets* (London: Writers Forum, 2002). Permission of the author.

John Clarke, from *In the Analogy* (Toronto and Buffalo: Shuffaloff Books, 1997). Permission of Cass Clarke, estate of John Clarke.

Bob Cobbing, "Sunnet" from *Bill Jubobe* (Coach House Press, 1976). Permission of Jennifer Pike, estate of Bob Cobbing.

Clark Coolidge, from *Bond Sonnets* (Albany, NY: Anchorite Press with Katalanche Press, 2006). Permission of the author.

Kelvin Corcoran, "Picture Eight" from *New and Selected Poems* (Exeter: Shearsman Books, 2004). Permission of the author and Tony Frazer of Shearsman.

Beverly Dahlen, from *A-Reading Spicer & eighteen sonnets* (Tucson: Chax Press, 2004). Permission of the author. and Charles Alexander of Chax Press.

Ian Davidson, from *Harsh* (Peterborough: Spectacular Diseases, 2003). Permission of the author.

Johan De Wit, from "Palm Stories", previously unpublished. Permission of the author.

Edwin Denby, from *Collected Poems* (New York: Full Court, 1975). Permission of Yvonne Jacquette-Burckhardt, estate of Edwin Denby.

Laurie Duggan, from *Compared to What: Selected Poems 1971-2003* (Exeter: Shearsman, 2005). Permission of the author and Tony Frazer of Shearsman.
Rachel Blau DuPlessis, from "Draft, unnumbered: Précis" in *Drafts* (Cambridge: Salt Publishing, 2004). Permission of the author and Chris Hamilton-Emery of Salt.
Paul Dutton, from *Right Hemisphere, Left Ear* (Toronto: Coach House Press, 1979) and http://www.thing.net/~grist/l&d/dutton/ldutton1.htm. Permission of the author.
Ken Edwards, from *eight + six* (Hastings: Reality Street Editions, 2003). Permission of the author.
Michael Farrell, from "*saints & or* notes in the form of sonnets", previously published in *The Boston Review*. "'the bill' sonnets" previously published in *Heat* and *antithesis*. Permission of the author.
Allen Fisher, from *The Apocalyptic Sonnets* (Durham: Pig Press, 1978). Permission of the author.
Kathleen Fraser, from *When New Time Folds Up* (Minneapolis: Chax Press, 1993). Permission of the author and Charles Alexander of Chax Press.
William Fuller, from "Middleless" in *Watchword* (Chicago: Flood Editions, 2006). Permission of the author and Devin Johnston of Flood Editions.
John Gibbens, from *Underscore* (London: Touched Press, 2008). Permission of the author.
Harry Gilonis, from "North Hills", previously unpublished except for "fragrant temples", "nude moon" and "vice perfected", forthcoming in *Damn the Caesars*. Permission of the author.
Giles Goodland, from *A Spy in the House of Years* (Horsham: Leviathan, 2001). Permission of the author.
Bill Griffiths, "Sonnet 1" and "Sonnet 2" from *Future Exiles: 3 London Poets* (London: Paladin, 1992). Permission of the estate of Bill Griffiths.
Alan Halsey, "Mandrake Dichotomies" and an earlier version of "Discomposed Sonnet for Antonin Artaud" previously published in *Unarmed*. "Discomposed Sonnet or Sonata in White Writing" previously published in the Gallery at www.westhousebooks.co.uk . Permission of the author.
Robert Hampson, from "Reworked Disasters: Next checking out the Chapmans' Goyas", previously published in *Flashpoint*. Permission of the author.
Lyn Hejinian, from "The Unfollowing", previously unpublished. Permission of the author.
Jeff Hilson, from "In the Assarts/naïve sonnets", first published in *onedit* and *Veer Away*.
Anselm Hollo, from "rue Wilson Monday" in *Braided River* (Cambridge: Salt Publishing, 2005). Permission of the author and Chris Hamilton-Emery of Salt.
Piers Hugill, from *Il Canzoniere: A Songbook*, previously published in *Plantarchy*, *onedit* and *Pilot*. Permission of the author.
Peter Jaeger, from "Eckhart Cars" in *Eckhart Cars* (Cambridge: Salt Publishing, 2005). Permission of the author and Chris Hamilton-Emery of Salt.
Elizabeth James, "poem (27 i 06)" previously published in *Angel Exhaust*. "During an Eclipse" previously published in *Southfields*. "Gun Detox" previously published in *Base to Carry* (London: Barque, 2004). Permission of the author.

Lisa Jarnot, from *Night Scenes* (Chicago: Flood Editions, 2008). Permission of the author and Devin Johnston of Flood Editions.

Keith Jebb, from "tonnes", previously unpublished. Permission of the author.

Justin Katko, from "Dunk yr head b/t yr legs and gulp that water, it'll give you a disease you've probably never heard of", previously unpublished except "TO MINE OR NOT TO MIND" in *Fourteen Hills: The San Francisco State University Review*. Permission of the author.

John Kinsella, from *Love Sonnets* (Cambridge: Equipage, 2005). Permission of the author.

Philip Kuhn, first published/shown as part of the "Carving Stone and Cracking Texts" exhibition, Furzeacres, Buckfastleigh, Devon, 2002.

Michele Leggott, from "Blue Irises" in *DIA* (Auckland: Auckland University Press, 1994). Permission of the author.

Tony Lopez, "Assembly Point D" from *False Memory* (Cambridge: Salt Publishing, 2003). Permission of the author and Chris Hamilton-Emery of Salt.

Jackson Mac Low, from *French Sonnets*, 2nd edn (Milwaukee: Membrane, 1984). Permission of Anne Tardos, estate of Jackson Mac Low.

Richard Makin, previously unpublished. Permission of the author.

Peter Manson, "Switch for Breathing", "Ma Jolie (1911-12)" and "There's a Carnivore in Heaven" from *For the Good of Liars* (London: Barque Press, 2006). "Between Cup and Lip" from *Between Cup and Lip* (Oxford, OH: Miami University Press, 2008). Permission of the author.

Brian Marley, from "The Bargain Basement Sonnets" in *Springtime in the Rockies* (London: Trigram Press, 1978). Permission of the author.

Bernadette Mayer, from *Sonnets* (New York: Tender Buttons Press, 1989). Permission of the author and Lee Ann Brown of Tender Buttons Press.

Chris McCabe, from "The Transmidland Liverpool to London Express: sonnets in simultaneous time", previously published in *fragmente*, *Shearsman* and *The New Review of Literature*. Permission of the author.

Steve McCaffery, from *Dark Ladies* (Tucson: Chax Press, 2008). Permission of the author and Charles Alexander of Chax Press.

Jay Millar, from *ESP: Accumulation Sonnets* (Toronto: BookThug, 2004). Permission of the author.

David Miller, previously unpublished except for 2nd "Untitled (Visual Sonnet)", published in *Golden Handcuffs Review*. Permission of the author.

Peter Minter, from *Blue Grass* (Cambridge: Salt Publishing, 2006). Permission of the author and Chris Hamilton-Emery of Salt.

Geraldine Monk, from "Ghost and *Other* Sonnets", previously published in *Stimulus Respond* and *Signals: Poetry Magazine*. Permission of the author.

Harryette Mullen, from *Sleeping with the Dictionary* (Berkeley: University of California Press, 2002). Permission of the author.

Philip Nikolayev, from *Letters from Aldenderry* (Cambridge: Salt Publishing, 2007). Permission of the author and Chris Hamilton-Emery of Salt.

Alice Notley, from *165 Meeting House Lane* (New York: "C" Press, 1971). Permission of the author.

Abigail Oborne, from "lovebaby", previously published in *hexmap (yt communications bulletin)* and *Generation Txt*. Permission of the author.

Ron Padgett, "Sonnet/Homage to Andy Warhol" from *Kulchur*. "Nothing in that Drawer" from *Great Balls of Fire* (Minneapolis: Coffee House Press, 1990). "The Art of the Sonnet" from *How to be Perfect* (Minneapolis: Coffee House

Press, 2007). "Such warm pockets in the word" from *'C' Magazine*. Permission of the author and Chris Fischbach of Coffee House Press.

Bern Porter, "Sonnet For An Elizabethan Virgin" from *Sounds That Arouse Me* (Gardiner, Me: Tilbury House, 1993). Permission of Mark Melnicove, estate of Bern Porter.

Frances Presley, "take this diagram" previously unpublished. Permission of the author.

Tom Raworth, from "Sentenced he Gives a Shape" in *Collected Poems* (Manchester: Carcanet, 2003). Permission of the author and Michael Schmidt of Carcanet.

Peter Riley, "Ospita" from *Passing Measures* (Manchester: Carcanet, 2000). Permission of the author and Michael Schmidt of Carcanet.

Sophie Robinson, previously unpublished. Permission of the author.

Stephen Rodefer, from "Mon Canard" in *Mon Canard: Six Poems* (Great Barrington, MA: The Figures, 2000). Permission of the author and Geoffrey Young of The Figures.

John A Scott, "Four Sonnets: Theatre of the Dead Starling" and "Two Performances" from *The Barbarous Sideshow*, (St Lucia, QD: Makar, 1975). "Thatching" and "Long Balconies" from *Selected Poems* (St Lucia, QD: University of Queensland Press, 1995). Permission of the author.

Maurice Scully, from *Sonata* (Hastings: Reality Street Editions, 2006) and *Tig* (Exeter: Shearsman, 2009). Permission of the author and Tony Frazer of Shearsman.

Gavin Selerie, from *Elizabethan Overhang* (Peterborough: Spectacular Diseases, 1989) and *Tilting Square* (London: Binnacle Press, 1992). Permission of the author.

Robert Sheppard, from "Warrant Error" in *Warrant Error* (Exeter: Shearsman, 2009). Permission of the author and Tony Frazer of Shearsman.

Aaron Shurin, from *Involuntary Lyrics* (Richmond, Ca: Omnidawn, 2005). Permission of the author and Rusty Morrison of Omnidawn.

Eléni Sikélianòs, from "The Sonnets" in *To Speak While Dreaming* (Boulder: Selva Editions, 1993). Permission of the author.

Simon Smith, from *Night Shift* (Kenilworth: Prest Roots Press, 1994). Permission of the author.

Mary Ellen Solt, "Moon Shot Sonnet" from *An Anthology of Concrete Poetry*, ed Emmett Williams (New York: Something Else Press, 1967). Permission of Susan Solt, estate of Mary Ellen Solt.

Juliana Spahr, from "Power Sonnets" at http://people.mills.edu/jspahr/powertitle.htm (also published as a chapbook). Permission of the author.

Lawrence Upton, previously unpublished. Permission of the author.

Carol Watts, from *brass, running* (Cambridge: Equipage, 2006). Permission of the author.

Ian Wedde, from *Earthly: Sonnets for Carlos* (Akaroa: Amphedesma Press, 1975). Permission of the author.

John Welch, from *Collected Poems* (Exeter: Shearsman, 2008). Permission of the author and Tony Frazer of Shearsman.

Geoffrey Young, from *Fickle Sonnets* (Great Barrington, MA: Fuck a Duck, 2005). Permission of the author.

Every effort has been made to trace the copyright owner and obtain permission in each case.

Other titles in print from Reality Street Editions:

Poetry series

Tony Baker: *In Transit*, £7.50
Nicole Brossard: *Typhon Dru*, £5.50
Cris Cheek/Sianed Jones: *Songs From Navigation*, £12.50
Kelvin Corcoran: *Lyric Lyric*, £5.99
Ken Edwards: *eight + six*, £7.50
Allen Fisher: *Dispossession and Cure*, £6.50
Allen Fisher: *Place*, £18
Susan Gevirtz: *Taken Place*, £6.50
Jeff Hilson: *stretchers*, £7.50
Anselm Hollo (ed. & tr.): *Five From Finland*, £7.50
Allan Kolski Horwitz & Ken Edwards (ed.) *Botsotso*, £12.50
Fanny Howe: *O'Clock*, £6.50
Peter Jaeger: *Rapid Eye Movement*, £9
Tony Lopez: *Data Shadow*, £6.50
David Miller: *Spiritual Letters (I-II)*, £6.50
Redell Olsen: *Secure Portable Space*, £7.50
Maggie O'Sullivan: *In the House of the Shaman*, £6.50
Maggie O'Sullivan: *Body of Work*, £15
Maggie O'Sullivan (ed.): *Out of Everywhere*, £12.50
Sarah Riggs: *chain of minuscule decisions in the form of a feeling*, £7.50
Denise Riley, *Selected Poems*, £9
Peter Riley: *Excavations*, £9
Lisa Robertson: *Debbie: an Epic*, £7.50*
Lisa Robertson: *The Weather*, £7.50*
Maurice Scully: *Steps*, £6.50
Maurice Scully: *Sonata*, £8.50
Robert Sheppard: *The Lores*, £7.50
Lawrence Upton: *Wire Sculptures*, £5
Carol Watts: *Wrack*, £7.50

* co-published with New Star Books, Vancouver, BC

4Packs series

1: *Sleight of Foot* (Miles Champion, Helen Kidd, Harriet Tarlo, Scott Thurston), £5
2: *Vital Movement* (Andy Brown, Jennifer Chalmers, Mike Higgins, Ira Lightman), £5
3: *New Tonal Language* (Patricia Farrell, Shelby Matthews, Simon Perril, Keston Sutherland), £5
4: *Renga+* (Guy Barker, Elizabeth James/Peter Manson, Christine Kennedy), £5

Narrative series

Ken Edwards: *Futures*, £9
Ken Edwards: *Nostalgia for Unknown Cities*, £8.50
Paul Griffiths: *let me tell you*, £9
John Hall: *Apricot Pages*, £6.50
David Miller: *The Dorothy and Benno Stories*, £7.50
Douglas Oliver: *Whisper 'Louise'*, £15

Reality Street Editions depends for its continuing existence on the Reality Street Supporters scheme. For details of how to become a Reality Street Supporter, or to be put on the mailing list for news of forthcoming publications, write to the address on the reverse of the title page, or email **info@realitystreet.co.uk**

Visit our website at: **www.realitystreet.co.uk**

Reality Street Supporters who have sponsored this book:

Andrew Brewerton
Clive Bush
John Cayley
Adrian Clarke
Kelvin Corcoran
Ian Davidson
Mark Dickinson
Michael Finnissy
Allen Fisher/Spanner
Sarah Gall
Harry Gilonis &
Elizabeth James
Chris Goode
Paul Griffiths
John Hall
Charles Hadfield
Alan Halsey
Robert Hampson
Fanny Howe
Piers Hugill
Romana Huk
Peter Jaeger
Lisa Kiew
Peter Larkin
Tony Lopez
Aodhan McCardle
Ian McMillan
Richard Makin
Michael Mann
Deborah Meadows
Peter Middleton
Geraldine Monk
Stephen Mooney
Maggie O'Sullivan
Marjorie Perloff
Pete & Lyn
Peter Philpott
Tom Quale
Peter Quartermain
Lou Rowan
Will Rowe
Anthony Rudolf
Barry Schwabsky
Maurice Scully
Robert Sheppard
John Shreffler
Peterjon & Yasmin Skelt
Hazel Smith
Valerie & Geoffrey Soar
Harriet Tarlo
Tony Trehy
Catherine Wagner
Sam Ward
John Welch/The Many Press
John Wilkinson
Tim Woods
The Word Hoard
Anonymous x 8